Ethics and Anthropology

Ethics and Anthropology

Ideas and Practice

Carolyn Fluehr-Lobban

ALTAMIRA
PRESS
A division of
ROWMAN & LITTLEFIELD
Lanham • Boulder • New York • Toronto • Plymouth, UK

Published by AltaMira Press
A division of Rowman & Littlefield
4501 Forbes Boulevard, Suite 200, Lanham, Maryland 20706
www.rowman.com

10 Thornbury Road, Plymouth PL6 7PP, United Kingdom

British Library Cataloguing in Publication Information Available

Library of Congress Cataloging-in-Publication Data

Fluehr-Lobban, Carolyn.
Ethics and anthropology : ideas and practice / Carolyn Fluehr-Lobban.
pages cm
Includes bibliographical references and index.
ISBN 978-0-7591-2186-7 (cloth : alk. paper)—ISBN 978-0-7591-2187-4 (pbk. : alk. paper)—ISBN
978-0-7591-2188-1 (electronic)
1. Anthropological ethics. I. Title.
GN33.6.F58 2013
301—dc23
2013020742

∞™ The paper used in this publication meets the minimum requirements of American
National Standard for Information Sciences Permanence of Paper for Printed Library
Materials, ANSI/NISO Z39.48-1992.

Printed in the United States of America

To anthropology students and their teachers, who together will construct an ethically conscious anthropology in the twenty-first century

Contents

Chapter One

Introduction

Ethics is not merely a subject to be considered when seeking approval of research proposals by institutional review boards; ethics *is* anthropology. Anthropology, as the comprehensive science of the study of our species, represents a totality of research possibilities for the cultural, biological, historical, and linguistic study of humanity. Although formal consideration of the ethical and moral aspects and consequences of research came late and as a result of crises in the field, nonetheless there has been a thoughtful and vibrant discourse in anthropology in the United States and in the world about the methods and ramifications of anthropological research in an ever more-complex and -challenging world. American anthropology in the twenty-first century is not what it was at the time of the early studies of the American Indian in the late nineteenth and twentieth centuries, and postcolonial world ethnography and ethnology is not what it was when European powers ruled much of the world. Global media has eradicated most old boundaries, creating a transformed context of international research.

Anthropology's conscience regarding ethical research was forged in the experiences of its practitioners and by multiple controversies and crises of those practices that are discussed in this book. The most recent code of ethics of the American Anthropological Association (2009) was begun in the controversy over the employment of anthropologists in military and intelligence work in the wars in Iraq and Afghanistan, almost an exact replay of the crisis involving anthropologists and the Vietnam War two generations earlier. Perhaps this is the normative expectation—that people take notice more in the alleged breach of ethics than in the ordinary, day-to-day practice of the profession. But the lessons of these episodes and resulting discourse are highly instructive, and, to rephrase an old axiom, anthropologists who do not learn (and profit) from their history are doomed to repeat it.

FOR STUDENTS IN TWENTY-FIRST-CENTURY ANTHROPOLOGY

It is important to treat the various codes discussed in this book not as a professional version of the Ten Commandments but as tools to be used for guidance and active decision making in advance of the onset of research and at every subsequent stage of research through publication or dissemination. It is far more important to reflect on the various principles—do no harm, practice informed consent, transparency, and collaboration—and their application through active consideration during the execution of research, and then of writing and publishing research results. It is vital to state at the outset that thinking about and planning ethically conscious work should be a part of every professional act and activity.

It may be asked, Who is an anthropologist? For consideration of ethics this can be minimally defined as anyone doing anthropology, including pre-professional students and professional anthropologists wherever they may be working or carrying out research. But lacking any formal means of determining who is or who is not an anthropologist, the question remains an open one.

AND FOR THEIR TEACHERS

Students are not only the future of the discipline but also its conscience, since the relationship between ethical conduct and sound research has never been clearer. The codes of ethics that the American Anthropological Association (AAA) has adopted since 1971 have often been viewed as inadequate tools for education, deliberation, and decision making in regards to ethical practice in anthropology (American Anthropological Association 1971; 1991; 1998; 2009). They need to be studied and discussed, preferably in group, collective settings with a range of examples along a continuum of best to worst practices.

INSPIRATIONAL CORE OF AN ETHICALLY CONSCIOUS ANTHROPOLOGY PRACTICE

Ethics continues to be the arena in which anthropologists debate who we are and what we aspire to be. Discussions of ethics have been buffeted by politics in the United States since the first code of ethics was forged for the AAA during the Vietnam War era (1971) and the first code for the Society for Applied Anthropology reflected on its practice after the Second World War (1949). In the most recent period it has been the relationship between anthropology and the military that ignited controversy once again, resulting in a hyper focus on the Human Terrain Systems in which only a handful of anthropologists actually participated. The heated discussions that ensued were deflected or postponed with the AAA's creation of a task force to revise the code of ethics, always a good idea to revisit as a matter of course but a reality that tends to mirror the politics of the moment. This time the task force wisely decided to follow the example of other academic and professional groups that have generated principles that both summarize a philosophy of ethical conduct yet also, in their discussion and debate, foster an active engagement of the anthropologist with the environment of research or application of anthropology and the inevitable issues that arise in the multiple interactions anthropologists have with other humans.

GUIDING PRINCIPLES OVER ENFORCEABLE STANDARDS

In 2009 the AAA adopted a set of "guiding principles" as the alternative to its previous codes that had set forth relevant topics and suggestions over matters of principles in ethics. The development of a set of guiding principles for anthropologists followed established trends in other professional fields and the social sciences. The enunciation of principles may be viewed as superior to previous prescriptive, seemingly legalistic, codes, and the lack of a "do's and don'ts" approach is intended to provide a framework for the individual anthropologist to engage in a process of *active* decision making involving appropriate ethical conduct in a given set of circumstances. Guiding principles do not offer comprehensive solutions to every practical problem, but they enable the anthropologist to ask most of the right questions and seek to resolve them using the framework that such principles provide. Guiding principles articulated around fundamental concerns regarding harm, openness and informed consent, or public dissemination of research are rendered more real than merely theoretical through a process of discussion and debate of their meaning. The use of guiding principles shifts the burden of ethical decision making to the individual anthropologist, best carried out in advance of accepting a job, research contract, or academic research sponsored by private, government, or nongovernmental groups.

These core principles are to (1) do no harm, (2) be open and honest regarding your work, (3) obtain informed consent and necessary permissions, (4) weigh competing ethical obligations due collaborators and affected parties, (5) make your results accessible, (6) protect and preserve your records, and (7) maintain respectful and ethical professional relationships (American Anthropological Association 2009).

Nonetheless, fundamental issues are still debated, such as the relationship of science to government, and the concern of anthropologists with social-justice issues and the inevitably unequal relationships that exist between overwhelmingly Western researchers and their "subjects" or participants.

Anthropologists will continue to search for appropriate and efficacious outlets to express these concerns outside of professional organizations.

A FOUR-FIELD APPROACH

There is a clear historic bias in the American anthropology codes that treat the subfield of cultural anthropology as the totality of anthropology. This began with the Society for Applied Anthropology's first codes in 1949 and later the American Anthropological Association's in 1971, which delineated the first responsibility as being to the "people studied." *People* can certainly be interpreted as humans in their biological, historical-archaeological, linguistic, and cultural selves. In the 1998 AAA code, specific reference was made to the primary responsibility to the "people, species, and materials they study and to the people with whom they work" (AAA 1998, A1). Despite increasing specialization, American anthropology has struggled to retain its historic four-field approach, and considerable effort has been made to reflect this in the AAA's codes. The current guidelines and principles are intended to address "general contexts, priorities, and relationships [that] should be considered in ethical decision making in anthropological work" (American Anthropological Association 2009). Section A of the current code reiterates that language: "responsibility to people and animals with whom anthropological researchers work and whose lives and cultures they study." The specific responsibilities enunciated are (1) harm avoidance for people and animals worked with or studied, (2) respect for well-being of humans and nonhuman primates, (3) work for the conservation of the archaeological record, implying both human fossil and material culture, and (4) active consultation and the development of a working relationship with affected individuals and cultures (code A.1). This wording is intended as more than a symbolic bow to the subfields; it is a present-day reminder that American anthropology remains a holistic and integrated science and that ethical standards basically do not vary across the subdisciplines.

The professional organizations of the subfields of physical/biological anthropology, archaeology, and linguistics have generated their own respective statements or codes of ethics. This fact discloses the centripetal and centrifugal forces that exist within American anthropology, unlike international parallel organizations of anthropologists that are in the main serving sociocultural researchers. This holism is both a disciplinary and pedagogical strength, as it strives to maintain the comprehensive and indivisible study of humanity. With respect to ethics, this also makes the point that ethics are ethics irrespective of either disciplinary or subdisciplinary specialty.

BIOLOGICAL/PHYSICAL ANTHROPOLOGY:
RESEARCH WITH HUMANS

Only since 1998 has the AAA's code included a "four-field" approach that specifically addressed some concerns that physical anthropologists confront; however, its language speaks more to the animals studied than to human biomedical or physical anthropological research. Missing, for example, is reference to a myriad of issues related to human DNA or biomedical research, to forensic anthropology, or to the collection, use, or ownership of human genetic materials. Biological anthropology is not methodologically unified; rather it borrows methods from biomedical and ethnographic research and from ecological and historical fields in studying the evolution and natural diversity of our species (Marks 2005, 29).

The code of ethics of the American Association of Physical Anthropologists (AAPA) was approved in 2003, and it closely resembles and is clearly derived from the AAA's 1998 code of ethics. In many instances the same words are employed, with credit to the source, and the overall intent of "do no harm," and responsibility to the "people and animals" studied is the same. In its introduction physical anthropology says that "for moral and practical reasons, the generation and utilization of knowledge should be achieved in an ethical manner" (American Association of Physical Anthropologists 2009, II).

BIOLOGICAL PROPERTY

With the advances in understanding through the Human Genome Diversity Project (HGDP) and the irresistible temptation to make a commodity of human cell lines, the matter of the ownership of human tissue has become an ethical issue. Perhaps the best-known case of "biological property" came from a blood sample taken by a medical anthropologist from a Hagahai man from New Guinea for which consent was given for the stated purpose of "scientific research." The man (whose identity is not revealed) raised a claim when it was learned that the cell lines from his blood sample taken for the HGDP were about to be patented by the National Institutes of Health (NIH). After the patient protested, the patent application was temporarily withdrawn and a follow-up study of what the Hagahai understood of the research project revealed that Hagahai community members were confused about the use intent of the blood samples, believing they were for diagnosis and not to be taken outside of the country. Jonathan Marks relates the story:

> Who could fault them for concluding that once researchers had what they wanted (HTLV-1 sample) then the Hagahai were no longer of interest? The Hagahai cell line is now available to the public at American Type Culture

Collection as ATCC, number: CRL-10528 Organism: Homo Sapiens (human)
for $216 (value in 2005). (Marks 2005, 37)

The whole episode raised serious ethical challenges as well as legal and
human-rights issues.

PRIMATOLOGY

The AAPA code defines physical anthropology as a "multidisciplinary field
of science and scholarship [that] includes the study of biological aspects of
humankind and nonhuman primates." In the latter respect, where the ethical
treatment of the primate animals that some physical anthropologists study is
referenced, the code is surprisingly nonspecific about the field in ethics of
animal rights. The AAPA code simply asks primatologists "to respect the
well-being of humans and nonhuman primates" (American Association of
Physical Anthropologists 2009, III.1). This could be because animal rights
are protected in other nonanthropological codes to which animal researchers
are bound, such as the Association for the Study of Animal Behaviour, which
published its "Guidelines for the Use of Animals in Research" in 1991
(183–86).

Anthropological methods are more field and less laboratory oriented, and
this methodological difference has important ramifications. In the general
ethics codes governing research with animals, it is axiomatic that animal
research must always be justified, alternatives to the use of animals is preferred, and the number of animals studied be kept to the minimum necessary.
The use of less-sentient animals is preferred to vertebrate animals. There is
an embedded bias in favor of greater protection of animals closer to humans,
such as primates, over the "less sentient," lower-order vertebrate and inverte-
brate animals. Animal-rights activists might describe this as "anthropocen-
trism"—treating animal rights from a human point of view, but this has not
been an issue articulated in anthropology.

ARCHAEOLOGY

There are areas of overlap in American four-field anthropology. Forensic
anthropology may be better known in popular culture due to the television
series *Bones*, which features a forensic anthropologist, but also is increasingly important in international human-rights investigations of past abuse and
atrocities under repressive governments. For example, the Guatemalan Forensic Anthropology Foundation continues to exhume bodies from the civil
war waged between 1982 and 1983, because of which charges of genocide

and crimes against humanity have been levied against its former dictator (Malkin 2013).

There is no specific archaeology subfield code within the code of the American Anthropological Association, but this is likely because there are extant codes of ethics for other professional associations, the Archaeology Institute of America (AIA), the World Archaeological Congress (WAC), and the Society for American Archaeology (SAA). These codes have tended to be formulated with the interest of the protection and preservation of historic material culture derived from archaeological work rather than the human descendants (regarded as "stakeholders") of the creators of these ancient cultures. For the most part archaeologists began their ethical statements sparked by the issue of the ethical treatment of human remains, initially raised by American Indians in response to the Native American Graves Protection Act (NAGPRA) (National Park Service 1990), the first of a series of federal acts and regulations to address human remains. All of the previous acts dealt with land, archaeological site, and object ownership (Morenon 2003, 113–14). Issues have also been raised by the study of the human-fossil record, including the study of ancient remains, where there have been ethical and moral objections raised by contemporary descendants. In the United States the impact of NAGPRA regulations favored the rights of indigenous people, at times, over the interest of scientists in their study.

At its meeting in Barquisimeto, Venezuela, in 1990, the World Archaeological Congress adopted "Principles to Abide By," with special sections devoted to the "Amazon Forest People," human remains, and sacred objects, each of which had caused controversy and prompted the council's action. The principles followed the 1989 "Vermillion Accord on Human Remains" that itself was likely modeled on the U.S. NAGPRA model regarding the repatriation of cultural property of indigenous peoples as well as the sensitive issue of the disposition of skeletal remains housed in museums and departments of anthropology. The wording "respect for the mortal remains of the dead shall be accorded to all, irrespective of origin, race, religion, nationality, custom and tradition" included respect for the wishes of the dead when knowable, the local community, and the protection of the scientific-research value of skeletal, mummified, and other human remains (including fossil humanoids) to be reached through negotiation.

These principles reflected the emerging standard at the time of "partnership" with local stakeholders, whereby archaeologists were encouraged to establish equitable partnerships and to include, whenever possible, representation of indigenous peoples in research funding and authorizing. The principles' articulated rules included obtaining informed consent from all stakeholders; not removing material culture items/objects without the express consent of the stakeholders; and obliging members to employ and/or train indig-

enous people in archaeological methods and use them for funding and monitoring projects.

The most recent cases of ethical lapse or misconduct involved the looting
of the Baghdad Museum over several days when the U.S. invasion of Iraq
was under way. The Baghdad Museum, with its World Heritage (a UNESCO
designation) collection of Mesopotamian antiquities, was looted by professional and amateur thieves, with some of the most famous treasures apparently stolen deliberately. The international illegal trade in antiquities unfortunately continues and is apparently difficult to eradicate, despite considerable
efforts made by global policing. Of some fifteen thousand objects stolen,
only about a third have been returned, including some but not all of the most
treasured objects. The rest remain in that underground marketplace where
middlemen and dealers buy and sell the antiquities that eventually end up in
the world's great museums where the tale of their acquisition is rarely if ever
told. When a museum visitor sees the phrase "provenance unknown," it is a
fair assumption that the object was acquired in at least a partially illicit trade.

Given the history of generalized looting of what are now recognized as
other World Heritage sites, and the robbing of lesser sites as well, access to
some archaeological sites is being curtailed or denied. There is a temporary
moratorium on opening new archaeological sites in Iraq, and others have
restricted access for nationalist and scientific reasons. The Chinese government has adopted a position of not granting permission for foreigners to
conduct archaeological excavations, preferring to exert full national control
over their national heritage. This caused some concern in global archaeological circles, as the Three Gorges Dam of the Yangtze River was constructed
by 2009 and opened in 2012 without archaeological partial excavation or
conservation. As a result, an estimated 1,300 archaeological sites were
flooded, including that of the previously unknown Ba civilization, estimated
to be a four-thousand-year-old site from which bronze masks had been un-
earthed during construction, which is now lost under the 185-meter depth of
the reservoir behind the world's largest dam. While dam construction displaced 1.3 million people, it is estimated that over a million Chinese were
lost to catastrophic floods over the previous century, thus immediately raising a complexity not immediately obvious if the focus had been solely
trained on archaeological considerations.

Patriotism and everyday ethics of the Egyptian multitudes were on display at Cairo's Tahrir square during the fall of the Mubarak regime: Despite
days of lawlessness, the Egyptian National Museum, located in the middle of
the square, was nonetheless protected. Even attempts by looters to enter the
museum through the roof were thwarted, and all but a few were kept from
entering the museum. As related by a friend who was an official at the
museum at the time, the would-be thieves were amateurs, heading for the
museum gift shop before being ejected.

PREHISTORY AND HISTORY

I am of the generation of students profoundly affected by the Vietnam War experience, and I had begun to get involved with the principles and practice of professional ethics when the first initiatives to modify the AAA's 1971 code began in the Reagan era of the 1980s, with an effort particularly to change—and, I believed, weaken—the "paramount responsibility to the people studied." I began to engage with professional ethics in this context, when changing economics and demographics meant that for the first time more anthropologists were employed in applied, practicing positions outside of the academy and many were not employed at all. By 1984 an ad hoc group had formed within the AAA in which I held a responsible position for monitoring the proposed changes to 1971's principles of professional responsibility (PPR), changes that were viewed as more favorable to the nonacademic, practicing anthropologists who were working for clients and could not always uphold the "paramount responsibility to the people studied." A new generation challenged the traditional dominance of academic anthropology and formed the National Association of Practicing Anthropologists (NAPA) in the 1980s. Some of these anthropologists were CEOs of their own consulting firms and lobbied within the AAA for modification of the 1971 statement.

I realized that a unique history of the discipline of anthropology could be ascertained through the lens of an emerging discourse on ethics. My first edited volume on the subject was *Ethics and the Profession of Anthropology: Dialogue for a New Era* (1991). It was in that same year that I was fortunate to be a resident at the Institute for Applied and Professional Ethics at Dartmouth College in the state of New Hampshire. The institute had been founded by prominent philosopher Bernard Gert and an activist group of physicians who had formed an ethics board within the medical school's regional hospital. I was told that I had attracted their attention in my proposal to become a fellow in the institute because I had related that there was no existing language on *informed consent* in our code, the PPR of 1971. I believe they were astonished—and probably saw an opportunity for intervention.

After that year of residence, spent in seminars with professionals from major fields outside of anthropology—particularly the biomedical fields, journalism, philosophy, and business—I gained an invaluable understanding of the principle that *ethical principles, standards, and practices are supradisciplinary*—that is, that *ethics are ethics*, irrespective of claims of disciplinary exceptions or exemptions. In this spirit, in 1994 I published what I believe to be the first article on informed consent in American anthropology, "Informed Consent in Anthropological Research: We Are Not Exempt."

LINGUISTIC ANTHROPOLOGY

Generally speaking, anthropologists studying languages and conducting research outside of the United States have followed the ideas and protocols of the ethics statements of general cultural anthropology or applied anthropology. There is a history of Christian missionaries combining their theological studies with anthropology in order to become more culturally sensitive and to translate the Bible into local languages. In many cases this is the context in which a nonliterate people became literate in the mission schools of an English-, French-, or Portuguese-speaking missionary. The Summer Institute of Linguistics at Indiana University has been a major training ground for such linguistic anthropologists.

Some of the many issues of ethics that linguistic anthropology raises are comparable to archaeological ones in the recording and preservation of "endangered languages"—recognized as those whose speakers number under five thousand persons. In addition to the archaeological record is the physical anthropological record, the study of the history of human origins and migration, which can be studied through language. Documenting linguistic diversity is fundamentally linked to cultural distinctiveness and preservation. The recognition of distinctive indigenous peoples' languages is key to recognition of their rights as sovereign peoples in nations where they are national minorities. Important examples of language and cultural identification and recognition can be found in the United States and Canada, in Australia, in South Africa, Russia, China, and Japan. In this respect, critical decisions can be made as to the choice of a writing system and the range of cultural-linguistic orthography from which a selection is made. The dominance of European languages globally often means the adoption of Latin characters, while in Asia, Chinese or Russian orthography may be selected for the purpose of transitioning the indigenous language to that of the dominant national culture. It is well to recall that the great Sequoia of the American Cherokee invented an alphabet and published a newspaper in the Cherokee language in the hope that they would be viewed as "civilized" and not subject to the treatment of other Indian groups, including removal from their native lands of the southeast.

PAST IS PRESENT IN ETHICAL CODES

A critical review of the history of the discipline in which issues of ethics have been discussed, voted on, resolved, contained, or deferred can be chronicled. This work is intended to be not a comprehensive study of the history of anthropological ethics but a thematic treatment of that history and the issues that have been raised and the principles derived during periodic crises and other developments within the discipline. As might be expected, much of that history is informal, unrecorded, and part of the oral tradition of the field, a great wealth of information yet to be mined by future historians of anthropology. For the most part, this review deals with the recorded history where there is sufficient material for the purpose of the more-formal history of ethics and professionalism in anthropology.

The acknowledged first statement on anthropological ethics is the Society for Applied Anthropology's 1949 *Report of the Committee on Ethics*. Tellingly, it was developed in discussions beginning in 1946 immediately in the wake of the Second World War when anthropologists worked for various branches and agencies of the U.S. government. The report referred to "principles . . . applying to the practice of applied anthropology as an addition to the anthropologist's own code of ethics [that] governs his behavior as a private individual, a citizen, and as a scientist in peace and in war." Rather than a clearly enunciated set of principles, the report emphasized the interrelatedness of the social institutions that anthropologists study and consideration of the effects of the work of anthropologists on the societies they study. The final paragraph reads:

> Applied anthropologists accept as a code of ethics: To advance those forms of human relationships [that] contribute to the integrity of the individual human being; to maintain scientific and professional integrity and responsibility without fear or favor to the limit of the foreseeable effects of their actions; to respect both human personality and cultural values; to publish and share new discoveries and methods with colleagues; those are the principles [that] should be accepted and [that] should be known to be accepted by all those who work in the disciplines affecting human relationships. (cited in Washburn 1998, 59)

The following is the first set of issues raised within the American Anthropological Association, found in the principles of professional responsibility, generated in 1971, around these recurrent themes:

1. Boas and social scientists as spies; intelligence-related research: 1919; 1967; 1970
2. Human Terrain System controversy: 2007–2009
3. Secret or clandestine research: 1967; 1968; 1990; 1998; removed in 1990 and restored in 2009
4. Appropriate relationship between anthropologist and government-intelligence research: 1967; 1971; 1990; 1998 (removed in 1998); (restored in 2009). General approval changed during the Vietnam War but was restored in 2009 with the caveat that "government work cannot compromise ethics" (American Anthropological Association 1998, II.c).

5. Responsibility to "people studied": 1971, paramount responsibility to the people studied; 1990, first responsibility is to "those whose lives and culture anthropologists study" retained; 1998, primary ethical obligation to "the people, species, and materials they study"; 2009, similar language, adding responsibility "is superior to seeking new knowledge," and specifies collaborative, reciprocal relations with the people, animals, and cultures studied

6. Responsibility to sponsors of research: 1971, sources of funding should be publicly communicated, and freedom of research should not be constrained; 1990, added responsibility to "clients and sponsors," with new reference to anthropologists working for government agencies and private business; 1998, researchers must be open with funders, colleagues, persons studied, and all parties affected by research; 2009, specified, but no reference to "sponsors" of research

7. Responsibility to public and science: 1971; 1990; 1998; 2009

The AAA's new professional code of ethics, "Principles of Professional Responsibility" (PPR), with its five new principles, published in 2009 more than four decades after the first code with the title, reflects the trend toward greater use of universal standards found in professional codes of ethics. The principle to "do no harm" and the practice of informed consent are part of every professional code of ethics, whether in the biomedical fields or in the social-behavioral sciences, including anthropology.

It is often surprising to new students of anthropology that statements on ethics, codes of ethics, and enunciations of principles came later to the profession than in the other social sciences. In Great Britain social anthropology developed as a relatively unself-conscious field closely tied to British colonialism. Classic designations in political anthropology, such as "acephalous" and "cephalous" societies, were created as analytical tools for use in colonial administration and indirect rule. French social anthropology during colonialism mirrored this reality, with neither expressing many substantive or critical reservations based on ethics or morality. In the wake of postcolonial independence of their former colonies, European intellectuals have taken up the multiple, complex legacies of colonialism and filled in the gaps left by the absence of the perspective of the ethnographic other during the decades of colonialism that lasted from the late nineteenth through the mid-twentieth centuries.

The first set of principles put forth a number of issues that have proved to be enduring. These include statements about secret or clandestine research leading to overarching concerns about the appropriate relationship between anthropologists and governments. Proper ethical relations with the people studied and with sponsors of research were also enunciated. Very little that is truly new has been said since the PPR first laid out this basic formula of responsibilities as seen in the latest version of the AAA code with the principles regarding harm, honesty and openness, informed consent, relationship with all parties affected by research, and public dissemination of research results.

COMPARABLE HISTORIES IN THE SOCIAL AND BEHAVIORAL SCIENCES: THE VALUE OF PERSPECTIVES FROM OTHER PROFESSIONS AND ASSOCIATIONS

There is no exceptional case for ethics in anthropology. Anthropology is part of the social sciences, and archaeology can be considered a branch of history, as biological anthropology may be viewed as a brand of human biology or medicine. As a complex discipline and profession with special methods and cross-cultural contexts, it is nonetheless part of science for which the rules of conduct and ethics apply. Fundamentally principles of ethics and of morality vary little by chosen field or practice. If anything, because of the lack of international oversight and rigorous and enforced standards of research conduct, anthropologists have been shielded from ethical accountability; this de facto reality is changing rapidly because of the internationalization of codes of conduct and the globalization of human-rights standards.

There is a perhaps unsurprising comparability between the history and content of discussions about ethics in the profession of sociology in the United States and that of the AAA. The more dramatic contrast exists with the American profession of psychology.

The American Psychological Association (APA) was founded in 1892 at Clark University at about the same time that Franz Boas founded the anthropology department at Clark University in 1889. For psychologists World War II proved transformational for the profession, in that it expanded dramatically from a membership of a few thousand to tens of thousands as the G.I. Bill trained many new professionals in clinical and abnormal psychology. The new National Institute of Mental Health expanded as well, along with new professional opportunities in public schools linked to testing.

The current membership of the APA hovers around 150,000, compared to the AAA's approximately ten thousand. The APA's first code of ethics was adopted in 1953 as "Ethical Standards of Psychologists." It was reviewed in 1977, and in 1979 it changed its name to "Ethical Principles of Psychologists" and then, at the time of its last revision in 1992, to "Ethical Principles of Psychologists and Code of Conduct." In 2010 its only amendment was issued in the substantive revision that the APA code of ethics could not be used to "justify or defend violations of human rights." This occurred in the context of allegations that professional psychologists may have been present at the interrogations of prisoners at Guantánamo and in the military prisons during the wars in Iraq and Afghanistan.

The APA code contains both "principles" and "standards," their basic structure for several decades. Since the AAA has just adopted the concept of principles over any prescriptive statements, it is worth reviewing the long-standing principles of the APA. These include: (1) beneficence, (2) fidelity and responsibility, (3) integrity, (4) justice, and (5) respect for people's rights and dignity. While the principles relate more to matters of morality, the APA standards are intended to address matters of professional responsibility. These include (1) resolving ethical issues; (2) competence, including discussion of the discipline's boundaries; (3) human relations; (4) privacy and confidentiality; (5) advertising and other public statements; (6) record keeping and fees; (7) education and training; (8) research and publication; (9) assessment; and (10) therapy (American Psychological Association 2013).

The American Sociological Association (ASA) was founded in 1905, and their first code of ethics was adopted during the same time period as that of the AAA, in 1970, and for the same motives. It was the unethical research methods of sociological researchers—notably a rather infamous surreptitious study of homosexuality in public restrooms coupled with the suggestion of the involvement of social scientists in the Vietnam War—that prompted the drafting of the code. It has been the rule that the ASA code should be reviewed and revised, if needed, every five years. They also have adopted principles: (1) professional competence; (2) integrity; (3) professional and scientific responsibility; (4) respect for people's rights, dignity, and diversity; and (5) social responsibility. What is noteworthy as a difference in outlook or emphasis is a specific injunction to "make sociological knowledge public and to serve the public good." The principle of professional and scientific responsibility contains the caveat that "while endeavoring to be collegial, this must never outweigh their shared responsibility for ethical behavior" (American Sociological Association 1999).

The ASA retained a complaint and grievance procedure for enforcement of its code of ethics through its Committee on Professional Ethics (COPE) with sanctions of withdrawal of privileges or termination of membership, although the whole process, including final determinations, are confidential.

The American Political Science Association began its exploration of professional ethics in 1967 at the same time as the other social sciences and in 1968 created a Standing Committee on Professional Ethics. At first envisioned as an educational body to protect the rights of political scientists, that first committee evolved into the Committee on Professional Ethics, Rights and Freedoms in 1989. Their latest *Guide to Professional Ethics in Political Science* (2012) enumerates ten principles of professional conduct, related more to education and relations with students, publication, and tenure and promotion than to field research. One brief section concerns research on human subjects, which references the federal Common Rule (effective as of 1991 and adopted by fifteen major federal agencies, including the NSF and the Department of Health and Human Services), in which "possible risk to human subjects is something that political scientists should take into account" (ASPSA Committee on Professional Ethics, Rights and Freedoms 2012).

INTERNATIONAL EXAMPLES

It is appropriate and reassuring that international discussions of ethics are parallel and reinforcing to the discourse about the ethics of social research in the United States (Caplan 2003). The Economic and Social Research Council (ESRC) of the United Kingdom has developed six principles and minimal requirements for the ethical conduct of research, with extensive explanation for the framework's implementation. A first "minimum requirement" is that ethics must be addressed in every proposal and that a complaints procedure is always in place. The framework acknowledges in its introduction that the research environment is "fast moving" and that new situations arise that cannot be covered in a single document. They suggest a "living document" for the framework, an excellent suggestion. The principle aim of ethics review (take note, those who think this may be no more than a formality or a hurdle to be jumped) is to "protect all groups involved in research: participants, institutions, funders, and researchers throughout the life of the research and into the dissemination process" (Economic and Social Research Council 2005).

The key principles of the ESRC code are comparable to those found in American-based professional associations in the social sciences: transparency, confidentiality, informing of research participants of the possible risks of the research, voluntary participation free of any coercion, avoidance of harm in all instances, independence of research free of any conflicts of interest (ibid.).

Canadian research agencies developed a heightened consciousness for work with its indigenous peoples, especially after the creation of the autonomous region of Nunavit. The shift of agency to control of research by the indigenous communities themselves is mirrored in a comparable agency that American Indians in the United States have adopted in their sovereign Tribal Research Boards that preserve their right to final review of all proposals to conduct research on tribal lands. These are discussed in detail in the chapters on informed consent and moral anthropology and ethics.

MAJOR ISSUES AND DEBATES IN THIS BOOK

Doing No Harm versus Avoiding Harm

The "do no harm" language is recent in American social-science ethics discourse, appearing for the first time in the AAA's 1998 code. The concept of harm has been a driving force in codes of ethics and in human-rights discourse. It is nearly impossible for an anthropologist or any social researcher to guarantee that no harm will come to people they study as a direct or indirect result of their research, activity, or publication of their work. Harm is a complex concept that has inadequately been explored in the discipline, and some argue that it may be subject to considerations of cultural relativism. Likewise, there is a difference between the principle to do no harm and the latest language used in the AAA code of ethics—to "avoid doing harm." Avoiding harm and doing no harm are different, as avoiding harm may also mean the prevention of harm or reduction of harm, whereas avoiding harm does not mean that *no* harm will result from the research or application of anthropology.

Doing No Harm versus Doing Some Good

What does the anthropologist or student preparing for research need to think about when consulting the code and applying the principle to do no harm in research? Which populations or segments of populations—vulnerable people, for example—need to be considered? The federal government took the lead in this area in 1979, sponsoring *The Belmont Report*, which recognized only the following vulnerable populations: "racial minorities, economically disadvantaged, the very sick. Given their dependent status and their frequently compromised capacity for free consent, they should be protected because as subjects they are easily manipulated" (The National Commission for the Protection of Human Subjects of Biomedical and Behavioral Research, Office of the Secretary 1979).

The vulnerable subjects that the Bioethics Advisory Commission's guidelines specify must have institutional-review-board (IRB) approval before research can be conducted are children, prisoners, pregnant women, the mentally disabled, or economically or educationally disadvantaged persons, all of whom thus require additional safeguards to be included in any study in order to protect their rights and welfare.

Anthropologists have a broader range of "subjects" to consider when the "do no harm" standard is addressed in their research, both for its cross-cultural and international reach but also for the primary method of participant observation that the discipline employs. Vulnerable populations may include indigenous peoples in the United States and around the globe; all women and girls in highly patriarchal societies with specific human-rights considerations of domestic and family violence; cultures practicing "female circumcision"; or a host of persons in other states of vulnerability—such as those living in Sudan's Internally Displaced Camps, where I have conducted research, and whose rights as "research subjects" have been as diminished as nearly every other basic human right. Vulnerability will be addressed in detail as a special subject for anthropologists in chapter 3 on informed consent.

Another major issue when considering harm in research is the canon of cultural relativism in anthropology. As the experts on the subject, anthropologists should be at the forefront of the discussion of what is harm, offering the multiple perspectives of cultural difference and similarity that can be documented. Are culturally normative customs that result in harm—such as various forms of female circumcision or culturally acceptable forms of homicide—less harmful or morally acceptable? Philosophers have debated the issue and have mainly decided the issue in terms of assertions of universal rights of humanity that do not and cannot sanction any predictable harm being carried out under the general justification of cultural norms. American law has not looked with favor on "the cultural defense" in cases involving harm to persons. It is my view that these gaps can be bridged through constructive dialogue with professions that treat the subject of harm most seriously—medicine and law—and that intercultural conversations and negotiations can also be productively carried out using the unique cultural perspectives of the anthropologist.

Informed Consent in Anthropological Research as a Process

Initial resistance by anthropologists to the informed-consent forms required by IRBs has given way not only to acceptance of the required protocols but also to an active engagement with what it means to "do anthropology" and how to best apply informed-consent standards to the occasionally unique populations that we study. The discourse on informed consent has extended to recognized vulnerable populations, such as indigenous peoples; ethnic, racial, gender, class, and other social and political minorities; and victims of human-rights abuses.

Informed Consent without Forms or Formalism: Issues of Legal-Ethical Accountability

One of the first hurdles to be overcome was obtaining informed consent without the necessity of using signed forms, as some anthropologists work with nonliterate or illiterate populations, in a variety of global settings and in the United States. I argued in 1994 that informed consent in anthropological research can and perhaps even should be obtained without the use of the legalistic forms that have dominated the application of the doctrine in the United States. Indeed, a primary reason for the previous rejection of informed consent in anthropology was the standard requirement of proof of consent through the use of such forms. Clearly the forms do not ensure harm prevention. For example, it was alleged that the use of informed-consent forms by some American biomedical researchers studying AIDS vaccines in Haiti in the late 1990s may have created a legal carte blanche whereby researchers were fully protected without sufficient accountability while the vulnerable research population was placed at risk. The informed-consent form did not mention why the study was being conducted, nor were the participants apprised of the potential risks (Fluehr-Lobban 2000b, 41–42).

GLOBALIZATION OF RESEARCH

In the current globalized world, is it possible to speak only for and to national groups of anthropologists? Clearly not. We have become a globalized profession by virtue of a common discipline and a transformed context of research in the international arena. But can we speak to all anthropologists and not just American anthropologists? *Should not global research be met by global ethics* or a vigorous discussion and debate of what our universal standards of ethical conduct are? Would American anthropologists in the current climate of research, framed today by matters of national security and the Global War on Terror, freely enter into and participate in such a global debate? Would European anthropologists, who have resisted what are perceived to be litigious American codes of ethics (Pels 1999), embrace a global discourse on professional ethics? Have non-Western anthropologists achieved agency in the international discourse of ethics and professionalism, or is this yet another piece of the unfinished business of colonialism and its fallout? These are all questions worthy of broader discussion—in the classroom, on the Internet, and in professional meetings.

Anthropologists have engaged with the discourse on global human rights and have helped to shape emerging standards and how they might impact anthropological research. But this discourse has not reached any consensus in anthropology as to what, if any, global standards exist in our culturally relative worldview. I have argued that human-rights advocacy is a moral choice but not an ethical imperative (Fluehr-Lobban 2006a). Other professions have attempted to reach this sort of consensus, such as The American Psychological Association Presidential Task Force on Psychological Ethics and National Security (2005), and they could not reach any consensus on what constitute universal human-rights standards and, thus, their role in their code of ethics. Lacking national—not to mention global—consensus on matters of professionalism and ethics in the current era of globalization and professional ethics means that anthropologists must first and foremost be educated about the complex realities of global research and be prepared to negotiate resulting ethical responsibilities and competing interests among local, national, and global forces. This is much easier said than done and requires continuous consideration of the implications of all acts of research and their local and global responses.

PROFESSIONALISM: WHO IS AN ANTHROPOLOGIST? WHAT IS ANTHROPOLOGICAL RESEARCH?

Neither the umbrella organization of the AAA nor any of the professional cultural, archaeological, or biological anthropological associations are licensing associations; thus alleged misconduct cannot be sanctioned by loss of a license to practice. This reality has shaped the education model for the various codes of ethics that have been constructed. And thus the associations are structurally often unable to make definitive statements about the ethical conduct of anthropologists. The exception to this general rule was the case of the Human Terrain System, in which participation by anthropologists was judged to be unethical in formal statements by the AAA in 2007 and 2009. This is discussed in depth in chapter 5's discussion of moral anthropology— and, by extension, judgments regarding immoral anthropology. The major professional associations of anthropologists are constitutionally unable to sanction anthropologists alleged to be engaging in acts that result in harm or abuse to the people studied, or any alleged misconduct. Lacking any formal licensing process, other than professional degrees of practitioners and the informal sanctioning by relatively small segments of a professional community, the ethical environment is relegated to education, guiding principles for study, and occasional admonition for alleged wrongdoing.

What boundaries exist between what is and what is not anthropological or between who is and who is not an anthropologist? This question has not been answered by professional associations of anthropologists. As has been debated in other social-science disciplines, such as psychology—where a distinction has been drawn between professional psychologists and counselors—the definition of who is a professional anthropologist and by which standards, ethical or professional, she or he is bound is in need of discussion and debate. In other professions, drawing on more stringent medical-biological models of ethics, such as in the medical fields, professional conduct and standards are defined and enforced to the extent that professionals are required to report misconduct.

So what anthropology is and who anthropologists are, are addressed in chapter 7. Is anthropological training sufficient to convey anthropological credentials, and at what level of education—bachelor's degree, master's, or

Ph.D.? Are all persons holding degrees in anthropology anthropologists? When persons holding degrees in anthropology are employed as anthropologists, is this sufficient? Are persons who hold anthropology degrees and work in national security or in the Global War on Terror, and may or may not have been hired specifically as anthropologists, anthropologists or defense and intelligence workers? The *Report of the American Psychological Association Presidential Task Force on Psychological Ethics and National Security* affirms that "when psychologists serve in any position by virtue of their training, experience, and expertise as psychologists, the Ethics Code of the American Psychological Association (APA) applies" and therefore they are professionals (The American Psychological Association Presidential Task Force on Psychological Ethics and National Security 2005, pt. 1).

It has been argued that anthropologists become "dual professionals" when they are both professional anthropologists as well as soldiers, intelligence officers, or government bureaucrats (Selmeski 2008). Anthropologists may be acting as dual professionals when they apply their expertise to asylum cases in a personal decision to become advocates—that this is a moral choice, not an ethical responsibility—or are employed as cultural experts by governments. As with the arena of human rights, there are few moral universals, and anthropologists may see themselves as acting in an equally moral way when they apply their expertise to national security and intelligence as to issues of gender, race, or class inequities in the Third World.

Secret-Clandestine Research

Philosopher George Lucas aptly describes anthropology's "misguided if not pathological obsession with secrecy" (2009, 179). It is a key component of his "litany of shame" in which anthropologists tell the story of professional ethics. It begins in 1918 with Franz Boas—when it is conveniently forgotten that he had been censured by the Washington Anthropological Society, the precursor of the AAA professional association. Boas opened the debate about anthropologists using the profession and its credentials as a cover for spying, as information had come to his attention in the context of World War I. Boas's censure was only rescinded in 2005 through a resolution introduced and approved by the AAA membership. The association had structurally disempowered itself in 1998 from censuring any anthropologist for any reason, having removed the "Grievance Procedure" from its code of ethics in 1998, substituting it with an education mandate.

The 1971 PPR was clear about "no secret research" and warned against anthropologists working for any government, one's own or that of the fieldwork site. A significant index of changing times is that the AAA's 1998 code of ethics was silent on the issue of secret research but stated that "anthropological researchers must be open about the purpose(s), potential impact(s), and source(s) of support for research projects with funders, colleagues, persons studied or providing information, and with relevant parties affected by the research. Further, researchers should disseminate their findings in timely and appropriate ways" (American Anthropological Association 1998). In the current context of American wars in Afghanistan and Iraq and the Global War on Terror, debates about anthropologists working with or for national-security agencies and the issue of "secret research" has resurfaced. These issues were investigated and scrutinized by the two ad hoc AAA Commissions on the Engagement of Anthropology with the U.S. Security and Intelligence Communities, 2007–2009. The commissions were charged with providing information and/or recommendations on the following:

1. varied roles practitioners and scholars are playing in intelligence and national-security agencies
2. the state of AAA's existing guidelines providing guidance on such involvement
3. the key ethical, methodological, and practical/political challenges faced by anthropology in current and future engagement (Nuti 2006)

The two final reports of these commissions are discussed in chapter 2's discussion of military anthropology. Anthropologists engaging in national-security research where secrecy is a condition of work are no different from anthropologists working in a traditional ethnographic context where secrecy is demanded by the people studied, such as the study of "secret societies."

COLLABORATIVE RESEARCH: A SHIFT FROM RESEARCH "SUBJECTS" TO "PARTICIPANTS"

As mentioned in chapter 5, participatory-collaborative research is acknowledged as having been derived from feminist research that developed modified, or nonhierarchical, methods for their research. The premises for this approach to research include consultation with and incorporation of the research population into the research design, methodology, and outcomes of research. Some following this method do not publish their work until it has been read and critiqued by the research participants. Taken to its logical end, the lines between researcher and researched are ideally minimized. This significant shift is worthy of its own chapter in this book and is treated more fully in chapter 5.

The debate in anthropology over accountability for ethical research methods moved from an initial grievance/censure model, adopted in 1971 in the heated period of the Vietnam War, to an "education mandate." This move to replace the "stick" with the "carrot" offered a model whereby the code of ethics itself was to be taught, debated, and modified, if necessary, through a vigorous discourse in undergraduate and graduate education and among AAA professionals. It is an understatement to relate that the promise of the education mandate has not been fulfilled in the years since the code was ratified in 1998. It is still true that few programs of anthropology have systematic training in ethics and that the old maxim remains true that anthropological ethics gain attention in their breach. The most recent best/worst case proving the point was the allegation of wrongdoing by anthropologist Napoleon Chagnon and geneticist James Neel for their decades of research among the Yąnomami made by Patrick Tierney in his 2000 book *Darkness in El Dorado: How Scientists and Journalists Devastated the Amazon* (1). At such times, and only at such times, are the conference halls filled with eager "students" of ethics. And the discourse is reactive, personal, and often far from the principles of professional practice that need to be addressed in these "teachable moments."

In the context of the current wars in Iraq and Afghanistan, the debate over the grievance/censure-education models has reignited.

QUESTIONS FOR DISCUSSION

1. Does a four-field ethics code still make sense for the increasingly specialized discipline and profession of anthropology?
2. What can anthropologists learn from the codes of ethics of other disciplines?
3. Should professional anthropology associations restore or initiate a grievance model for their codes of ethics?

Chapter Two

What Does It Mean to "Do No Harm"?

DO NO HARM: COMPLEXITIES OF ETHICS FOR ANTHROPOLOGISTS

"Do no harm" is the gold standard of professional ethics, descending from the oft-cited physicians' ethical mantra to "first, do no harm," in Latin *primum non nocere.* The "do no harm" admonition is drawn from biomedical ethics and was first enunciated in the 1847 work *Physician and Patient* by Worthington Hooker. Do no harm has been interpreted as beneficence or nonmalfeasance, meaning that it may be better to do nothing than to risk creating a situation where more harm than good might take place.

The "do no harm" principle is the first one enunciated in the latest AAA principles, adopted in 2009. It is described as a primary ethical obligation to avoid doing harm to the "lives, communities, or environments they study or may be impacted by their work" (American Anthropological Association 2009, A.1). Not only is harm to be avoided, but the principle also implies an obligation to weigh carefully the consequences and impacts of researcher work on others. Moreover, the significance of this obligation can mean that research that is uncertain about compliance with the intent of the "do no harm" principle may result in a decision to not undertake the research or to discontinue it in consequence.

WHAT IS HARM?

Harm has not been defined in anthropology, nor has it been adequately defined in the allied social and behavioral sciences. Should anthropologists try to formulate a universal, culture-free definition of harm? Anthropologists work in cross-cultural gray areas of absolute rights and wrongs, and harm is inevitably judged as right or wrong by culturally differentiated moral systems.

Harm is mostly about morality. Anthropologists grapple with ethical dilemmas and take responsibility for the inevitable ambiguities that characterize their research, but ideas about harm dwell in the realm of morality and in culturally based ideas of right and wrong. If, however, a transcultural definition of harm is to be developed in the social sciences, of all the disciplines anthropology is the right one to ask the questions about its relativist or universal conception and meaning. Human-rights organizations have little difficulty with the question of harm, especially after Western consciousness was changed in the wake of the Holocaust of the Second World War. A universalist view would state that all humans possess the same human rights as a matter of natural law, while a relativist view would add that harm is subject to cultural interpretation and what the "reasonable person" in a society would judge as harmful.

The general principles of biomedical ethics, where the "do no harm" principle originated and continues to predominate, include (1) respect for autonomy, (2) beneficence, (3) nonmalfeasance, and (4) justice. Beneficence and nonmalfeasance are the obvious expressions of the avoidance of doing harm in biomedical research. Respect for autonomy and justice speak to the social dimensions of research and the avoidance of doing harm built on an open and transparent methodology. Philosopher Bernard Gert defined morality as "an informal public system applying to all rational persons governing behavior that affects others and includes the moral rules, ideals, and virtues and has the lessening of evil or harm as its goal (2004, 137–39).[1]

A major theme in anthropology codes has been that the first obligation of the anthropologist is to the "people studied," implying that harm prevention or avoidance is a major concern (American Anthropological Association 1971). Subsequent discussion of this 1971 first principle complicated this basic theme and led to enunciation of ethical obligations to clients or those who employ anthropologists, and to the profession.

Harm is a complex concept, and doing no harm and avoiding harm are different. *Avoiding harm* means the prevention or reduction of harm but does not mean that *no* harm will ever result from research or the application of anthropology. Would all anthropologists or their research participants agree what harm is? This is unlikely, making its discussion—where there is agreement and where there is disagreement—fruitful. What does the anthropologist or student reading the "avoid harm" section of the code need to think about when applying this principle in research? Does harm prevention apply to healthy adult populations or mainly to the many categories of vulnerable populations common in federal regulations—women, children, the sick, and others?

Increasing well-being may be a better general guide in research, but then the accusation of anthropology becoming a branch of international social work can be levied. Gert argues that *"moral judgments can only be made about those who know what kind of behavior morality prohibits, requires, discourages, encourages, and allows.* Harm is, thus, a central moral concept and is what rational creatures seek to avoid in their common human concerns with death, pain, disability, loss of freedom, and loss of pleasure. 'Common' morality is far more concerned with prohibiting or discouraging evil/harm than with requiring people to enhance good or benefits" (2004, introduction).

There is a difference between harm and wrongdoing. Harm can often result from well-meaning acts and unanticipated consequences. Moreover, degrees of harm can be debated by anthropologists, and harm mitigation and amelioration is increasingly addressed in disciplinary practice. There are difficult cases to negotiate that are discussed in this chapter that include conflicting ideas of *good*. A well-known case involves an anthropologist's knowledge of the danger of leaded pottery in Oaxaca where the principle of trust and secrecy within the community about the content and method of their valued pottery conflicted with the moral choice of the clear harm of lead poisoning to the health of the community. Or in Sudan, the intention of lessening harm included documentation by NGO workers of the systematic rape of Darfur women and anthropologists who aided them. This documentation in some cases resulted in greater harm to victims when the publicly known victims were blamed and shamed for their loose morals. Female circumcision or "female genital mutilation" is discussed in this chapter as a complex cultural terrain for the assessment of harm, to girls as well as women, for which anthropology can be of great assistance in the analysis of changing moral and cultural norms. In the end, the greatest sensitivity and skill is required to negotiate such complex ethical-moral terrain. An example that students and American readers can relate to is the "right to life"/abortion conflict in the United States, where individuals from different moral and ethical positions can and do disagree, sometimes respectfully, at other times angrily and violently. The ethically conscious anthropologist engages respectfully with local normative beliefs while practicing her or his craft and makes personal decisions regarding his or her own life.

PRIMARY AND SECONDARY HARM

I propose a distinction between primary and secondary harm. *Primary harm* is that which affects the people studied—including both direct traditional-fieldwork projects and those removed from direct-fieldwork contact. Primary harm results when a researcher intentionally deceives the people studied about the real intent of research—for example, taking blood samples from an indigenous people for pharmacological or cell line sale and use when the research was explained as a kinship and ancestry study. *Secondary harm* relates to harm done to professionals, in this instance anthropologists. Alleging harm to the scholarly or personal reputation of an anthropologist accused of professional or fieldwork-related misconduct is one example of a secondary harm. In a moral system for anthropology, primary harm is that to which anthropologists first turn in consideration of the consequences of engagement with the people studied. Secondary harm addresses the professional standing of an anthropologist who, for example, placed herself at odds with a powerful agent that impeded or halted her research or applied project for its own motives.

The first AAA ethical code stated that anthropologists' "paramount responsibility is to those they study" (American Anthropological Association 1971, 1). A consistent feature of anthropologists' codes of ethics is that professionals bear responsibility for the integrity and good reputation of the discipline (American Anthropological Association 1971, PPR 3; American Anthropological Association 1998, B.2). As anthropologists grapple with defense and intelligence engagement, this primary responsibility to the people studied may help to clarify both professional ethics and common morality. Anthropologists could assert that *primary harm* is that which affects the people studied, including projects removed from direct-fieldwork contact, and that *secondary harm* addresses harm to anthropological professionals. It would be to the primary harm to the people studied or affected by research or application of anthropology that anthropologists would first turn to in consideration of the consequences of any engagement. Attention would be drawn to vulnerable populations not specifically mentioned in any anthropological code of ethics, such as those most affected by war and chronic conflict, refugees (primarily women and children), internally displaced persons, and victims of human-rights violations, as well as their defenders, and indigenous peoples who may or may not be officially protected by their governments.

Attempting to prevent or lessen harm by acting on behalf of the people they study is ethical for anthropologists and is likely to be unquestioned if requested by the people themselves through informed consent. Advocating on behalf of the people studied *without* their consultation risks being paternalistic, or maternalistic, as a majority of anthropologists are women. I have argued that such advocacy is a moral choice but *not* an ethical responsibility (Fluehr-Lobban 2006a). The present AAA code reflects that "anthropologists may choose to move beyond disseminating research results to a position of advocacy is a choice. This is an individual decision but not an ethical responsibility" (American Anthropological Association 2009, C.3).

Respecting the autonomy of people studied, including their right to *not* be studied or to not be the subject of certain research—such as recruitment of religious militants or counterinsurgents—must be respected in the ethical conduct of research. Acknowledging this right may lead to a decision to not engage or not research particular topics, meaning that the anthropologist gives up freedom in research for the greater good of the paramount responsibility to the people studied. Violations of this core principle would be an example of a primary harm.

Secondary harm to professionals in a moral system for anthropology addresses the professional standing of an anthropologist who, for example, placed herself at odds with a powerful agent that impeded or halted her research or applied project for its own motives. Often the dominant consideration of the major ethical controversies in anthropology have involved secondary harm to anthropological professionals, the anthropologists allegedly involved with counterinsurgency research in Camelot and Vietnam, and the anthropologist centrally involved in the *Darkness in El Dorado* and his supporters who focused on harm to the anthropologist over the Yanomami.

Do Less Harm: Avoidance of Harm, a Key Standard

Philosophers have been most active in an exploration of the meaning of harm while anthropologists have not attempted to resolve the question of a universal definition of harm. As mentioned, one definition of harm focuses on an act by one human upon another resulting in death, pain, disability, loss of freedom, or pleasure (Gert 1988, 47–49). How this Western-derived definition of harm can be applied in the myriad cultures across the globe that anthropologists study is challenging at the very least and thus far has not been attempted. It is possible—though not specifically researched or demonstrated cross-culturally—that most humans would agree that death, pain, and disability are rejected or to be avoided. "Loss of freedom or pleasure" is more problematic, as ideas of freedom and pleasure are highly culturally variable.

Philosopher John Rawls enunciated a number of "natural duties" for all humans that extend beyond "do no harm" to what might be described as "do some good." His duties include a duty to "not be cruel; to help one another; to practice justice; and to abide by a duty of mutual respect" (Herman 2000). By these philosophical considerations anthropologists should not only avoid harm as professionals but also practice justice.

An Anthropological Definition of *Harm*

What would constitute a working definition of harm for anthropological purposes? Ethnographically, the answer would be *whatever a particular culture defines as a harmful act*. However, defining harm in a way that is cross-culturally valid is not easy. Body tattooing is accepted in Western and Polynesian cultures but forbidden in Islamic culture. Ideologically, harm would be defined by the cultural prescriptions of acceptable and unacceptable death, pain, or disability—backed by human and supernatural (religious) sanctions. Many cultures inflict pain as part of initiation rites or rites of passage. Disability, in the form of religiously sanctioned amputations, is an accepted part of legal interpretations of Islamic criminal law.

When a code of ethics asks professionals to do no harm, it can be asked, How can harm be operationally defined in both theory and practice in order to make this a useful principle? For anthropologists the theory should be culturally responsive and the practice ideally one that applies principle to practice and utilizes a method of consultation with research participants and colleagues for consideration of ethical options and, ultimately, decision making.

Since the absolutism inherent in the admonition to do no harm is both idealistic and unrealistic, it is better to explore meaning and the applications of harm to the anthropological experience. A moral interpretation of doing no harm would concentrate on avoidance of harm to the most vulnerable segments of the population—for example, women, children, the aged, or targeted ethnic minorities. The application of specialized cultural knowledge that anthropologists possess is an obvious means of avoiding harm. But avoidance of harm for whom? For which individuals or groups, for what intended purpose(s), is this knowledge deployed?

The complexities of harm in a variety of culturally relative contexts are in the early stages of discussion by anthropologists, led by concerns with universal human rights. An entire spectrum of harmful human practices—from culturally legitimated homicide, to domestic and family violence, to female circumcision, and more—can be profitably debated. A line of distinction has been drawn between anthropologists who see human-rights advocacy as a moral and professional responsibility (Turner's and Graham's chapters of Goodale 2009) and those who see such advocacy as a moral choice but not an ethical obligation (Fluehr-Lobban's and Cowan's chapters of Goodale 2009). At this point the space between obligation and choice is not viewed as a case of moral right and wrong but, rather, more a matter of reasonable persons who happen to be anthropologists disagreeing. Anthropologists have asserted, but not debated sufficiently, "good" or "bad" cultural practices and the appropriate interventions that might be advocated or applied. By contrast, human-rights advocacy groups have made clear moral choices. Western feminist campaigns unilaterally label *female genital mutilation* (FGM) what anthropologists and indigenous communities have referred to as *female circumcision*. FGM has become a legal ground for female asylum seekers in U.S. courts, a move clearly intended to reduce harm.

All manner of government and nongovernment organizations have been called to account for their actions and use of anthropological information. The potential for harm resulting has been most often raised for government contractors. The case of an emerging "military anthropology" has been the most problematical. Might it be asserted, for example, that the only moral and ethical engagement for anthropologists working in military applications is to work with or for projects and missions whose intent is to reduce, ameliorate, or prevent harm or further harm?

Research Post–September 11, 2001, and Do No Harm

In the context of the Global War on Terror, what does it mean in practice to avoid harm or wrong? Fear and suspicion arose that anthropologists may have played a part in the "intensive interrogation" or torture of suspected terrorists. Heated public debates of right and wrong followed, where American security interests were threatened. The war in Iraq, launched in response to false accusations of weapons of mass destruction, and the arrest, detention, and torture of Iraqi prisoners at Abu Ghraib prison were emotionally debated in the United States.

The revelation by Seymour Hersh that *The Arab Mind*, written by Israeli anthropologist Raphael Patai, was the source for cultural information in interrogation at Abu Ghraib caused some anthropologists to reflect on the potential dire consequences of their research and publications. Documented acts of cultural humiliation, such as forcing detainees to wear women's underwear or to simulate homosexual acts (Greenberg and Dratel 2005), suggested a cultural menu drawn from sources like Patai's, where sexual honor and shame was a centerpiece of his analysis. It is a well-understood fact that anthropologists, along with every other social scientist or writer, have little to no control over how their writings are applied in social engineering or policy decisions. But in this case it was the journalists who took the lead—as was the case with the *Darkness in El Dorado* controversy. It was revelations by Seymour Hersh in the *New Yorker Magazine* that *The Arab Mind* was a major source for cultural knowledge in the use of tactics and interrogation at Abu Ghraib (Hersh 2004, 1). The AAA's *Anthropology News* appropriately solicited comment, but those who responded focused on the general silence of the social-science community. Floyd Rudmin (2004) argued that part of the "do no harm" admonition calls on researchers to anticipate that their findings might be abused and take effective steps to prevent or stop the abuse. What those steps would be is unclear, as published works are in the public domain and not subject to control of their use. Rudmin further argued that professional codes of ethics override demands of employers to perform unethical acts. As it turned out, no direct anthropological connection was disclosed to the allegations of participation in torture.

Can an anthropologist working as a military contractor or subcontractor as part of an intelligence team be assured that her research will do no harm? Moreover, where is the locus, or loci, of responsibility in the room of interrogation or in the defense-strategy meeting? Is it distributed among several or all of the consultants resulting in a dispersal of responsibility effectively amounting to nonaccountability? It is troubling that anthropology and anthropologists did not participate in this public debate perhaps because there was no "smoking gun" for anthropological involvement. It fell to the later AAA condemnation of the Human Terrain System (HTS) to oppose the misuse or abuse of anthropology in the Global War on Terror.

The world changed after September 11, 2001, and certainly the research climate was affected, especially for Muslims in America and around the world and those anthropologists who study these people, myself included. Trust is a critical component of the relationship that anthropologists develop with their "informants"—intentionally using this old referent for information providers because of its double meaning for both intelligence and anthropology. Fearful of the anti-Muslim climate that might develop, some Muslim communities closed ranks while others—especially American-born Muslims—sought to educate their fellow Americans about the real Islam and dispel the stereotype that it is a violent and aggressive religion. Some commentators made good use of anthropological perspectives to sort out "good Muslims" from "bad Muslims" (Mamdani 2007). To the credit of the American people and the strength of the doctrine of religious freedom on which the country was established, the climate of hate that many feared would take hold or become rampant did not, less a few well-publicized controversies—for example, over the construction of a mosque at Ground Zero.

Now, more than a decade after the traumatic events of 2001, two wars having been waged in its wake, the atmosphere can still be intensely political and emotional and fewer anthropologists have ventured into this charged arena to carry out studies of Islam and Muslims abroad or at home. It may not be too far-reaching to suggest that the environment of research has been fundamentally altered and that loss of trust is its primary victim. But when so much harm was inflicted and suffered in the decade since 9/11, could it be otherwise?

I have written about my own case studying Shari'a and Islamism (politicized Islam) in Sudan (Fluehr-Lobban 2012), when I entered a transformed research environment after fifteen years' absence due to the extremes of Islamism that were prevailing. Despite the previous decades I had devoted to conducting research in that country, when I returned I was coming from America, which was alleged to be anti-Islamic, and thus I was someone potentially not to be trusted. I wrote about the challenge of research in this environment:

> Among entrenched Islamist functionaries with whom I was not previously acquainted I was held with a mixture of curiosity, suspicion, and mistrust.

Whereas in the past access to courts and observation of cases was open without formal permission, during this period of research such access required written permission or high-level verbal approval. In one case I was admonished by a high-level administrator in the judiciary about the "agendas" of Westerners—whom he presumed to be human-rights investigators—coming to Sudan and documenting their version of the "truth" irrespective of the facts. In some cases barriers and difficulties were erected such that permission to observe court sessions was effectively denied. (Introduction)

At the core of the loss of trust and its restoration is the "do no harm" imperative. Although anthropological researchers do not perceive themselves to be powerful, they do most often come from powerful countries, and that "baggage" is not light. And, of course, the question of harm to whom is raised. Were I capable of inflicting harm on the ruling circle of military Islamists, would I have been less guilty than had I inflicted harm on any of the ordinary people with whom I continuously interacted? This matter ties in well with chapter 4's discussion of openness and transparency in research. When the research goals, funding, methodology, and findings are openly shared with research participants and the cards are plainly laid on the table, so to speak, informants or subjects are able to make their own personal decisions about collaborating or not with the research as it is carried out. This happened to me so many times in the post–9/11 context of research that recounting each would be difficult. Suffice it to say that the research population in Sudan was literate, global, connected to the Internet, and sophisticated about the politics of research and many of the most sophisticated were women with clear personal agency. The terms and limits of research were often laid out in a first interview—"I can talk about this, but not that" or "You need to talk to so-and-so for that information," or "This conversation is not for quoting me personally." And in my search for data, for example, on the number of limb amputations carried out in the country during the height of the initial Islamist surge from 1983 to 1985, the response "that data is not available" said it all.

Harm Amelioration Using Cultural Knowledge

A growing emphasis on the obligation to consider the well-being of civilian casualties in modern warfare using cultural knowledge of indigenous payments for loss of life and limb has become an accepted part of the wars in Iraq and Afghanistan. The payment of blood money (*dia*) as compensation for harm and loss has become a regular feature of the counterterrorism and counterinsurgency military operations in these Muslim countries where remote-warfare technology has replaced traditional warfare and where harm to civilian noncombatants has become a part of these twenty-first-century wars. New drone weapon-delivery technology increases the chances of civilian casualties and confounds ethical decision making and responsibility as the human is removed from direct combat and the intimate experience of warfare. In these cases the United States has a strategic, and inevitably ethical, desire to ameliorate harm from its military operations that relies on the local cultural tradition of the payment of *dia*, monetary compensation in Islamic law, for loss of life and disability. However, minimizing harm to civilians caused by drone strikes requires lifting the veil of secrecy that shrouds the CIA-led drone program (Holewinski 2013, 20). This is a complex, evolving area of military ethics.

DO NO HARM IN ARCHAEOLOGY

Harm prevention or amelioration in archaeology mainly focuses on the preservation, protection, and proper care of material cultural heritage. Museums are the centerpiece of this ethical arena and provenance—the legal acquisition of antiquities—as the central question of ethical conduct. Because there is often a high market value attached to antiquities, especially from the classical civilizations of the Middle East, Europe, Asia, and Central and South America, an often-elaborate illicit trade has developed. There is hardly a major world museum that has not had controversy or been involved on both the ethical and unethical sides of the antiquities trade. Added to this is the postcolonial increased demand for the return or repatriation of objects historically taken from colonized areas by their colonizers or by agents under their protection, considered looted or stolen by indigenous authorities. Some of the more famous examples include the Elgin Marbles (Parthenon) removed from Greece by Great Britain and on prominent display at the British Museum, as well as some of the most famous of Egyptian treasures, the bust of Nefertiti at the Berlin Egyptian Museum and the Rosetta Stone at the British Museum, acquired by Great Britain after it defeated the French for control of Egypt in 1803. U.S. museums have a greater percentage of Mesoamerican antiquities that have also received requests for the repatriation of objects of national cultural heritage. A few items have been repatriated, but for the most part museums involved with such high-visibility objects have taken the position that they are the lawful owners of the objects. In other cases of "less-valuable" objects, museums have entered into partnership and sharing agreements with national entities seeking repatriation of the museum object.

The sale of most antiquities is legal, but the illegal trade (also known as the black market) is of ethical concern. Artifacts are often transported from an illegal source through a middleman, generally unsuspecting (or knowing) collectors, and museum and antique dealers. There has been a call to dry up the demand that fuels the illegal sales along with the trend to repatriate artifacts thus traded. The harm to nations' cultural heritages caused by the international illegal trade in antiquities unfortunately continues and is apparently difficult to eradicate despite considerable effort by global policing. The most dramatic recent case of looting took place during the conquest of Baghdad in the early weeks of the American war in Iraq. Prewar plans for protection of Iraq's World Heritage Mesopotamian sites were not fully carried out, and, specifically, the Baghdad Museum was not protected during the early days of the Iraq War. On April 8, 2003, inadequate preparation left the front and rear entries of the museum unprotected. Looters, apparently thieves with specific shopping lists, descended between April 10 and 12, taking among of the museum's most famous objects, such as the Sumerian Ur "golden harp" and the "princess's gold diadem." According to museum officials, over 3,100 jars, vessels, and pots were stolen. A subsequent attempt by looters was curtailed and an investigation launched by a special U.S. team headed by Marine Col. Matthew Bogdanos. The inquiry concluded that, although no U.S. forces had engaged in looting, there were three separate thefts over four days. Of some of the fifteen thousand objects stolen, only about a third have been returned, including some but not all of the most treasured objects. U.S. Customs recovered the largest percentage. The rest remain in that underground marketplace where middlemen and dealers buy and sell the antiquities that eventually end up in the world's great museums or private collections where the tale of their acquisition is rarely if ever told. When a museum visitor sees the phrase "Provenance unknown" on a display placard, it is a good bet that the object was acquired in at least partially illicit trade.

In 2010 Google created a virtual copy of the Baghdad Museum's collections, called the Virtual Museum of Iraq. The museum did not reopen until November 2011. In 2012 an estimated ten to twelve thousand items were still missing, according to museum director Amira Euidan, about forty to fifty of which are of the greatest historical importance according to UNESCO, the global monitor of world heritage since its 1970s Convention on Antiquities. The United States has no comprehensive agreement but separate ones, which ban sales of antiquities from Canada to Central America and Europe.

Patriotism and everyday ethics of the Egyptian multitudes were on display at Cairo's Tahrir square during the fall of the Mubarak regime: Despite days of lawlessness, the Egyptian National Museum, located in the middle of the square, was nonetheless protected. Even attempts by looters to enter the museum through the roof were thwarted, and all but a few were kept from entering the museum. As related by a friend who was an official at the museum at the time, the would-be thieves were amateurs, heading for the museum gift shop before being ejected.

Looters take advantage of wartime and social chaos. It is alleged that the ongoing Syrian civil war is funded in part by sales of antiquities and that smugglers and antiquities dealers were active in Lebanon as well. All of Syria's seven World Heritage sites and countless museums have been looted or damaged by the civil war. The Hague Convention for the Protection of Cultural Property in the Event of Armed Conflict is at best well-meaning, but the opportunity that conflict presents and the ill-gotten gains to be made are sufficient to keep this underground trade alive.

Military Anthropology and Harm Reduction

Today a subfield slowly emerges that was unthinkable before September 11, 2001. Anathema to the discipline and largely a legacy of the Vietnam War era for the alleged "secret and clandestine" research that working for the military meant, anthropologists had long averred employment with the military. However, with the acknowledged importance and relevance of cultural interventions in counterinsurgency and in conventional military operations in Iraq and Afghanistan, the demand for cultural knowledge has grown, especially after some embarrassing and harmful errors in these war and conflict zones. Serious cultural misjudgments occurred early in the Iraq War involving female modesty at security checkpoints and misinterpretations of religious elements, such as believing the dawn call to prayer was a battle cry, a story related to me by a student and former Marine deployed during the early days of the U.S. siege of Baghdad. Most of these costly and even deadly basic errors have subsequently been addressed with the application of cultural and anthropological knowledge—the use of female security personnel in the former case or basic education in the Muslim religion in the latter. The value of social science in reducing harm in these military settings was aided by the endorsement of General David Petraeus, who holds a Ph.D. in political science and has command experience in both war zones, and the activism of anthropologist Montgomery McFate, who advised the counterinsurgency program.

American anthropologists Rebecca Goolsby (2012), Paula Holmes-Eber (2008 with Barak K. Salmoni), Robert Rubinstein (2012), and others have pioneered in this field. The lead anthropologist in the promotion of social-network analysis, Goolsby laid the basis for government funding of research in conflict reduction. My husband, Richard Lobban, was the recipient and principal investigator for a multiyear research grant on conflict reduction in Sudan, funded by the U.S. Office of Naval Research. The sole purpose of the research is analysis of the root causes of chronic conflict in Sudan—a country that experienced twenty-two years of civil war ending in separation into two nations—as well as analysis of the allegations of genocide in Darfur and the estimated two million deaths resulting from these conflicts.

Some military anthropologists were surprised at the highly developed ethical concerns among officers for the well-being of Iraqi and Afghan people. Goolsby relates that a learning curve regarding transparency was necessary due to security concerns but that transparency was achieved and rigorous ethics training instituted. She was the lead anthropologist on the development of the Human Terrain System (HTS) but left the program due to its shift away from research and toward human intelligence.

At the time of the revelations of abuses that took place at the Abu Ghraib prison in Iraq, there was fear that anthropologists may have been involved directly or indirectly with the documented torture of detainees. This proved not to be the case but prompted an examination of ethical issues involved with detention and interrogation under American authority. The 2004 *Schlesinger Report* by an independent panel of review of DoD detention operations admitted to serious ethical challenges. "Effective interrogators must deceive, seduce, incite, and coerce in ways not normally acceptable for members of the general public" (Greenberg and Dratel 2005, 974). The report acknowledges that the tactics used in Abu Ghraib interrogations challenge American values and raise a red flag for the improvement of ethics education. The matter of implied consent is treated in a novel way—that persons who engage in suspected insurgent or terrorist activities may be said to have "consented" to arrest and possible imprisonment with the foreknowledge that they are engaging in criminal acts (ibid.).

Anthropologists working in "compartmentalized" or modeling projects cannot be sure that they are not indirectly contributing to harm. They might be persuaded that they are lessening harm by offering their expertise to projects in conflict or postconflict zones because of their long-term involvement with the people and region under question. Anthropologists may not be any surer that they are not contributing to harm or that they are lessening harm when they work for humanitarian NGOs.

Understanding the mission, methods, and likely outcomes of any project is key to ethical decision making. Before deciding to engage in a government or nongovernment project in which anthropological knowledge or expertise constitutes only a part of the whole, the ethically conscious anthropologist would (1) seek information that enables her to evaluate the overall project mission in relation to lessening harm to studied populations, (2) review the project's methods in terms of the risk of potential harm, and (3) be assured that adequate, external review of the project has been conducted.

Acknowledging the controversies of anthropologists working with the military, the editors of the 2012 volume *Practicing Military Anthropology: Beyond Expectations and Traditional Boundaries* ask their readers to see military as "more than the Human Terrain Teams" headlines (Rubinstein, Fosher, and Fujimura). Recalling personal attacks on their work as "war criminals" at an AAA meeting, they ask that fellow members of their discipline see them as professionals and not just tools or technicians of the state and its foreign policy waged through wars. They describe their work as complex and multifaceted in the post–9/11 world, mostly taking place in noncombatant positions or as educators in military undergraduate and postgraduate academies. The training of military personnel in cultural sensitivity to local populations is crucial to harm amelioration in war zones. Indeed, anthropologist-archaeologist Laurie Rush has expressed her personal concern that such cultural-sensitivity training may increase the potential for harm for the soldiers she teaches, in that it may result in their letting down their guard in dangerous contexts.

Critical of this new field is David Price, who writes in *Weaponizing Anthropology* that the United States has become a security state after 9/11. The "intelligence scholars" of the "Bush Terror Wars" have been replaced by the "Obama counterinsurgency wars" (Price 2011, 2). The current era of "small wars"—insurgencies in a variety of global contexts—needs anthropological knowledge in order to be effectively countered. "The military does understand that anthropology is not just a product; when practiced ethically, anthropology can be transformative" (ibid., 3).

Price is correct about the transformative power of the anthropological method of participation and observation in a culture that relies on long-term, intimate, and intensive relationships of mutual trust. That trust in a conflict zone where there are enemies and allies is extremely difficult and may in many cases be impossible to initiate, cultivate, and maintain. It is akin to intimate, long-term relationships between blacks and whites in the United States, extremely difficult but not impossible.

Nonetheless some of the best ethnographies and analyses of the Afghan conflict are by anthropologists (Barfield 2010; Coburn 2011). These are critical and instructive regarding U.S. policies and options in these chronic conflict zones. Barfield argues that the American focus on democracy and women's rights as countrywide policy is misplaced (except perhaps for domestic consumption of an unpopular war), as this is viewed as anti-Islamic. It would be better to introduce these reforms in the cities where they would be well-received and allow a natural process of diffusion from urban to rural areas take its course. Moreover, a simplistic or mechanical use of anthropological knowledge is counterproductive, such as fetishizing Islamic practices beyond their normative cultural practice. A former student assigned to work with inmates at Guantánamo related to me that non-Muslims were required to wear white gloves when handling copies of the Qur'an, an absurd idea for a Muslim. Barfield notes that the Human Terrain Team's analysis of a shattered "tribal" structure was ignored as policy evolved to "engage" with tribal society that forms the fabric of Afghan society (Star 2011).

Some anthropologists are pacifists; others may have conscientiously objected to military service. Others are employed by the military, including my own work in military education since 2010. If acting as a cultural adviser in U.S. military operations is a violation of anthropological ethics, then how and in what contexts is this the case? I am unconvinced that the emerging subfield of a "military anthropology" is fundamentally different from what we are already practicing as anthropologists or that it is a violation of our professional ethics. Moreover, we perform a disservice as a discipline if we continue to engage in discourse that labels anthropologists good or bad whenever controversies arise. Such arguments and differences are bound to continue as the field of anthropology expands and shows its real power as the integrated study of humanity in all of time and space. This great conceptual power of the discipline is itself harmed every time anthropologists blame and shame one another rather than rise to the challenge of a relevant field for the multiple issues of the twenty-first century.

The Human Terrain System and Do No Harm

The Human Terrain System (HTS) was developed as a U.S. Army program to apply cultural knowledge to the "human terrain" in conflict zones in Iraq and Afghanistan. After media attention featured an HTS female anthropologist embedded with combat troops in Afghanistan in October 2007, a furor erupted in American anthropology that resulted in the creation of an investigative commission to explore issues of anthropological engagement with defense and intelligence agencies. The issues and reports of the two Commissions on the Engagement of Anthropology in U.S. Security and Intelligence Communities (CEAUSSIC I and II) will be discussed in chapter 5's discussion of moral anthropology.

During the furor I was recruited to teach anthropology and African studies at the Naval War College, near where I live in Rhode Island. Military officers in my classroom questioned why anthropology had condemned the HTS program that they so valued. They complained that in Iraq and Afghanistan they needed more, not less, cultural advice and that professional anthropologists and social scientists were needed, not just local interpreters. They stressed the designated nonlethality of the program and its role in harm reduction, telling stories of HTS cultural advisers interpreting religious activities as nonviolent when there was a default military fear of any public gatherings of Afghans or Iraqis. They hinted at the potential increase of harm with the lack of competent cultural advisers. I began to see this latest polarizing controversy in anthropology and ethics as "white hats versus black hats," where the likely truth was somewhere in between. The anthropology profession had every right to be concerned that the discipline would be associated with combat missions when the essence of the anthropological method is long-term relations of trust, and the anthropologists and other social scientists who worked for the HTS program saw their work as meshing U.S. defense and intelligence goals with concerns for the human populations affected by these missions. The unfortunate defense language—"human terrain"—certainly appeared to make objects of the humans affected by U.S. military-intelligence operations.

Two contradictory lines regarding harm developed, one viewing embedded anthropologists, or other social scientists, as harm doers and the other as harm reducers. The stated mission of the Human Terrain Team (HTT) model is clear about the nonlethal engagement of the HTT members and the application of cultural knowledge for the prevention of harm to American troops and to local communities although much of the criticism centered on possible lethal targeting using anthropological knowledge. Intentional and unintentional harm are widely differentiated in world law, with the former justified when further harm is prevented. But communities are complex, often-heterogeneous entities where predicting harm is imprecise.

Acting with little knowledge of how the HTTs were operating, this type of engagement by anthropologists was rejected by the AAA Executive Board in 2007, based on the view that HTTs contradict the essence of anthropological method of long-term relationships of trust and that their direct connection to combat places them in the realm of military intelligence. Three social scientists were killed in HTS operations, adding to the general view that HTS work was to be avoided. But, in fact, only a handful of anthropologists have been employed in HTS work, in disproportionate relation to the attention that the program received in the profession. A moral view to do no harm may be developing in the profession whereby ethical conduct by anthropologists working with the military occurs only when anthropologists are deployed in operations where the mission intent is to save lives.

DO NO HARM AND MILITARY ENGAGEMENT:
A VIEW FROM PSYCHOLOGY

Anthropology and psychology both have the potential of being force multipliers in the field and moral dividers in the two professions.[2] Psychologists and anthropologists have formed associations of concerned professionals (The Network of Concerned Anthropologists, Psychologists for Social Responsibility) over applications that might result in harm. Military psychology has been a recognized and accepted branch of the American Psychological Association (APA), largest of the professional associations, and psychologists have been in and around interrogation rooms.

There are differences between psychology and anthropology—mainly, studies of the individual in psychology and of community in anthropology, and from these derive different ethical responsibilities toward individual versus group ethical concerns. American psychology developed a close relationship with the military in World War I and World War II, leaving a legacy of psychologists in the military functioning as an organization. Military psychology exists as a legitimate division of the APA primarily because of its supportive role in managing personnel. The Veterans Association, for example, employs 5 percent of all clinical psychologists. The demand for psychologists and anthropologists exceeds available job opportunities, and the Global War on Terror and the wars in Iraq and Afghanistan have greatly increased the demand.

The APA directly collaborates with national-security agencies in policies and programs fostering operational psychology in the War on Terror, including psychologist-assisted interrogations. However, the American Medical and Psychiatric Associations take an arms-length stance, forbidding their members to assist in interrogations but not pursuing allegations of abuse.

Without learning from controversial episodes like the Human Terrain Team and without a sanctioning body in our main professional association, we will continue to do as we have always done—respond to questions of ethics interrogated by special task forces, such as the recent *Darkness in El Dorado* controversy, or reviewed by special commissions, such as CEAUS-SIC I and II. Absent any legal or quasilegal process, alleged violations of ethics end up being used mainly for pedagogical purposes, which is, perhaps, how they are best used. Undoubtedly, this will be the case for the "HTS Controversy" and may, this time, inform future debates, but past history does not ensure that this will be the outcome.

DO NO HARM AND MY IRB RESEARCH PROTOCOL IN SUDAN, 2007 TO 2009: PREVENTION/AMELIORATION OF HARM IN SUDAN CONFLICT ZONES

After fifteen years of not conducting research in Sudan due to chronic civil war and multiple human rights abuses, I resumed research in the country when a peace agreement was being forged in 2004 and was signed in 2005. I was funded for this research by the U.S. Institute of Peace, and since the USIP is funded by the U.S. Congress I was subjected to U.S. sanctions against Sudan and to full institutional-review-board (IRB) protocol for my research project on the sensitive subject of the role of Shari'a in Sudan's Islamism. What struck me—or impressed me—most was the protocol for my conduct of research that was advanced by the IRB of my home institution: U.S. sanctions prevented my taking any electronic equipment into the country, including my laptop, or hiring any Sudanese for any purposes. The IRB worked creatively with me on these, and all issues were resolved with my accommodations to the sanctions, but the IRB panel was most concerned with the protection of my research subjects. They feared that some might be harmed by the mere fact of working or collaborating with an American, and they developed a stringent protocol for my active and continuous use of informed consent, especially in research with the most-vulnerable populations I intended to study: women in Shari'a family-law cases and non-Muslims in camps of the Internally Displaced. They asked me to describe my research goals, funding, and the likely use of the findings with every individual or group with whom I met. This was at variance with the relaxed and informal style of research I was accustomed to in Sudan, where casual conversations and everyday interactions were the substance of my ethnography. However, we all realized that the nature and conduct of research in the region had been fundamentally altered since September 11, 2001.

CULTURAL RELATIVISM AND HARM

Cultural relativism asserts that, since each culture has its own inherent integrity with unique values and practices, value judgments should be withheld or suspended until cultural context is taken into account. What members of one culture might view as strange, inappropriate, or forbidden may be acceptable and unquestioned in another culture. For example, free versus restricted social mixing between the sexes varies greatly across cultures, as do marital ideas and practices. Religious ideas regarding customs are variable and can be permissive, indifferent to them, or condemning. Cultural universals are few, including, for example, the incest taboo against sexual relations within the nuclear family and most—but not all—forms of homicide. The universal mandate to do no harm to another human being can nonetheless justify culturally acceptable forms of homicide, such as infanticide or senilicide (the killing of a newborn or aged person) or "honor killings," where the greater harm of damage to the reputation of an individual or family justifies the killing of one of its own (usually a male killing a "dishonored" female family member). Since the Universal Declaration of Human Rights was introduced to the global community by the United Nations in 1948, the idea of universal human rights has presented a challenge to cultural relativism. Universal human rights and cultural relativism are not philosophically or morally opposed to one another. The terrain between them is fluid and rich, and ethically conscious anthropologists seek to explore this territory and make considered judgments about seeming conflicts between them.

Even the most experienced anthropological field worker must negotiate the terrain between universal rights and cultural relativism with caution, to avoid the pitfalls of scientific or discipline superiority. The anthropologist is capable of hearing, recording, and incorporating the multiple voices that speak to issues of cultural specificity and universal human rights. When various perspectives are taken into consideration, still in the end a judgment may have to be made when harm is a factor.

Harmful Cultural Traditions

When cultural traditions are deemed harmful by international human-rights standards—such as female circumcision, domestic violence, or the use of culture to justify violence against others—the balance of weighing risk and benefit to humans might be easier to determine. However, where detection of potential harm is more nuanced, it may be wise to consult with other professionals, including nonanthropologists—and with "native" cultural agents in the field site. It may be fair to assert that reasonable, impartial persons from different cultural backgrounds would likely agree what projects, methods, and outcomes have the potential for causing harm, or for lessening it when the specific cultural context is considered (Fluehr-Lobban 2008d). The "reasonable man"—apart from the now-archaic gender reference—was asserted by anthropologists who study law cross-culturally, thus proffering the idea that legal norms sanctioning acts resulting in harm—intentional or unintended—are close to universal.

Where is the locus of professional ethics in this discussion? We can ask, Is it equally ethical to take either a relativist or a universalist position in the case of female circumcision? If we apply the standard "do no harm," and if ethnographically the anthropologist knows that varying degrees of harm result from the different forms of female circumcision currently in practice, then what is the responsibility of the anthropologist? Are there negotiable degrees of harm that frame an answer?

Example #1: Domestic Violence across Many Cultures

The cultural "right" of a man to discipline, slap, hit, or beat his wife (and often, by extension, his children) is widely recognized across a myriad of different cultures throughout the world where male dominance is an accepted fact of life. Indeed, the issue of domestic violence has only recently been added to the international human-rights agenda, but it is firmly in place since the Vienna Conference of 1993 and the United Nations Beijing Women's Conference in 1995. This relatively new dialogue intersects at a point where the individual rights of the woman clash with a potential cultural defense of a man practicing harm and is a dialogue that anthropologists could inform and enrich tremendously with their firsthand knowledge of community and family life. Violence against women, against children, against people, is neither acceptable on moral grounds nor defensible on cultural grounds, although an examination of its many expressions and facets is very useful knowledge for both social science and public policy. The future development of a cross-cultural framework analyzing domestic violence would serve both scientific and human-rights work.

Violence against women and children is a global problem not limited to individual cultures or regions. Often Latin America and the Middle East are unfairly stigmatized as bastions of unbridled male authority and violence, but the international statistics on this crime bear witness to its transcultural presence. Overwhelmingly "domestic" violence is perpetrated by husbands on wives—although there are cases in every culture of husband battering, often retaliation by wives, and of familial violence where male relatives "discipline" their female members. There can be little debate that violence, or its threat, causes both emotional and physical harm.

Male physical and verbal control over women likely emerged with the rise of the state and the necessity of the strict control of female reproduction that was linked to the rise of private property and the desire that wealth transmission take place through "legitimate" heirs, only possible through male kin and others' control of women's sexuality. Concomitant with the rise of the state was also a male monopoly of coercive force and instruments of violence with their nearly exclusive exercise of power through weapons, armies, and warfare. For Western culture, male dominance was enshrined in the Roman paterfamilias doctrine, later expressed and supported in Judeo-Christian and Islamic ideas of the dual cultural mode of male superiority/ responsibility for women. A very large proportion of the world's people is influenced by these ideas regarding male authority over women.

Domestic or family violence is a greatly underreported offense across the globe, including in the United States, where it is often neither subject to cultural critique nor universally criminalized. There are few laws protecting women and children from violence, and where there are such laws, there may be ignorance or reluctance on the part of police and judges to use the laws against family members. There is often denial beyond the familial level to official state denial, and violence against women and children is diminished as a "lesser" form of violence. The activist mantra that "there is no excuse for abuse" became a global slogan, rejecting any "cultural-defense" arguments that might exclude such gender-based forms of violence. These include the following well-known cases:

- Rape was recognized as a strategy of war only after the war in Bosnia. Rape and gang rape were used as explicit strategies of war, resulting in an international consensus that rape constitutes a war crime against humanity.
- Sexual and gender-based violence (SGBV) was among the most persistent crimes committed in Darfur after Bosnia. Victims were reluctant to report abuses from cultural shame, fear of retaliation, and lack of confidence in local and state authorities prosecuting these crimes. Despite repeated calls for greater protection of civilians in villages and IDP camps, there was little change and at times reprisal for raising the issue of SGBV.
- A major obstacle to establishing accountability is the insensitive and often intimidating treatment of victims of sexual violence by local authorities,

including international humanitarian agencies. This is both a cultural and political problem, leading to the "culture of impunity" described by international NGOs.

- In chronic conflicts, women and children are the most vulnerable persons, without weapons, absent male kin, or unprotected by state and local government.

THE LIMITS OF CULTURAL RELATIVISM: CULTURAL RELATIVISM, AND DOING NO HARM

When cultural traditions are deemed harmful by international human-rights standards, ethical decisions and the balance of weighing risk and benefit to humans might be easier to assess. However, where detection of potential harm is more nuanced, it may be wise to consult with other professionals and with cultural agents in the field site. Reasonable, impartial persons from different cultural backgrounds would likely agree what projects, methods, and outcomes have the potential for causing harm or for lessening it when the specific cultural context is considered.

Cultural relativism can be taken to extremes when it comes to morality and ethics. Some argue that, since cultures vary and each culture has its own unique moral system, we cannot make judgments about right and wrong in comparing one culture to another. Thus, one cannot reject any form of culturally acceptable homicide—for example, infanticide, senilicide, or "honor" killing of women in Mediterranean and Middle East societies for alleged sexual misconduct—on moral grounds because cultural acceptance or condemnation are equally valid. An extreme relativist position is actually a form of absolutism with which few anthropologists would agree. Anthropologists did not defend Nazi genocide or South African apartheid with cultural-relativist arguments, and many have been critical of relativist defenses especially of Western practices they see as harmful, such as cultural institutions emphasizing violence. The truth about our complex world of cultural difference is that moral perplexity abounds. The ability to accept that another person's or culture's position with which one disagrees is nevertheless rational or intelligible lays the basis for fruitful discussion of differences.

Relativism can be used as a way of living in society with others. An egalitarian relativist sees all human beings as moral agents with equal potential for making ethical judgments. Though moral judgments in and of themselves are not scientific, they can be socially analyzed. That is, relativism and universalism in cultural values or practices (including international standards of human rights) need not be opposed morally, but they can be discussed, debated, and assessed by the social sciences, including anthropology.

The ground between universal human rights and cultural relativism in regard to military and national security is as yet unexplored terrain for anthropologists. "National" security may presume the primacy of the culture of one's nation over another. Cultural relativism rejects this notion, and anthropologists may act with a sense of great, or even greater, responsibility for the culture(s) of the people they study over their national culture. The transnationality of anthropologists is welcome in a globalized world, but it can be a contradiction for the ethically conscious anthropologist considering engagement with national-security agencies. Consideration of the project's mission and a weighing of the overall potential benefits and risks to the people studied *primarily* and to the discipline and profession of anthropology *secondarily* aids in decision making.

Relativist Challenge to Universal Rights: Islamic Societies and the West

In the conflict between cultural relativism and universal rights, the cultural area with which I am most familiar is where the West meets the Islamic world. The highly politicized context of this often-oppositional discourse and occasional real warfare reminds us of another kind of cold war between the United States and the Soviet Union. The subjective perceptions of morality and immorality, of right and wrong, on both sides can be so powerful that objective discourse and cultural negotiation may seem impossible.

Islamic governments from Iran to Afghanistan to Sudan have claimed cultural and religious immunity from international human-rights standards. For example, the perceived Islamic responsibility to protect women by re-stricting their activities has been asserted in defense of public morality. This stand has been criticized in the context of Western human rights and femi-nism. Islamic philosophers and political activists may deny that a woman can be a head of a family or a head of state. Their position violates international standards of women's rights and human rights, particularly as outlined in the United Nations 1979 Convention on the Elimination of All Forms of Dis-crimination against Women. Muslims in several states, however, have disre-garded the advice of these religious figures when they made Benazir Bhutto prime minister of the Islamic Republic of Pakistan and Tansu Çiller and Sheikh Hasina the respective heads of state in Turkey and Bangladesh in recent decades.

Cross-Cultural Definitions of Harm: *Darar* in Islamic Law

The concept of *darar* in the Arabic language and in Islamic family law translates as *harm* or *abuse* and is broadly applied in Islamic law (Shari'a) and specifically in three different cultural settings I have studied in Sudan,

Egypt, and Tunisia (Fluehr-Lobban 1987). *Darar* comes from the same root as the word used to describe a strike or a physical blow (*darab*). However, *darar* in Muslim family law as a ground for divorce has been interpreted to include both physical harm and emotional harm, the latter usually described as insulting words or behavior.

The divorced husband often does not acknowledge the harm, as is frequently the case with abusive husbands in other countries where the "right" of a husband to discipline a wife is a cultural norm. A relativist position might attempt to split the difference here between the cultural right of the husband to discipline a wife and the wife's right to resist. Moreover, the relativist's position would be upheld by cultural institutions and persons in authority—judges, for example, with the legitimate right to enforce the norm of "obedience" of wives.

Example #2: Stoning for Adultery in Sudan and Nigeria

Islamic law has criminal punishments for specified forms of theft and morals offenses, such as fornication and adultery. These punishments are known as the *hudud* (meaning "to the limits") and include lashing and stoning for the latter and limb amputations for the former. Few Muslim states apply these punishments, and they are frequently a part of political Islamizing states such as Afghanistan under the Taliban, Northern Nigeria, and Sudan during their militant Islamist phases. Shortly after this political Islamization of its law, Sudan began applying the harsh punishments of amputations for theft and threatened use of the penalty of stoning for adultery. In predominantly Muslim northern Nigeria a comparable trend toward Islamization occurred in the first decade of the twenty-first century with twelve of its northern states making Shari'a provincial law. In both cases these moves exacerbated Muslim-Christian relations, intensifying the civil war in Sudan and resulting in widespread and deadly rioting in Nigeria.

Applications in Sudan and northern Nigeria of the punishment of stoning for the crime of adultery raised fresh questions about violence and discrimination against women as well as the limits of cultural relativism. Shari'a courts in both countries have sentenced women to be stoned to death for convictions of adultery or fornication. In each of these cases national and international women's and human-rights groups condemned the stoning sentences as cruel and inappropriate by international human-rights standards. In both Sudan and Nigeria, convicting women of adultery and sentencing them to stoning resulted in similar protests, where either the sentences ended up being overturned or were not meted out. The intent appeared to be use of fear of application rather than carrying out the sentences.

Human rights, cultural relativism, and the ethics standard of harm all intersect in these examples. Anthropologists would test the limits of their relativism to defend stoning and other *hudud* sanctions. Harm clearly occurs as pain is inflicted in any potential application of the sentence; harm also occurs particularly to women as they and not their partners are penalized as offenders. The fact that the penalty of stoning has not been carried out in either country suggests that the severity of potential harm that the punishment inflicts, combined with human-rights activism, has restrained those authorities empowered to apply it.

Rape in War and Chronic Conflict: Darfur

Rape is acknowledged as a tool of war, a recognized war crime, and a crime against humanity. An anthropologist's role may be to assert cultural knowledge that a woman who has been raped requires anonymity and that her need for secrecy must be respected, even by powerful NGOs with a vested interest in reporting such crimes. The intent is to respect the autonomy of those we study, or on whom we apply our knowledge, including respecting their right to *not* be studied. Violating secrecy in such cases would be gravely harmful and unethical.

Example #3: Female Circumcision/"Female Genital Mutilation"

One of the most culturally and emotionally charged battlegrounds for the cultural relativist to confront the universal human-rights advocate has been the issue of harm resulting from female circumcision (FC) or female genital mutilation (FGM). The former term is used in the African cultural context where it is widely practiced, while the latter term is the invention of Western feminists. The issue has pitted Western feminists against African traditionalists, and it has been debated by religious scholars.

Western and indigenous female doctors and anthropologists have studied and commented on the question (El-Dareer 1982; Gruenbaum 2001; Abdel Halim 2006; Abusharaf 2006). These studies have added a critical dimension to the debates as they are both ethnographically grounded and give a voice to the supposed victims regarding harm done to them. Abdel Halim (2006, 27–28) cites descriptions of female circumcision by Western feminists who use language such as *torture, barbaric,* and *mutilated female bodies.* She argues that FC culturally establishes a woman's social identity, bringing with it bargaining power, and offering a sense of inclusion in society. Indeed, one of the worst insults in Sudanese society is to call a man "a son of an uncircumcised woman." Abdel Halim's interviews with Sudanese women in America in which they are given full voice indicate that many deny permanent harm such as lack of sexual fulfillment as a result of FC or infibulation.

Gruenbaum argues that not only are Western condemnations ineffectual, they also provoke strong defensive reactions (2001, 25). She wisely adds that naïve or ill-informed condemnations can lead to a judgmental ethnocentrism contributing to prejudice that can be harmful if acted on.

Prevalent in African Islamic societies, female circumcision is also found in non-Muslim, African contexts and is rare in Islamic contexts outside Africa. There is no consensus among Muslim scholars or African Muslims about whether female circumcision is mandated by religion. Religious interpretation in the Sudan as early as 1939 determined that female circumcision is only "desirable" (*manduh*), not compulsory (Fluehr-Lobban 1987, 96), while in 1994 the late Grand Sheikh of Al-Azhar Islamic University in Cairo, Gad al-Haq Ali Gad al-Haq, called female circumcision "a noble practice [that] does honor to women," for which he was sued by an Egyptian human-rights group (Sipress 1995, 25). His chief rival, the Grand Mufti of the Egyptian Republic, said that female circumcision is not part of Islamic teaching and is a matter best evaluated by medical professionals (ibid.).

The concept of harm has been the driving force behind the feminist, medical, psychological, and cultural opposition to female circumcision. I wrote about my personal struggle with the practice in Sudan, which exposed me to the ideology and justifications for female circumcision, as well as the harmful medical effects that can result. Chronic infections are common from the use of unsanitary instruments used to cut the clitoris in various stages, a procedure that is described as "light." The lightest cutting procedure involves an incision of the tip of the clitoris, while the most extreme form of the operation removes both the labia majora and minora as well as the clitoris. Sexual intercourse after marriage and childbirth are rendered more difficult and painful. Despite the practice being outlawed under colonialism in 1946, it continues to be practiced, although the most severe form is declining in usage.

For a long time I felt trapped, on the one hand, between my anthropological understanding of the custom and the sensitivities about it among the people with whom I was working and, on the other hand, the largely feminist campaign in the West to eradicate what critics saw as a harmful custom. To ally myself with Western feminists and condemn female circumcision seemed to me a betrayal of the value system and culture of the northern Sudan. But as I was asked to comment over the years on female circumcision as an "expert" I came to realize how deeply I believed the practice to be both harmful and wrong. In 1993 female circumcision was one of the cultural practices pronounced harmful by delegates at the historic Vienna Human Rights Conference. They opined that female circumcision was a violation of the rights of children as well as women who suffer a lifetime of consequences from what was done to them as a child.

What changed my view away from the conditioned relativist response was the international, cross-cultural, interdisciplinary dialogue that placed female circumcision on a level of such harm that whatever social or cultural good it represents (in terms of sexual propriety and marriage norms) is out-weighed by the harm it poses to the more basic rights of women and girls. Moreover, active feminist agitation against female circumcision within the Sudan has fostered the kind of indigenous response that anthropologists like, as the anthropologist would prefer not to agitate themselves, not wishing to appear to be among the ranks of the Western feminists who had patronizingly tried to dictate the "correct" agenda to women most directly affected by the practice. Women's and human-rights associations in the Ivory Coast and Egypt, as well as the Sudan, have also called for an end to female circumci-sion, while the Cairo Institute for Human Rights reported in 1995 the first publicly acknowledged marriage of an uncircumcised woman. In other words, a broad spectrum of the human community had come to an agreement that genital mutilation of girls and women is wrong.

HUMAN RIGHTS, HARM, AND INTERNATIONAL CONTEXTS: "NO (CULTURAL) EXCUSE FOR ABUSE"

Violence and injustice are transcultural phenomena. This is true of human-rights violations whether they are in the form of arbitrary arrest, detention and torture inflicted by the state, or female circumcision imposed by custom. Moreover, many international progressives have taken an active role in eval-uating the contemporary legitimacy and relevance of cultural practices ar-guing for the retention of useful traditions and the abandonment of practices that inflict harm or injury. Ethnic scarification in much of Africa has all but disappeared among peoples for whom this practice was routine only a few generations ago.

Using the standard of harm, it is increasingly evident that attempts to justify the control of female sexuality—whether using aesthetics, cleanliness, respectability, or religious ideology—increasingly are being questioned and rebuked in different cultures and cannot be sustained as a justification for the continuation of a harmful practice, whether domestic violence or female circumcision. The Women's League of the African National Congress in South Africa has its organizing mantra for its campaign against all forms of violence against women: "There is no excuse for abuse."

During the Fourth World Conference on Women held in Beijing in 1995—the last global conference on women to be held—positions on wom-en's rights expressed by some Muslim activists diverged from some of the global-majority feminist views. Debates over sexual and reproductive health and over sexual orientation as universal rights of women met with opposition not only from Muslim nations, like Iran and Egypt, but also from the Vatican and other Catholic representatives at the conference. In the end, disagree-ments were aired that proved not to be destructive of any final pronouncements, and there was frank acknowledgment that reasonable persons (and, by extension, cultures) could disagree. This is a relativist solution to different views about "universal rights" of women. But consensus was achieved on a host of other issues, including (1) opposing all forms of violence against women, (2) opposing female genital mutilation, and (3) identifying rape during armed conflict as a war crime and, in certain cases, a crime against humanity. Relativism expressed with respect to the religious sentiments of some delegates eased the negotiated terrain and permitted dialogue that achieved consensus on many other points while allowing reasonable difference to be asserted on other matters.

It is my view that these gaps can be bridged through intercultural conversations and negotiations. I have argued elsewhere that *when reasonable persons from different cultural backgrounds agree that certain institutions or cultural practices cause harm, then the moral neutrality of cultural relativism must be suspended.* In such conversations the old legal-sociological idea of the "reasonable man" (read *reasonable person*) may be helpful. Reasonable persons can and do agree that harm can be identified and intervention can result.

DO SOME GOOD/INCREASE HUMAN WELL-BEING

Is it an ethical responsibility for an anthropologist to apply her or his knowledge to human-rights concerns? I have argued that such engagement is a personal choice but not an ethical responsibility; however, anthropologists can and do disagree. Anthropologists are also citizens who are activists and nonactivists and have no special obligation to be one or the other. My engagement on the side of asylum seekers is a part of my moral-political system and is a personal choice, and I do accept compensation for professional service provided. Laura Graham argues that anthropologists who study people suffering human-rights abuses and forms of social injustice have an ethical obligation to seek ways to improve these conditions (2009, 200). Moreover, she adds that anthropology as a humanistic field has an obligation to promote social justice, especially in indigenous, vulnerable, and marginalized communities. The difference between us is that of a personal moral responsibility rather than a professional obligation.

According to Gert (2004, 9), the basic goods that humans seek are pleasure, freedom, ability, and consciousness. The primary reason to act morally is that someone else will be harmed if you do nothing, which is not necessarily altruism but is a fundamental concern for the well-being of others. One does not act morally when acting on one's own behalf. A person sees these moral rules as a part of natural law, or the natural human condition.

While avoidance of harm has been the key concept in the development of ethical guidelines in medical and biological research and also in federal regulations regulating research in the behavioral sciences, the corollary considering the possibility of doing some good is less explored. Philosophers have refined concepts of harm and benefit; however, the discussion more frequently occurs around the prevention of harm rather than the promotion of benefit. The idea of the promotion of benefit to the people anthropologists study has been a subject of some debate. The subfield of applied anthropology has a strong tradition built on the idea that anthropological knowledge can be used for social benefit. The divide between so-called pure and applied research has narrowed, and indirectly codes of ethics make a necessary "good" and a professional responsibility for the dissemination of research results.

There is a growing sensibility in the United States of a civic duty to report harm—neighbors who witness or hear evidence of domestic violence are duty bound as citizens to report the abuse to the police. This provides a new perspective that knowledge of harm may not be something that can be personally or morally dismissed. Is it the duty of an anthropologist to report harm? Is the standard the same as for the asylum cases with which I work? That legal standard that needs to be met in my affidavits in support of asylum seekers is the fear of or actual existence of a threat to the life or well-being of an individual.

Some codes are becoming explicit about the obligation to contribute to the communities in which they work. The ethics guidelines devised by the linguistics department at the Max Planck Institute for Evolutionary Anthropology mandate that "wherever possible researchers ensure that they contribute to the communities in which they work as a part of normative practice, only to be excepted in 'truly unusual conditions.' Such contributions for linguists include documentation of the language in an accessible way; development of a writing system for the language; [and] training for members of the community studied in linguistic anthropological methods, transcription analysis, literacy, audio-visual recording" to create an indigenous group of experts (n.d., principle 5).

The negative admonition to do no harm can be positively challenging to the researcher to do some good. In its online discussion of the "do no harm" principle carried out by the AAA group tasked with rewriting the ethics code, a cautionary note was struck that is reminiscent of cautionary remarks about the danger of paternalism/maternalism that might cloud ethical discussions (Fluehr-Lobban 2006a). They wrote that

> while anthropologists welcome work benefitting others or increasing the well-being of individuals or communities, determination regarding what is in the best interests of others or what kinds of efforts are appropriate to increase

well-being are complex and value-laden and should reflect sustained discussion with those concerned. Such work should reflect deliberate and thoughtful consideration of both potential unintended consequences and long-term impacts on individuals, communities, identities, tangible and intangible heritage, and environments. (American Anthropological Association 2010)

Where is the precise locus of professional ethics in this discussion? We can ask, Is it equally ethical to take either a relativist or a universalist position using the case of female circumcision? If we apply the standard to do no harm, and if ethnographically the anthropologist knows that varying degrees of harm result from the different forms of female circumcision currently in practice, then what is the responsibility of the anthropologist? Are there negotiable degrees of harm that frame an answer?

Understanding the mission, methods, and likely outcomes of any project in which anthropologists become involved, a key to ethical decision making is reflection on the admonition to do no harm.

DO SOME GOOD: PRIMATES

Outside of anthropology, nonanthropological guidelines for research with animals recommend alternatives to the use of animals in research, with the substitution of computer models, for example. The use of various species of animals also should be justified as research subjects with an emphasis on the animal(s) suffering a minimum of pain and distress (Koppelman 2012). Since anthropologist primatologists prefer research in natural settings, where they feel they can best study primate behavior, the issue of pain and suffering should be minimized. However, primatologists working in the field stress an added responsibility to the human communities in which they work and their relationships to the local primates. Primatologists can act to resolve potential conflicts between conservation/management plans and the local human population (Mackinnon and Riley 2010). For ethical field primatology, much like the transcultural social anthropological research that is mainly observational, ethical practice is a matter of self-monitoring.

Mackinnon and Riley emphasize the concept of "sustainable community ecology" as an ethical imperative, especially for the primate field schools that train future primatologists and anthropologists. This discourse is contextualized in the fact that the extinction rate of nonhuman primates is now approaching 50 percent, and so the call for their own code has become urgent, but that code—in true anthropological form—should reflect both nonhuman and human community considerations (ibid.).

CONSULTATION WITH COLLEAGUES AND CULTURAL SPECIALISTS

Ideally decision making occurs in a group process where the relevant disciplinary, cultural, and government-agency stakeholders are at the table. Professional ethical and personal moral lines could be more clearly defined through a process of communication where a road map for military and national-security engagement, or nonengagement, would be developed. Consultation with professionals in related disciplines who have been grappling with issues of engagement is recommended (e.g., psychology), as well as those that have been historically "engaged" without serious controversy (e.g., political science and international relations).

Perhaps the best advice comes from the cultural information providers themselves and from one's disciplinary colleagues. To this end a new Friends of the Committee on Ethics has been formed within the AAA with a mission to offer informal, private advice from a group of experienced professionals to potential engagers, or to those who have other inquiries about anthropological ethics.

Consultation of the Codes and Experiences of Other Nations

The "Framework for Research Ethics" of the United Kingdom's Economic and Social Research Council (ESRC) contains a detailed discussion of risk assessment that is their focus rather than definitions or interpretations of what is harm. While harm avoidance is a key principle, risk is more explored. Risk should be minimal as "the dignity and autonomy of research participants is to be respected at all times" (Economic and Social Research Council 2005). Risk must be realistically assessed with the insistence that research ethics be included in every proposal and that the environment of research be likewise assessed. In the "Frequently Asked Questions" section of the group's website the question is raised, "Can all risk be avoided?" to which the response is "No," especially in longitudinal, qualitative, and cross-cultural circumstances where every possibility cannot be anticipated. Moreover, at times it is desirable to expose research participants to risk if the anticipated benefit of the research outcome outweighs the risk. Vulnerable populations must be identified and issues appropriately addressed so far as is possible. And Internet research that poses many new dilemmas for ethical research requires full ethical review for possible risks as well as benefits.

CONCLUDING REMARKS

Consideration of the possibility of harm resulting to the participants in anthropological study, at every stage, is at the core of an ethically conscious approach to research. Thus it should be a first consideration undertaken in an active, not passive approach, to ethics. In your consideration of potential risk and harm, consult broadly, and discuss matters of concern with peers, colleagues, and responsible persons in official regulatory institutions, such as review boards, and the research participants themselves. Do not be shy about raising difficult questions or feel guilty before you have started. Do not overworry about causing harm to your research participants as by applying protocols of full informed consent and transparency you are doing your best to engage in ethically conscious research. The previous discussion of harm and its complex set of issues is not intended to curb research but to encourage a key part of its ethical conduct summarized in the challenging admonition to do no harm.

QUESTIONS FOR INDIVIDUAL REFLECTION OR GROUP DISCUSSION

1. Is harm an absolute moral and ethical concept? Is it even possible to do no harm in research?
2. Should harm be considered along a continuum of greater or lesser harms? If yes, what factors should be taken into consideration?
3. Is the only ethical engagement for anthropologists to do some good rather than to do no harm?
4. Should anthropologists assert that *primary harm* is that which affects the people studied, including projects removed from direct fieldwork contact, and that *secondary harm* addresses harm to professionals? It would be to the primary harm that anthropologists first turn in consideration of the consequences of engagement.
5. Is advocacy a professional responsibility or a moral choice?
6. How should anthropologists treat harmful cultural traditions or specific acts of harm they encounter in their work?

Chapter Three

What Does It Mean to Obtain Informed Consent?

Language on informed consent was not included in an anthropological code of ethics until 1998, an example of historical weakness on the subject in mainstream American anthropology. Responsibility to "the people studied" and "secrecy in research" have greater depth in the history of ethics discourse. There has been a lag due to acknowledged resistance by some anthropologists to institutional review boards (IRBs) of their research where proof of informed consent was required and the formality of signed informed-consent forms was deemed inappropriate to anthropological research.

Informed consent as a standard in research developed in the wake of the revelations of the abuse of humans through medical experimentation in research in Nazi Germany during World War II. The largest literature on informed consent is in the field of medicine. Anthropology adds the cultural and cross-cultural components to informed consent, as well as the important issue of literacy (reading and signing informed-consent forms) to the evolving discussion of the meaning and application of informed consent.

Informed consent has been invoked more for its absence in recent intracollegial debates, such as in the *Darkness in El Dorado* (Tierney 2000) and Human Terrain System controversies. In many ways the politics of these controversies overwhelmed the importance of the issue of informed consent, and the treatment of these were two essentially missed opportunities to have a broader and deeper discussion about what informed consent in anthropology means. Philosophically, *informed consent might be interpreted as a professional responsibility or admonition that in research anthropologists will practice full disclosure, to the best of their ability, and that issues affecting participants regarding methods, use, or publication of research will be discussed with them in advance.*

However, what is "informed" in consent and what constitutes adequate, valid consent are questions that have been raised but not satisfactorily answered or explored for their contextual meaning in anthropological research. "Voluntary, noncoerced consent" was introduced during the Human Terrain System debates as specific language to oppose the program. What does "voluntary" mean, and why was the idea of noncoercion brought into discussion of anthropological ethics? These and a myriad other questions will be raised and addressed in this chapter.

INFORMED CONSENT AS THE GOLD STANDARD OF PROFESSIONAL ETHICS

Informed consent is the gold standard of professional ethics in both biomedical and social-science research. As a formal legal-ethical construct, it grew out of the 1972 Supreme Court case of *Canterbury v. Spence*, which articulated the principle for medical research; it has since evolved to represent the minimum standard for the ethical conduct of research. The primary context for informed consent was the need for protection in biomedical research and practice where there existed the potential for harm to humans as a result of the research or treatment. The principle quickly evolved into a doctrine with such legal potency and moral suasion that it became *the* standard by which biomedical research was conceived, funded, and executed. Failure to conform to informed-consent guidelines, monitored by IRBs from the mid-1970s, could easily translate into nonfunded research proposals or denial of applications for renewed funding. The principle of informed consent acquired such legitimacy that it came to be applied as a general principle not only to all biomedical research—whether or not it received federal funding—but also to the social and behavioral sciences after the publication of *The Belmont Report* in 1979. The legal and ethical standard demonstrating that informed-consent guidelines have been met has become a requirement for meeting IRB standards when reviewing any proposals involving human "subjects" or participants, including anthropological research.

DEFINITION OF *INFORMED CONSENT*

Informed consent has been defined as "the knowing consent of an individual, or a legally authorized representative, able to exercise free power of choice without undue inducement or any element of force, fraud, deceit, duress, or other form of constraint or coercion" (Department of Health and Human Services 1990).

Informed consent lies at the core of ethical principle and practice in Western biomedical and social and behavioral science and is acknowledged in the U.S. Common Rule as the cornerstone of federal regulation, whose supervision is the responsibility of the National Office of Research Oversight. This philosophical and cultural tradition was born more generally in the West out of the Nuremburg Code of 1947, the Helsinki Declaration of 1964 (revised in 1975), and the Federal Regulation of 1974 issued by the U.S. Department of Health, Education, and Welfare. These early declarations against human experimentation were generated not out of the post–world war examination of the unethical and immoral medical-research practices of the Nazi regime, but the American Tuskegee experiment. Conducted by the U.S. Public Health Service between 1932 and 1972, the Tuskegee experiment used human experimentation on poor, black sharecroppers in Alabama who were injected, without their knowledge or consent, with the syphilis bacterium in order to study the progress of this fatal disease, if untreated. The forty-year study is infamously unethical because the researchers knowingly failed to treat their subjects with penicillin, the known cure. Revelation of these details by a whistleblower led to major changes in U.S. law and regulation, requiring informed consent. Except for the American Psychological Association and its 1973 code, the other social and behavioral sciences, including anthropology, were generally slow to recognize the centrality of informed consent in *all* research involving humans.

Given this history, it may be surprising that the major professional association of American anthropologists did not introduce specific language on informed consent until authoring its 1998 code of ethics. In 1994 I wrote an article, "Informed Consent in Anthropological Research: We Are Not Exempt"—adding the nonexemption wording at the urging of philosopher Bernard Gert. The *American Anthropologist* rejected this article for publication, an indication that the consciousness in the discipline was still undeveloped, so I turned to the major practitioners' SfAA journal *Human Organization*, which did publish this call for inclusion of informed consent in anthropological codes of ethics. Indeed, the first professional statement on ethics was issued by the SfAA in 1949 as the *Report in 1949 of the Committee on Ethics of the Society for Applied Anthropology*, chaired by Margaret Mead. Reading that statement, it is clear that emphasis was placed on the integrity of the anthropologist and the "dynamic equilibrium of human relationships" the anthropologist should strive not to disturb rather than consideration of an ethical relationship with the people studied. The issue of responsibility to the subjects of research was developed first in biomedical research and then later filtered into the social and behavioral sciences.

Today the social sciences, including anthropology after 1998, have specific informed-consent language in their codes of ethics. *The Belmont Report* and the Common Rule for the Protection of Human Subjects for Behavioral and Social Science Research are the relevant federal documents that deal with anthropological research. Although covered under the rubric of "ethnographic research," the method pioneered by anthropologists, it is used extensively in nonanthropological studies.

The Belmont Report of 1979—the first statement about research ethics and professional responsibility for researchers in the social and behavioral sciences—sets forth the basic ethical principles that should guide responsible research. These are (1) *respect for persons*, (2) *beneficence*, with two complementary actions: the well-known exhortation to do no harm and the directive to maximize the possible benefits, and (3) *justice*, raising the fundamental questions, Who is equal, and who is unequal?

The Common Rule was developed by eighteen federal agencies for regulation of social- and behavioral-science research, and in it both "exempt" and "expedited" review for informed consent are detailed. Ethnography has been treated as exempt, depending on the topic and methodology of research. Research involving the observation of public behavior is almost always exempt, unless disclosure of information from the research could be used to harm the participants. Certain sensitive topics, such as the study of drug behavior, nonmainstream sexual practices, mental illness, or forms of family and domestic violence, require special consideration. Before informed consent became the acknowledged standard, a well-documented case in sociological research of the surreptitious observation and study of homosexual encounters in public bathrooms by one researcher was often taught as a negative example of unethical research (Humphreys 1970). Nonetheless, the study had its defenders who argued that the use of deception and lack of consent were the only ways to conduct this useful piece of sociological research.

As written documentation of consent may make the research appear suspicious, inappropriate, rude, or threatening, alternative forms of consent are covered in the Common Rule as special cases in which the overall success of the research can be endangered. Also, exemptions are made where written consent might harm the research participant, as in conditions often prevailing in the world's undemocratic nations. Moreover, women and minors have less agency globally in predominantly patriarchal societies, and it is often difficult to obtain informed consent from them. The best advice is to "do your homework" when planning a research design incorporating the necessity for ensuring informed consent. It is often up to the IRB to determine the form of informed consent to be obtained. Group consent is also addressed as appropriate to traditional societies and should present in an open meeting and be consultative.

Accepted exceptions to the Common Rule, thus allowing exemption from IRB review, include (1) research carried out in an educational institution involving educational practices, (2) research involving educational tests, surveys, questionnaires, and observation of public behavior, (3) research using existing data, if publicly available or unidentifiable, (4) research projects with demonstrable public benefit, and (5) taste and food-quality evaluation; in each of these cases, persons or an institution other than the researcher must determine that the research is exempt (National Science Foundation 2013). These exceptions are clearly marginal to the anthropological enterprise and are designed for American research.

DEVELOPMENT OF INFORMED CONSENT IN ANTHROPOLOGY

In November 2000, in response to allegations of misconduct on the part of the anthropologist most closely associated with the *Darkness in El Dorado* controversy, the Committee on Ethics of the American Anthropological Association was asked to address what constitutes valid and informed consent in anthropological research. The members of the committee prepared a briefing paper that began with reference to the 1998 code of ethics language: "Anthropological researchers should obtain the informed consent of persons being studied, providing information, owning or controlling access to material being studied, or otherwise identified as having interests [that] might be impacted by the research" (AAA Committee on Ethics, with Lauren Clark and Ann Kingsolver, 2000). Informed consent was recognized as "dynamic and continuous"—as a process begun in the project design and continued by way of dialogue and negotiation throughout the research. Informed consent was not interpreted in a legalistic way—as requiring signed forms, for example—but as expressing a spirit of openness and consultation with persons studied throughout the conduct of research. In the latest version of the AAA code of ethics, adopted in 2009, informed consent is treated thusly:

> Anthropological researchers should obtain in advance the informed consent of persons being studied, providing information, owning or controlling access to material being studied, or otherwise identified as having interests [that] might be impacted by the research. It is understood that the degree and breadth of informed consent required will depend on the nature of the project and may be affected by requirements of other codes, laws, and ethics of the country or community in which the research is pursued. Further, it is understood that the informed-consent process is dynamic and continuous; the process should be initiated in the project design and continue through implementation by way of dialogue and negotiation with those studied. Researchers are responsible for identifying and complying with the various informed-consent codes, laws, and regulations affecting their projects. Informed consent, for the purposes of this code, does not necessarily imply or require a particular written or signed form. It is the quality of the consent, not the format, that is relevant. (American Anthropological Association 1998)

In the present code, obtaining informed consent was framed in a context of transparency.

Anthropological researchers should obtain in advance the informed consent of persons being studied, providing information, owning or controlling access to material being studied, or otherwise identified as having interests [that] might be impacted by the research. It is understood that the degree and breadth of informed consent required will depend on the nature of the project and may be affected by requirements of other codes, laws, and ethics of the country or community in which the research is pursued. It is understood that the process of informed consent is dynamic and continuous; the process should be initiated in the project design and continue through implementation by way of dialogue and negotiation with those studied. . . . Informed consent, for purposes of this code, does not necessarily imply or require a particular written or signed form. It is the quality of the consent, not the format, that is relevant. (American Anthropological Association 2009)

How do you know that valid and informed consent has taken place? The AAA Committee on Ethics offered the following characteristics indicative of obtaining valid consent (AAA Committee on Ethics, with Lauren Clark and Ann Kingsolver, 2000):

- Engage in an ongoing conversation with research collaborators about the study and any potential risks or benefits that takes place at all stages of the research.
- Discuss with research participants the forms of documentation that you intend to use and how dissemination of results may affect them.
- Inform participants about their anonymity and the confidentiality and security measures used for all data, including digitized, visual, and material data.
- Establish a long-term mechanism for researcher and participants to remain in touch to express concerns or withdraw their data from the research.
- The form of official consent can vary. It need not be a signed form and can be written, audiotaped, or videotaped, and the person giving consent should be active in deciding which form of consent is used.
- These should be approved by the appropriate review board prior to recruiting participants or collecting data.

The standard of ensuring that informed consent has been obtained in social-science research has been broadly adopted. One example is the ESRC Research Ethics Framework of the Social Science Research Council of the United Kingdom, whose précis on informed consent adds to the above (1) competence to give consent and consent by proxy, (2) exceptions to informed consent, (3) where consent forms are not appropriate, (4) covert research, and (5) whether informed consent is always necessary. Thus, their definition of informed consent contains the requirements of being informed, voluntary, and competent. As such the research participant must be fully aware of and understand the following:

- what the research is about
- why it is being conducted
- who it is being conducted for and who is funding it
- what the purpose of the study is and what will happen to the results
- what is expected of them if they agree to participate and an understanding that the participant (1) does not *have* to participate and, (2) having agreed to participate, can withdraw any time without detriment

The ESRC document further considers the category of less than fully competent volunteers in research—for example, persons with mental disorders who may be willing to be participants but are not fully competent to give full and informed consent. Any preexisting relationship between the researcher and the potential participant should be evaluated, especially when the researcher is an authority figure. When working with communities care should be taken to ensure that *all* participants are informed and their participation is voluntary.

Exceptions in the ESRC protocol to the necessity to obtain informed consent are the usual ones accepted in the United States: (1) research on public behavior, like street or crowd settings, (2) where consent would compromise the participants, such as studying illegal behavior like drug trafficking, (3) where written consent puts participants at unnecessary risk.

Covert research, by definition, cannot involve informed consent and should only be undertaken where it provides unique data or where overt observation would alter the phenomenon being studied. Importantly, it should only be used where important issues of social significance are being addressed, such as forms of abuse. (Social Science Research Ethics n.d.).

Informed Consent and Secret Research

The 2009 AAA revised code of ethics restates the fundamental view that any research that by its design does not allow the anthropologist to know the full scope of a project (i.e., part of large projects known for government projects as "compartmentalized research") is ethically problematic, since by definition the researcher cannot communicate transparently with participants. Likewise singled out as problematic is the use of the old language of "secret or clandestine research" that deceives research participants about the sponsorship, purpose, or implications of the research. This is tied organically to informed consent as basic requirements for openness, honesty, and transparency in research (American Anthropological Association 2009).

The language of the 1998 code of ethics stated that informed consent—rather than being obtained once—is "a process that is dynamic and continuous" and is negotiated during the process of research and that in the end it is "the quality of the consent, not the format, that is relevant" (American Anthropological Association 1998, 2.4). The 2009 principles reiterate this language verbatim, without any revision or change (American Anthropological Association 2009).

Nonetheless, informed consent as a necessary component of the ethical conduct of research has still not been sufficiently debated such that the *practice of informed consent* is clear to students or researchers. In my view the following questions remain unresolved:

1. What are best practices in obtaining informed consent without the use of forms?
2. What recommendations are made for the use of appropriate language (English or another) and presentation of the research mission, its goals, and methods?
3. Will or will not an informed-consent form be used to have an "informed conversation" about the research, its source of funding, duration, and foreseeable outcome(s), including the negotiation of the terms of the researcher-participant(s) relationship and the unilateral right of the participant to withdraw at any time?
4. Without forms, how is verbal consent from research participants to be verified as sufficient? How is this documented? How to establish and review a system of accountability when consent is obtained without forms?
5. What additional consent is needed for the possible use of recording devices, audio-video taping, and e-mail messages?
6. How is verbal consent obtained and verified in a noncoercive manner and not the direct result of economic or power disparities between the researcher and researched?
7. When is collective informed consent appropriate? For example, among indigenous communities or studies of human relations in hierarchical communities where gender, minority status, class, or other status *disempower* individual or group participants?
8. How are Western-based individual rights balanced or in opposition to non-Western, collective rights? What are the best ways to conduct a two-way, open, and public conversation about informed consent?
9. What *proactive, special measures* should be introduced *to protect vulnerable populations* with regard to consent to participation in research, even that which is perceived as being in their best interests, such as victims of human-rights abuses?

10. How is confidentiality/anonymity, or acknowledgment, of participation negotiated with the research participants asking them explicitly about the precise nature of their participation, acknowledged or protected by anonymity?

Overall, it is the spirit, and not the form, of informed consent that matters in determining best practice. In most cases it is the conversation about informed consent that the researcher has with the persons to be studied that is most valuable in initiating and maintaining an open relationship between researcher and researched. The conversation about informed consent is the key that opens this door. These questions ask the researcher to be aware of the "native point of view" as a research participant and to acknowledge the potential paternalism/maternalism of the anthropologist in making assumptions about what is in the best interests of the people studied.

INFORMED CONSENT IN CODES OF ETHICS OF ALLIED SOCIAL SCIENCES

The American Psychological Association (APA) has the most detailed language on informed consent, a result of its lengthy history of research among American subjects and research designs that are experimental rather than observational. Language on informed consent appears in several sections of the extensive APA code that serves the fifty-thousand-plus professional psychologists in the United States. In its most succinct form it provides that

> when psychologists conduct research or provide services in person or via electronic transmission or other forms of communication they obtain informed consent of the individual(s) using language that is reasonably understandable to that person(s), except when conducting such activities without consent mandated by law or government regulation or as otherwise provided in this ethics code. (American Psychological Association 2013, sec. 3.10)

The Code of Ethics of the American Sociological Association (ASA) likewise contains an extensive section on informed consent with several subsections: (1) the scope of consent, (2) the process of obtaining informed consent, (3) for students and subordinates, and (4) for research with children. The basic language is similar to the APA:

> Informed consent is a basic ethical tenet of scientific research with human populations. Sociologists do not involve a human being as a subject in research without the informed consent of the subject or the subject's legally authorized representative, except as otherwise specified in this code. (American Sociological Association 1999, sec. 12.01)

Informed consent in social-science research is based on trust-building relationships. The general history of resistance in social science to informed consent is largely due to the derivation of the concept from biomedical research and the view of its inappropriateness to social research. Social-science research generally involves lower risk than biomedical or health-related research, and the methods are built around the incremental development of trust over longer-term relationships of respect with research participants. These differences may justify the use of novel approaches to the researcher-participant relationship that can support or replace informed consent" (Burgess 2009). These modifications can include verbal and unwritten consent, implied consent, group consent, or the waiver of any requirement for consent in certain minimal- or low-risk research.

Assessment of Adequate Consent

What is adequate consent, and how is it obtained in complex/compromised field situations? What is minimal/maximal informed consent? Anthropologists working for powerful agencies, such as the World Bank or US/AID, will need to follow their protocols. But how can informed consent be adequately documented in these often-complex environments in which they work? Some of the problems that might arise include:

1. Cultural barriers that impede agency required for informed consent (e.g., male consent seen as adequate for women and family members in patriarchal societies).
2. Consent with all manner of vulnerable populations; addressing consent (or adding to) the federal guidelines on this critical matter; to children, the incarcerated, and the "insane"; we could add, for example, vulnerable persons in chronic zones of conflict, human-rights activists, or their defenders.
3. The inability to obtain consent when conducting "remote ethnography," the study of culture at a distance without "informants." There are other examples where consent may not be achievable or applicable; this is a good subject for group discussion.
4. Reciprocal consent obtained in collaborative research; when is individual or collective consent appropriate? What to do when there are individual/community tensions? What is the difference between consent and assent?
5. What are the problems of self-reporting in informed consent where the researcher is also the reporter? What devices of researcher accountability can be devised?

Assessing the adequacy or validity of consent can be difficult because the standards of obtaining consent have been somewhat of a moving target as they have evolved over the decades since the concept was introduced into social-science research. Legal consent, "expressed" or implied consent, the use (or not) of written forms, and the variety and social differentiation among participants/subjects, including the challenging case of vulnerable populations, have all been specifically addressed. When assessing what is adequate consent, there is a degree to which it might be assumed or inferred, but it should always be obtained without any coercion. Assurance that there is no coercion by status, finances, relationship, or any other source should be assessed and then addressed by the appropriate IRB.

The transdisciplinary features of valid informed consent for which there is general agreement include (1) disclosure, (2) capacity, and (3) voluntariness. Any waivers are usually based on perceived or clear direct benefits to the participants resulting from the research. Disclosure to the participants, funders, and other stakeholders by the researcher ensures transparency in research funding, execution, and dissemination. "Capacity" to give informed consent has been defined as applying to persons who are capable of giving full, voluntary, and informed consent. Historically in the United States it has excluded children, mentally impaired individuals, the imprisoned, and subordinates in a superior-subordinate relationship. Voluntariness reinforces the free and open participation of the researched individuals or populations.

INFORMED CONSENT IN RESEARCH AMONG VULNERABLE POPULATIONS RECOGNIZED IN FEDERAL REGULATIONS: ADDING ANTHROPOLOGICAL PERSPECTIVES[1]

Research populations recognized as vulnerable federal regulations and thus as requiring IRB approval include: *children, prisoners, pregnant women, the mentally disabled, or economically or educationally disadvantaged persons* who, by virtue of their status, require additional safeguards to be included in the study in order to protect the rights and welfare of these subjects. The federal guidelines recognize "special classes" of subjects in need of protection. A subsection among these special classes is on international research that extends the protections in the federal guidelines to *all* human subjects in research carried out by Americans, thus, by implication, not just Americans as subjects. Absent any agreed-on international code for the protection of subjects in the conduct of research, the federal guidelines require approval in advance by the appropriate IRB to ensure that there is an equivalence of protections in the host nation to the federal guidelines. These are mandated if the research is funded by a federal agency, such as the Department of Health and Human Services. From personal experience I can relate that this is much better in theory than in practice.

Vulnerability is one of the least-examined concepts in research ethics (Levine et al. 2004). The historic focus has been on the limitations to capacity to give informed consent. Social-science interpretations have focused on incapacity as resulting from unequal power between politically or economically disadvantaged groups and investigators or sponsors, such as a research professor and their students. So many new groups are now considered "vulnerable," especially in international research, that some ethicists argue that the idea has lost practical and theoretical force. Anthropologists and international researchers would acknowledge that victims of human-rights abuses, persons living in refugee camps or those for the internally displaced, women and girls hurt by harmful cultural practices (domestic violence or female circumcision), child soldiers and forced laborers, trafficked persons for slave labor or the sex trade, persons financially coerced to sell their human organs, and a host of other groups comprise a diverse and concerning variety of vulnerable persons in the places and contexts where anthropologists carry out their research.

To complicate matters further, classifying groups as vulnerable may have the effect of stereotyping them and may not reliably protect them from harm (Levine et al. 2004). Moreover, the label itself may suggest lack of agency, which is not the case among many so-called vulnerable people who have successfully agitated on their own behalf, such as many indigenous peoples. This may be more evident in the biomedical fields where AIDS research participants, for example, have been stigmatized, such as was the case for Haitians. But such stigmatizing of vulnerable research populations generally has not been the case for anthropology, although the criticism of exploiting research populations has been made in the *Darkness in El Dorado* controversy. Moreover, no discipline is better situated than anthropology to explore international, cross-cultural dimensions of vulnerability and consent.

In 1979 *The Belmont Report* recognized only the following vulnerable populations:

> Racial minorities, economically disadvantaged, the very sick. Given their dependent status and their frequently compromised capacity for free consent, they should be protected because as subjects they are easily manipulated.

As mentioned, generally missing from the federal regulating bodies is an awareness or acceptance of international contexts of research and research among subjects who are not Americans. A selected review of biomedical research in the post-HIV era—where much U.S.-funded research takes place outside of the United States in AIDS-pandemic countries—also failed to take note of this international reach of American research. In the December 2000 recommendations from the National Bioethics Advisory Commission, *Ethical and Policy Issues in Research Involving Human Participants* (a group composed almost entirely of medical professionals and lawyers), it was established that extra protection for vulnerable populations is essential, but the definition of who and what constitute vulnerable groups did not include any mention of the international populations that many anthropologists study.

Research with high-profile vulnerable populations, such as HIV-positive persons, requires a multilevel and multiphased approach to consent given at the times of pre-enrollment, enrollment, and the study's continuation—in other words, in all phases of research (Woodsong, Abdool Karim, and Colletti 2004). The main issue is the participants' comprehension of the study, its goals, and its link to prevention.

The 2000 U.S. Bioethics Commission described the following *new* categories regarded to be distinct, ethically relevant types of vulnerability:

1. *Cognitive vulnerability*: prospective research participants who are insufficiently able to comprehend information, deliberate, and make decisions. Mentioned as examples of "situational cognitive vulnerability" are emergency situations or where prospective participants and investigators speak different languages. Mere agreement does not constitute sufficient informed consent (Faden and Beauchamp 1986, 277–78).

2. *Institutional vulnerability*: when prospective participants have capacity but are subject to the formal authority of others who may have independent interests in whether the prospective participants agree to enroll in the research study (AIDS research in Uganda and Haiti, for example). Safeguards should be in place to ensure participant voluntariness and that it is fair and immune from the influence of institutional authorities.

3. *Deferential vulnerability*: similar to the previous case, but the subordination is informal and not defined by formal hierarchies (e.g., based on gender, race, or class inequalities, or inequalities of power and knowledge as in doctor-patient relationships).

4. *Medical vulnerability*: potential participants with serious health conditions for which there are no satisfactory standard treatments, thus increasing the risk that they will be exploited. Participants must be fully and accurately informed and expectations of success carefully explained.

5. *Economic vulnerability*: undue inducements to enroll, need safeguards

6. *Social vulnerability*: diminished capacity to consent by belonging to undervalued social groups. Care should be taken to structure the informed-consent process so as to reduce stereotyping and empower prospective participants.

The report continues to reflect the bias of American-based research with no specific reference made to an international, cross-culturally complex research environment. However, anthropologists can interpret the new list of vulnerable participants from their own varied research perspectives. Cognitive vulnerability for researcher participants speaking languages other than that of the anthropological researcher is a clear application to anthropological research. Deferential, economic, and social vulnerabilities also link to anthropological research but need to be applied to the specific conditions and locations of cross-cultural research. The list of at-risk populations that anthropologists study is a lengthy one, beyond those already mentioned, and includes not only the world's indigenous peoples but also all manner of relatively powerless and disadvantaged people in international contexts that would qualify as socially, economically, medically, institutionally, and deferentially vulnerable.

Not only do the government reports reflect a clear American bias, but they also fail to take into consideration the large amount of federally funded research that takes place in relatively powerless and economically vulnerable countries around the world where multiple contexts of vulnerability apply. While the American reports acknowledge comparable vulnerable populations in the United States—for example, African American and Latino populations—and are mindful of the harm and lack of protection of African American men in the notorious Tuskegee research example, they fail to extend regulation beyond the U.S. borders. Complaints have been raised by aboriginal peoples about the patenting of human genetic material (Guha 1998), and there have been complaints from Haitian, Kenyan, and Ugandan circles about the conduct of research among HIV-positive patients in their countries (Fluehr-Lobban 2000b). And in the United States, Native American tribal research boards have restrained biomedical as well as cultural researchers who seek unfettered access to "tribal" peoples.

INDIGENOUS ASSERTION OF CONTROL OVER RESEARCH THROUGH INFORMED CONSENT: BIOLOGICAL PROPERTY; BLOOD SAMPLES AND INDIGENOUS RIGHTS TO OWNERSHIP

Complaints were raised about the ownership of DNA as early as 1995 when the U.S. government became the first nation to patent the DNA of a Hagahai man from Papua New Guinea (Fluehr-Lobban 2003d, 99–100). The man was infected with a cancer virus yet did not develop cancer, presumably because his DNA conveyed some immunity from the leukemia-causing virus.

Beyond these cases is the matter of the ownership of blood and cell lines generated in genetic research with differentiated responses from tribes, the evolved standard being partnership with tribes, although some tribes have resisted citing examples of misuse of blood samples. The American Indian Havasupai tribe is a case in point. The tribe agreed to participate in an Arizona State University Diabetes Project that studied possible links between genetics and diabetes. The researchers did not find a link and then passed the blood samples on to researchers studying schizophrenia, migration, and inbreeding among American Indians but without their secondary consent. The tribe only found out about the unauthorized change by accident when a tribal member attended a lecture at ASU. The tribe filed a lawsuit against the Arizona Board of Regents for civil-rights violations, mishandling of blood samples, unapproved research, and violation of confidentiality promises. After a lengthy legal battle, the Arizona Board of Regents and the tribe reached a settlement of $700,000 in compensation for misconduct. Funds for a health clinic and school and the return of the blood samples were negotiated in an out-of-court settlement, leaving no legal precedent. In the suit the tribe claimed lack of informed consent for the secondary studies, as consent had been given orally to the diabetes study but not to the subsequent studies. The Havasupai also argued that (1) genetic studies need not depend on biological samples, (2) human-migration studies, for example, can be done through linguistic analysis, (3) the genetic studies are sensitive as they may undermine cultural beliefs about tribal origins, and (4) a study showing a high inbreeding coefficient may foster myths about Indian inbreeding and deficiency. As a matter of principle, tribes need more controls over the collection and management of blood samples for scientific research (National Congress of American Indians 2012).

The general guideline that the National Congress of American Indians established for the protocols governing genetic research among indigenous peoples of America is that approved research is that which benefits tribal people. Their policy balances tribal sovereignty with ethical considerations and shifts the balance of power and agency from the researcher to the researched.

Outside of the United States, the Canadian Institutes of Health Research (www.cihr-irsc.gc.ca) have guidelines for research involving aboriginal communities. An Aboriginal Ethics Working Group was established in 2004 as part of a broad strategy for consultation with aboriginal peoples in research. The working group generated fifteen articles including a core first principle of understanding and respecting aboriginal worldviews, including showing respect for the privilege of being granted sacred knowledge, the treatment of which must be incorporated into research agreements that have become standard in researching indigenous communities. Jurisdiction over research rests with indigenous communities, including (1) the option of participatory research, (2) free, prior, and informed consent, (3) research guided by the community, (4) research being of benefit to the community, (5) research supporting the education and training of aboriginal peoples, (6) that all proto-

cols should be understood, (7) that secondary use of biological samples requires specific consent from the donor and affected community, and (8) that
secondary consent may be obtained from the individual but not from the
community. Moreover, secondary research requires ethics-board review. In
the event that biological samples cannot be traced to a specific community,
the consent process should be renewed. Biological samples should be considered to be on loan unless otherwise specified in the research agreement.
Finally, indigenous communities should have the opportunity to participate
in data interpretation and review of the research's conclusions and recommendations, while acknowledgment and identification of the community and
participants should be at the discretion of the aboriginal community.

Marlene Brant Castellano summarizes the emerging research standard of
partnering with indigenous communities in conjunction with the Canadian
principle in tribal research that community, family, ceremony, and language
are respected and protected (2004). Among many collisions of worldviews
would be the Western view that the earth and waters are lifeless and that
mice are research objects, contrasting with the indigenous view that all life
forms are coinhabitants with humans on the planet, an integrated biosphere.
The fundamental question of who owns indigenous knowledge has been
raised and answered. Knowledge belongs to the tribe—it is a cultural creation of the tribe and can only be transmitted through authorized individuals.
The research protocols described here follow the activism of the panindige-
nous peoples' movements of recent decades and can be grasped by the increasing agency of aboriginal peoples and their reassertion of control after
centuries of colonization, mistreatment, and, in many cases, near genocide.
The community-controlled model of research is evident in medical research
that is necessarily participatory and shifts the balance of control toward those
being researched and away from the researcher.

INFORMED CONSENT AND THE
OWNERSHIP OF HUMAN TISSUE

The question of ownership of human tissue, also known as *biological property*, has been evolving in American law in close association with informed-
consent demands and protocols. Biological anthropologists Heather Walsh-
Haney and Leslie Lieberman have pointed to the balance of rights in postmortem organ donation between the individual, the next of kin, and science
(2005, 125). Yet some scientists and organ-procurement organizations pro-
ceed to harvest organs under the presumption of consent because a dead
person is not a federally recognized person capable of giving consent, and
perhaps following the principle of beneficence. A comparable scenario exists
in forensic work, where human remains are harvested without question and

without consulting the next of kin, with the express purpose of solving criminal cases (128). This vacuum has left the matter to state law.

The case of Henrietta Lacks (Skloot 2010), whose cells were harvested in 1951 and then released or sold to various scientific research organizations as HeLa, has recently come to public attention. The cell lines of Ms. Lacks, who happens to be African American, were part of the research used in the development of vaccines, cancer drugs, in vitro fertilization, and gene mapping and cloning without her or her family's consent (Skloot 2013, 4). The main issue discussed in the press was that Lacks's DNA sequence was published without permission in the online genetic-information source SNPedia, which is akin to Wikipedia. Thus the issue revolved around privacy and not the considerable corporate financial benefit derived from the patenting and use of the cells for many of modern science's most important breakthroughs. Apparently the descending family is proud of their ancestor's association with the research, but they want acknowledgment that HeLa cells are not anonymous and should be treated accordingly, meaning that consent needs to be obtained for the cells' future use. Moreover, the Lacks family seeks to work with scientific researchers to determine how best to handle the HeLa genome while working toward the creation of new international standards for ethical treatment of "immortal" cell lines, like Henrietta Lacks's. In 2013, in a landmark decision, the U.S. Supreme Court determined that human genes and DNA are "natural" and cannot be patented or owned by any research or commercial entity.

Donna Gitter (2004), legal authority on the ownership of human tissue, argues from her review of the American courts' legal decisions that the following new standards are recognizable trends in the law's evolution on the subject: (1) that consideration of equity militates in favor of compensation for research participants, (2) that such recognition would neither make commodities of human beings and their tissue parts nor erode notions of community, (3) that, nonetheless, the doctrine of informed consent is inadequate at present to protect research participants' interests in dignity and autonomy, (4) that this leads to concerns about scientists luring research participants with false promises and participants elevating financial concerns over health concerns but is still insufficient to deny research participants ownership interest in their own tissue, (5) that recognition of participants' property rights neither appreciably erodes notions of community nor discourages altruism, and (6) that a contractual property-rights model has both advantages and drawbacks. In short, this leading expert on property rights in human tissue argues for the rights of participants over that of the scientists, an egalitarian model in a hierarchical world of knowledge production and the high-stakes world of commercialization of human genetics.

Gitter concludes her argument with a proposal for congressional enactment of a hybrid property rights/liability law that recognizes this property interest of research participants in their body tissue, suggesting the creation of an international oversight body. As American models focus on the rights of individuals, international and cross-cultural dimensions and implications for genetic research are overlooked, and the model depends on negotiation of the terms of research by the participants who possess the agency of those who are fully informed of all risks associated with the research. The model offers the right to sue for damages resulting from any use of their genetic material without obtaining subsequent informed consent and entitling participants to compensation only if the scientists profit from the commercialization of their tissue. These terms, while in many ways quintessentially American, is unworkable and nonapplicable to many of the populations with whom anthropologists work, unless the anthropologist works diligently and collaboratively with the non-Western research participants. The suggestion of an international Human Genome Trust to prevent private ownership by private entities, with international body oversight, would be tasked with granting rights for patentable inventions (Gitter 2004, 343). Such a system recognizes the globalization of science and renders U.S. law compatible with widespread Europe. Opposition to commercialization of the human genome is difficult to achieve, as private ownership of human DNA sequences is already firmly entrenched in both the United States and throughout western Europe (344). A hybrid model that combines research participants' rights with international regulation of the use of the human genome provides a superior solution that keeps the incentive piece alive and "honorable and equitable treatment of human participants that would foster voluntary citizen participation in the United States and Europe with the anticipation that the model would be spread by these researchers to the non-Western world" (Gitter 2004).

An international market in human tissue already exists, and its ethical complexity has been discussed by medical ethicists, its dark, "black market" underside exposed by anthropologist Nancy Scheper-Hughes (2009). But not without controversy. With scientific advances, the increasing demand for human organs for transplantation, especially kidneys, has been matched by a scarcity unable to keep up with the demand. The ethically sound, altruistic donation of a kidney, or postmortem body parts, corneas, and even hearts, has given way to a market-driven trafficking of human kidneys from donors from poorer countries—especially India, the Philippines, and eastern Europe—to rich recipients in the West and oil-rich nations. Violent, repressive regimes associated with various experiences of "disappeared" resisters, such as Argentina and South Africa, have also been documented as participating in the harvest of human organs. The issue of informed consent is rendered technically irrelevant, as the organ donors agree to the necessary procedures out of desperate need. It is likely that the complications and risks are not fully disclosed, making deception a part of the arrangement. Scheper-Hughes herself engaged in deception to carry out her research, a subject that will be revisited in chapter 4's discussion of transparency. Scheper-Hughes argues that bioethics becomes the "handmaiden of free-market medicine" in this illicit, horribly asymmetric trade where ethics and informed consent slide down a slippery slope of market supply and demand operating in contexts of impunity and lack of accountability (Scheper-Hughes 2009). In the United States it is the most vulnerable classes of human populations—overrepresented Latino and African American racial and ethnic minorities from the poor—who are targeted. Scheper-Hughes laments the relative silence of anthropologists on the subject, and so she turned to the human-rights community, creating Organs Watch in 1999 with colleague Lawrence Cohen, perhaps drawing inspiration from the international watch-dog group Human Rights Watch.

Consent among Highly Vulnerable Research Populations

I conducted research in two of the seven Internally Displaced Camps that ring Khartoum, Sudan—Mandela/Mayo and Wad al-Bashir. Their respective names denote both the dependency as well as the agency of the people who reside in them. Mayo is the oldest camp, opened by the government of Sudan and named for the 1969 May revolution of President Jaafar Nimeiri, who went on to install the first camps for Sudan's internally displaced in the 1980s. Mandela is the same camp, renamed by its residents for South African liberator Nelson Mandela. The more recently established camp is Wad al-Bashir, which means the "sons/children of Beshir," the military president after 1989.

In order to conduct research in the camps I needed to obtain permission from the government Humanitarian Assistance Committee (HAC), which reviewed the list of questions that I submitted along with my personal documentation of passport and source of funding from the U.S. Institute of Peace. After one week my research assistant and I were granted permission to begin research, with the requirement that a representative from the HAC accompany us at all times we were in the camps and conducting interviews. After spending weeks with this person, he appeared to us to be more of a social worker than a government-intelligence agent. The small group that regularly traveled to the camps included a hired taxi driver, the HAC representative, my research assistant, Salma, and me. Typical of Sudanese culture and the informal resistance we encountered, we developed an excellent group rapport with the taxi driver—fascinated by the lives and stories he had heard in the camps—the government agent leaving us to conduct interviews in his absence, we researchers enjoying and documenting rich conversations revealing the humor, cynicism, and long-term objectives of the camps' residents.

Formal consent had been granted by the government HAC, without which we would have been barred from entering the camps. However, for every interview and group meeting that we held—whether with interned "tribal" chiefs (*Salateen*) or with women or youth groups organized in the camps— we described in colloquial Arabic or in English with translation to the local languages, Dinka or Fur (displaced residents were from conflict zones of southern Sudan and Darfur), and obtained verbal consent. Typically the oral consent was granted after we had described the research project, the funding source, and the likely outcome of publication in academic book(s) or articles. As some journalists had visited the camps, I needed to clarify that I was not a journalist when interviewees asked me to "tell the world" about their plight. Not a single interviewee asked to remain anonymous, reflecting an agency that likely stemmed more from a lack of fear than personal empowerment, and the cynicism that I quickly saw was the most common outlook. This was often expressed in jokes about the actions and motives of the government and of the police who supervised the camp residents' daily activities and move-ments. The most striking expression of their resistance was the brewing of beer and alcohol for sale inside and outside the camp, requiring police to alternatively turn their heads and conduct raids in which the brew would be confiscated—"for their consumption" was an oft-repeated comment de-livered with a hearty laugh.

To say that obtaining consent was informal is self-evident, but I have come to believe that a more realistic and candid form of informed consent was made possible as a result of the camp conditions, which allowed frank discussion of the goals and outcomes of research with little impact on lives already so deprived of freedom and human rights.

One of my former students, Kevin DeJesus, conducted his doctoral re-search in Palestinian refugee camps in Beirut, Lebanon, in 2005. His research and methodology was highly cognizant of the special vulnerable circum-stances of long-term camp residents, many if not most of whom had been born and raised in the camps. In particular his research highlighted the issue of memory, the act of remembering through interviews that induced, or were capable of inducing, psychological trauma in individuals and families. His 2005 research was on postcolonial, war-torn Lebanon; then in 2011 he stud-ied survivors of Khiam Prison and their families, who had endured extreme violence and physical, social, and psychological trauma that was indelibly imprinted in their lives and on their capacity to reinvent their lives (DeJesus 2011, 385).

DeJesus's research primarily dealt with three interrelated factors: volatil-ity, politicization and protection, and resulting ethical concerns prevailing in conflict zones. "Studying people who live with frequent acts of terror, kid-nappings, suicide bombers, and other operations by nonstate actors," he noted, and who live under "state-sponsored repression such as curfews, de-tention, and high levels of surveillance . . . presents unique circumstances of vulnerability," and "vulnerability is a pervasive condition in violently divided societies" (51). He went on to note that "the risk of harm to both research participants and researcher is an urgent concern to sponsoring academic institutions, and IRBs center on the plausibility of obtaining valid research data while ensuring that no harm comes to participants" (52).

Research participants who had been tortured raised with DeJesus the issue of learning to forget, learning to cope with memories (flashbacks), and desiring to let the world know of their condition. "I want people to know what they did," said one subject (386); a similar sentiment had been expressed to me in the Sudan camps. Moreover, the fact that the Lebanese state failed to protect these people meant that the victims remain vulnerable even once the described events have passed.

The extreme vulnerability of these research participants also exposed the researcher to the possibility of manipulation and misidentification. The Hezbollah organization believed DeJesus to be a spy, publicly labeling him CIA. He received threatening messages that ultimately ended his formal research. He then relied on the method of autoethnography, reflecting on the "tumultuous, ironic, and multiple layers of relational political and identity complexities. Under these conditions it was virtually impossible to build trust." DeJesus thinks that perhaps he was threatened because he had been studying former detainees at Khiam Prison, and his personal reflection was that imperfect engagement and research is better than no research or engagement at all. His circumstances called for a high degree of ethically conscious practice. He concluded his study with recommendations for supportive mental-health policy for future research of survivors of torture and with special advice for researchers, cautioning them to engage with caution and special consideration of the multiple layers of vulnerability of both research participants and researcher.

ANTHROPOLOGISTS' HISTORICAL RESISTANCE TO INFORMED CONSENT

The points made in this chapter and others to follow may help explain why anthropologists have historically given a lukewarm or indifferent reception to informed consent in their research methodologies and their ethical codes. Recall that there was a twenty-seven-year time span between the first AAA code of ethics in 1971 and the first appearance of informed-consent language in the 1998 code. The arguments used by anthropologists and other social scientists continue to challenge the utility and application of informed-consent regulations in social research.

The arguments include the assertions that informed consent (1) is difficult to obtain in ethnographic research as part of the trust-building relationship required, (2) does not lend itself easily to the methods of participant observa-

tion or other unobtrusive methods of research, (3) is an impediment to research participants behaving naturally, (4) cannot be explained or adequately
obtained in many settings where anthropological research occurs, such as in
non-English-speaking contexts or semiliterate, nonliterate societies, (5) is an
impediment to obtaining certain kinds of information about disapproved or
illegal activities, (6) would keep the researcher from having access to powerful subjects or those in closed settings where researchers would not normally
be admitted, (7) is an unreasonable burden, as the researcher cannot always
predict the course of fieldwork, (8) is a U.S. or Western concept and cannot
be fully explained in the context of cross-cultural research, and (9) is impractical in community settings or where it may be required to inform and acquire
consent from every newcomer to the research situation.

There is an anecdotal history of the resistance and even refusal of some
anthropologists to come before their university IRBs and defend their nonap-
plication of the essential components of informed consent in their research,
especially the often-required informed-consent form. Over the years IRB
chairs and committee members from across the country have complained
privately to me about this and have sought my advice.

IRB Challenges

Anthropologists and IRBs have differed over the interpretation and application of informed consent in low-risk ethnographic research. It has been
argued that the historical biomedical standard not only does not fit traditional
anthropological research but also that mechanical requirements to have research participants routinely sign consent forms is unnecessary and harms the
often informal, participatory nature of ethnographic research.

Anthropologist Lawrence Michelak of the University of California,
Berkeley, relates some complaints that suggest an overattention to the process of informed consent by IRBs rather than concentrating on its substantive
content.[2] In one case an anthropologist was required by the IRB to read a
long statement to each interviewee and have the interviewee sign the paper
indicating informed consent had been provided for the interview. Anthropologists' emphasis on trust building would find such a beginning to the research relationship awkward and off-putting. In other cases, consent forms
had been required for anonymous survey data, seemingly because the subject
of the research was alcohol use and public health. This is a case of the
informed consent becoming an end in itself rather than a means to the real
end of the intent of informing and gaining consent—written or otherwise—
from research participants.

Sometimes IRBs with a strong biomedical bias—at major research universities, for example—can view social-science research as neither rigorous
nor scientific. The potential and real importance of social science for its own

sake or for medical research may be undeveloped. IRBs are required to have a community member and an ethics member (such as a philosophy professor who teaches ethics, a priest, or an active member of a hospital IRB), and often these people know little about social-science research or its findings. Medical specialists may apply an inappropriate scientific model to social-science research. However, for anthropologists and for many other social scientists, a waiver of review can be decided by the IRB because overall ethnographic research is viewed by federal regulating agencies as low risk and this is often more appropriate (personal communication with Lawrence Michelak).

However, if the spirit and intent of informed consent simply means that the researcher should offer the fullest possible disclosure of the goals and potential uses of research *before* it is undertaken, then the application of informed-consent guidelines in anthropological research need not be as problematical as originally appraised or as continues to be imagined. First of all, since consent forms are *not* a necessary component for obtaining informed consent, the potential chilling effect on research that most anthropologists fear can be reduced or eliminated entirely. This basic information still seems to be a source of confusion within IRBs and a source of resistance from anthropologists and their students who may be advised to "get through" the IRB-approval process and then carry out their research as they see fit. Since so much of informed consent in anthropological research is self-regulated, education and discussion about the spirit and intent of informed consent is still needed. Acknowledging and addressing the challenges informed consent presents for anthropological research can result in an enhanced, more-open research environment in which both researcher and participant are made to feel more comfortable—and more ethical. It can even lead to greater collaboration in research.

INFORMED CONSENT AT THE HEART OF DEBATES OVER MILITARY ANTHROPOLOGY

Some of the world's most vulnerable peoples are found in military and combat contexts, and in the refugee camps that result from years of fighting. Anthropologists, for the most part, do not carry out research in these environments, although the camps of displaced persons can last for decades and become, in effect, slums surrounding the cities in the conflict-ridden nations. My 2007 research in camps for internationally displaced persons (IDPs) in and around Khartoum, Sudan, were instructive in regard to the flexibility needed for adequate and fully informed consent. Obtaining informed consent among war-weary, long-term-displaced, and highly cynical people meant engaging in a conversation about the intent and potential use of my research.

Many laughed at the irony of their free decision to participate or not in their prisoner-like conditions, but then they encouraged me to use their names and to accurately record their quotations, as they viewed me more as a journalist who could publicize their condition and fate. They were vulnerable people asserting agency in the only way they had at their disposal (Fluehr-Lobban 2012).

Informed Consent and the Human Terrain System

The assertion was made in the two CEAUSSIC Reports on the relationship between anthropologists and defense and intelligence that open, noncoerced informed consent was impossible for anthropologists potentially engaging with the Human Terrain Teams in the Iraq and Afghanistan wars (AAA Commission on the Engagement of Anthropology with the U.S. Security and Intelligence Communities 2007; 2009). This was at the heart of the overwhelming rejection of this form of professional employment in the two separate commission reports. I served on both of these two commissions. The final report of the 2007 commission cited informed consent as one of its central concerns for such engagement. The concept of informed consent "may be compromised, undermined, or rendered impossible" to obtain in settings where vulnerable populations are found and where consent may not be free, voluntary, or noncoerced (ibid. 2007, 25). In the second of CEAUSSIC's final reports (2009) the presumed lack of informed consent was again a central reason for condemning anthropological involvement with the HTS program, although the two commissions had never met as a whole with current or former HTS personnel.

In my view, judgment was passed against a defense and intelligence—not research—program that might employ anthropologists and other social scientists before a broadly based discussion of its mission, potential, and actual practice were investigated objectively. The presumption of doing harm—and not reducing or ameliorating it—and the presumed impossibility of informed consent—presuming a battlefield context and not the complex environment of intelligence work—resulted in the condemnation of the HTS program and of anthropologists associated with it. After four years on the two CEAUSSIC commissions I was left feeling uneasy about how a form of defense employment, essentially a branch of human-intelligence work, had been condemned, especially when we as a full commission had not met with HTS anthropologists or other social scientists to learn about the practice of the program in the different contexts of Iraq and Afghanistan. To me the episode was reminiscent of the ways that anthropologists—mostly forgotten now—had been vilified during the Vietnam War era when I was a student.

I decided to conduct research with former HTS workers and to discuss with them the issue of harm and informed consent when I was invited to write an article on ethics and the HTS program for a book coedited by Montgomery McFate (Lucas and Fluehr-Lobban forthcoming). McFate was the anthropologist at the heart of the HTS controversy and the person most publicly associated with the program. I took this as an opportunity to interview present and former HTS personnel, a conversation that was needed during the four years of the CEAUSSIC commissions. Through McFate and my own contacts at the Naval War College, I conducted interviews with eight former and present HTS members, only one of whom was an anthropologist, the others holding advanced degrees in political science and international relations. All were aware of the HTS controversy in anthropology, and many reported that they had discussed it in their ethics training prior to deployment. Each stressed the nonlethal core of the mission and the care taken to obtain consent and protect the confidentiality of their local contacts and of military personnel in theater. Although my interviewees offered many frustrations and complaints—consistent with public reports from former HTS personnel—each saw her or his role as harm reducing, operating with standards of informed consent, and no one saw their role as traditional academic researchers but as an employment opportunity (Lucas and Fluehr-Lobban forthcoming).

Montgomery McFate reported that HTS independently maintained a process for peer review of research, informed consent, and ethics training, consistent with what the interviewees report. In a personal communication she wrote,

> Since we had no resolution on exemptions from 32 CFR 219 from the JAG and recognizing that there was no single ethics code that applied to such a diverse group of social scientists, we began in 2008 to draft our own Guidelines for Professional Practice (GPP). We called it "guidelines" since the military is already bound by a code of regulations, the Uniform Code of Military Justice. The HTS GPP was signed in 2010. The GPP prohibits engagement in lethal targeting activities, participation in interrogations or interviews without full consent, and encourages publication of research results. The GPP also requires that HTTs provide informed consent and they respect interviewee/interpreter confidentiality. (personal communication, January 10, 2013)

All but one of the interviewed HTS workers indicated that discussion of ethics had been a part of their advance training and that in several cases specific study of the AAA code of ethics had been incorporated in their training. They reported that emphasis was placed on harm avoidance and reduction and on informed consent.

Already mentioned is philosopher George Lucas's (2009) analysis of American anthropology's tendency to blame and shame anthropologists associated with intelligence and defense work, chronicling the discipline's "litany of shame," recited each time a controversy arises to galvanize the discipline. I have often remarked that American anthropology most often discusses ethics at times of crisis, when allegations of wrongdoing by anthropologists is brought to broad public attention. The latter point is most telling as the HTS controversy was sparked by a front-page story in the *New York Times* (October 10, 2007), featuring "Tracy," an HTS anthropologist working in Afghanistan. The image of an anthropologist in military gear with soldiers at her side was riveting and concerning, sparking the first conversations about ethical malfeasance. To my mind this was comparable to the allegations raised by journalist Patrick Tierney, whose 2000 publication *Darkness in El Dorado* had been provocatively subtitled *How Scientists and Journalists Devastated the Amazon*. The subsequent controversy over Tierney's revelations pitted supporters and detractors of the anthropologist so accused against one another, and the lack of informed consent in the research was decried, although no language on informed consent existed in anthropology codes at the time. The controversy raged until the events of September 11, 2001, overwhelmed all discussion other than the implications of the attacks, and the overall context of American research in the Islamic world and in the world shifted seismically.

Informed Consent without Forms

Almost invariably when the subject of informed consent is discussed among anthropologists, the first objection raised is the requirement of a consent form. That anthropologists—accustomed to their informal, participatory methods—might administer forms to their "informants" or participants is anathema to traditional field-research methods. Anthropologists conducting research for clients under federal sponsorship must ensure that informed-consent guidelines have been met. In a research relationship with often relatively powerless, vulnerable participants outside of the West, the Western researcher may feel that she or he is exerting even greater influence over the relationship by introducing the need for a signed form into the research situation. One researcher working with non-Western women concluded that the informed-consent form had become a barrier that also symbolized the great chasm between the demands of research within the university environment and the system of trust already a part of the research collaboration. She described how her research participants resisted signing the forms and how she saw this as an assertion of *their* control over the ground rules for their voluntary participation in the research (Lykes 1989).

This telling, now historic, description of the failure of the use of informed-consent forms is one that most anthropologists would recognize and perhaps applaud for the agency expressed by these women, but the possibility of paternalism/maternalism with respect to decisions regarding risk, benefit, or potential harm to participants might be less easy to recognize. The value of open, collaborative research is that informed consent becomes a natural part of the development of the research project and relationship with research participants and informed consent can be ensured without the use of forms through a process of raising relevant issues that inform and thereby empower the participant. Voluntary participants already sense, or are actually conscious of, that power that flows from their cooperation with the research project. Paid participants, perhaps still a minority in anthropological research, enter into a relationship with researchers that is less ambiguous by being contractual and, therefore, is more open to all manner of discussion and negotiation of the research protocol, including informed-consent concerns.

Among vulnerable indigenous peoples—who are increasingly connected to global conversations about human rights, including the ethical conduct of scientists, researchers, journalists, and others who seek their collaboration—obtaining informed consent is not only possible, it is necessary. The documentation of that consent—whether from an individual or a group—may be recorded orally or in writing, using the language of the people studied as well as that of the researcher (Fluehr-Lobban 2000c). All research involving vulnerable populations must be reviewed not only by the relevant IRB but also by multiple layers of accountability—persons or institutions, including funders, national or tribal research boards, and the profession itself. Where it is determined that increased vulnerability exists, as with HIV-positive persons or refugee populations, the process and documentation of obtaining informed consent needs to be double blind, meaning that multiple parties with no vested interest in the research are consulted.

Terminology in Informed-Consent Protocols

Openness and full disclosure and the reference in social studies to "participants" instead of "informants" or "subjects" convey the shift of power and agency away from the researcher to greater empowerment of the persons agreeing to be a part of research. Models of collaborative research that incorporate informed consent are all components of anthropological research that is fully current with developments taking place in the world we study and the professions that study it. Informed consent may only be a convenient summary term for what has taken place in biomedical and social science research, but when its spirit is implemented it results in better researchers and better research.

CONSENT IN INTERNET RESEARCH

Internet research and virtual ethnography are topics that were not mentioned or explored in the latest AAA code of ethics, (American Anthropological

Association 2009), nor are they mentioned in any other anthropology code. Neither has the realm of cyber research been mentioned or discussed organizationally in any of the major bodies of professional anthropology. This is an important oversight, as anthropologists are among the prime candidates for increased Internet research with a global reach. The lesson that ethics is a continuous and evolving process is made again. Virtual ethnography can be expected to become more common as some research sites become unavailable due to international politics and greater agency on the part of subjects. Also, funding for anthropological research is not guaranteed, and as such the cyber world becomes an ever more fascinating locus of research. Needless to say ethical discourse of these new areas of research has been subject to accompanying lag.

Examining more-advanced European models reveals that at the end of the first decade of the twenty-first century ethical discourse for research using the Internet adopted the human-subjects model of ethical conduct—that is, Internet communication has been viewed as a new kind of community that approximates or resembles real communities that anthropologists and other social scientists study. However, British ethicists E. H. Bassett and Kathleen O'Riordan have argued that the human-subjects model is inappropriate for Internet research, as the Internet represents a new space and textual form from traditional human-subject research (2002). Moreover, informed consent is rendered meaningless and inappropriate as Internet space is public and consent protocols have been developed to protect the privacy and autonomy of individuals. Protecting anonymity and privacy in Internet research is problematical, and thus research participants enter into research relationships with a different set of assumptions than have characterized traditional research (Hamelink 2000).

Moreover, Internet research is not homogeneous, and it is reductive to consider it as such with a gloss of "online research." The Internet is a unique global medium that is differentiated minimally by language, culture, content, genre, and form, and its future directions and possibilities defy the imagination. Virtual communities constructed through websites organized around innumerable topics, interests, and missions create a whole new universe of research possibilities. "Virtual ethnography" and discourse analysis in computer-mediated communication are just two possibilities (Hine 2000; Markham 1998).While still novel in anthropology and the other social sciences, methods that incorporate the Internet as a research tool are gaining in use and acceptance. University professors initially skeptical or hostile to Wikipedia and other Web research resources for research papers have yielded to the increasing dominion of almost exclusive online research in the classroom. Moreover, online teaching and learning are increasingly either used as the virtual classroom supplements or even supplant the real classroom. Indeed, this may be the salvation of accessible postsecondary education in the United States.

The American Association for the Advancement of Sciences (AAAS) issued a report on Internet-research ethics (Frankel and Siang 1999) as a first effort to inform Internet research. It provides a valuable mapping of the issues and argues that the human-subject model already in use in research ethics can be adapted to Internet research. They viewed the Internet as a "site of community" invoking space as the primary paradigm and thus implying that all Internet research is human-subject research. This is severely reductive, as the Internet is a heterogeneous array of media that is far more than interpersonal communication in space. The "Internet as community" space model is likely a historical legacy of the pre-Web Internet. There is a need for the acknowledgment of the unique textuality of the Internet; a good example is Wikipedia, a diverse and dynamic but ever-popular research source. With Internet technologies being used to publish texts produced in a complex convergence of written text and other media and with the new globalized community that is the Internet, the research possibilities and ethical ramifications are indeed difficult to fathom.

The essential textuality of the Internet is likewise challenging for ethics (Bassett and O'Riordan 2002). Most of what is written is published in the traditional ways as a journal or book, and it is copyrighted. However, online bulletin boards, information exchanges, and chat technologies can be harmful, as the number of documented cyber-stalking cases reveals. The Internet is not private; it is by its nature public, and the ethical implications are immense. We would do well to recall that for many years anthropological research was viewed as generally exempt because of the overwhelming public context in which it occurs. The "text," as a reflection of the author, or as an object underlying copyright law—including the Internet of today—extends to Internet news stories, software, novels, graphics, textbooks, and e-mail. Texts that are not covered by copyright are those without such notice and those where the copyright has expired, and these texts are in the public domain. An Internet domain can be legally seen as the equivalent of a corporate trademark, although the case law lags behind Internet discussion of the topic.

Cases of alleged plagiarism become nearly impossible to adjudicate. Google Books has surprised many an author, myself included, with nearly complete versions of their copyrighted text available for free online while the book is still offered for sale as a printed text. The evolving position appears to be that when the research source is a written text, ethical guidelines may be viewed as unnecessary as the text itself is the subject. British students are not asked to engage with their textual item of research as would a sociology or anthropology student in studying humans. However, a case study involving an Internet gay magazine in the United Kingdom (Gaygirls.com) used a public bulletin board for postings, and the effects on LGBT humans became obvious for its potential violations of harm, informed consent, privacy, and anonymity.

The American Frankel and Siang report noted the importance for the delineation of public and private realms in the Internet, but these authors argue that, in fact, there is no such separation (1999). Their point is to acknowledge the essential hybridity of the Internet, that it is both public and private where neither virtual humans nor items or objects on the Net are distinct from those who write them. So is the Internet like a graffiti wall or a message board in a supermarket? Or is it more like a special-interest newsletter intended for group members only? Frankel and Siang caution that the hybrid model of relational ethics incorporating text, space, and the human-subject model really only has limited application and when it is applied as a "safe" default model it can in fact be unethical and unsafe.

Added to these concerns are issues of plagiarism and direct downloading from the Web so familiar to high school and university teachers. This practice resulted in the creation of websites for detecting plagiarism, such as Turnitin.com, where plagiarized term papers can be searched for direct quotations or for whole papers that have been downloaded and dishonestly represented as a student's own work. An interesting ethical effect would be students' knowledge that the tool is available, leading, presumably, to more honest student writing.

Is Consent Necessary, or Possible, in Internet Research?

The new environment of Internet research raises important questions about consent. British public-policy specialists argue that if consent is to protect people's privacy, which we no longer have, what is the point (Spicker 2007)? Privacy is not protected or respected in today's social-media world. Thus, seeking consent is not appropriate when the subject is public or when human rights are being violated and the public's right to know is a justification. Since there can be no reasonable guarantee of privacy, any member of the public, including journalists, not to mention social scientists, all can be observers of public behavior. Most social anthropologists maintain a first responsibility to research participants, but this supposes that research is a private matter depending on a trust relationship between researcher and participant, it is argued. They conclude that the case *against consent in Internet research* is based on (1) the impracticality of obtaining informed consent in public settings, such as at a football match, and (2) the effect of the method's effect on behavior when the participant knows he or she is being studied, as informed consent demands. In order to minimize this effect, no consent in public settings is required. Relying on consent may be morally wrong if the research is guided by other ethical concerns, such as enhancing the public good—for example, investigating the role of government in harm to humans or investigating criminal activities—thus morally justifying critical research in the public interest. Consent thus cannot always be taken as the default position. This view corresponds approximately to the early federal guidelines for anthropological research, which view it as largely "exempt from review" for the fact of its being carried out in the main in public places where consent is impractical or impossible. Certainly this new dimension of Internet research needs to be considered in the ethical guidelines of the professions.

AUTOETHNOGRAPHY AND INFORMED CONSENT

Autoethnography is "a form or method of research that involves self-observation and reflexive investigation in the context of ethnographic field work and writing" (Maré chal 2010). In the past this used to be called "insider ethnography," but it has evolved and is evolving, and its meaning is imprecise as a result. In some cases it is the self-reflexive writing of personal stories and narratives. This can be welcome as positive when historically suppressed voices, as those of American Indians and African Americans—are heard. A branch of Critical Race Theory is composed of narrative of such racially subordinated voices.

A more serious criticism is that of the knowledge production itself is subjective, that autoethnographers tend to reject the idea of social research as objective and scientific. Autoethnography is postmodern in its reflexivity and consequently has similar enthusiasts and critics as do postmodern theories. Autoethnography is not considered as mainstream by positivist or traditional ethnographers, yet it is gaining in popularity. Why this is the case has as much to do with the state of Western civilization—where the majority of anthropological knowledge is still created—as with the old realities of time and money. Autoethnography is less expensive and time consuming than traditional research that can extend for years in challenging cross-cultural environments. Theoretical questions as to how generalizable autoethnography is research are valid, as well as how much resonance such research has with the social collective. At its best it should stimulate cultural criticism, perhaps as sections of larger ethnographic works. Heewon Chang (2008), the pioneer of the field, worries about neglect of ethical standards regarding others when engaging in self-narratives as research.

Wolff-Michael Roth sees autoethnography as an emerging social-science method but cautions that it is more the writing of the self than the "ethno" part of ethnography (2009). At best it can be conceived of as a form of therapy; at worst, it is narcissistic. Elizabeth Dauphinee says that social researchers need to continue to distinguish between scholarship and storytelling (2010). Autoethnography does release the human self from the academic voice as the human context in research is often lost. She argues that purposeful autoethnography should have a place in her academic field of international relations. This would be the case for anthropologists as well, since their experiences as field researchers in cross-cultural contexts can be as instructive as their research. In my own study of the role of Shari'a in Sudan's quarter-century of Islamism (2012), I wrote an autoethnographic section in the book's introduction in order to contextualize the difficulties of rebuilding trust relations in a setting that was transformed by its isolation as a pariah nation. I discuss this in chapter 5's exploration of moral anthropology and ethical decision making.

Anthropologists have been helpful in distinguishing individual and group consent. While it is illogical to obtain consent from yourself in autoethnography, it is certainly important to make an examination of the self in relation to others when applying the method. One useful approach may be affording those mentioned in the research study to read and comment to drafts of the final product and to afford the opportunity to provide full and informed consent to the work. If the person does not agree with the findings, this does not mean that the researcher changes the analysis of the study.

There are few clear ethical guidelines in autoethnography as a method (Chang 2008). The main outstanding questions involve obtaining informed consent and protecting the privacy and confidentiality of persons described in the autoethnographic study. Such reflexive studies are personal, often in small social settings where the observations and data may well suggest the identity of persons described. The historical doctrine of informed consent is rooted in the autonomy and agency of others, and this may be difficult to observe in autoethnographic studies.

QUESTIONS FOR DISCUSSION

1. Should anthropologists be required to document informed consent in their ethnographic studies?
2. How can or should consent be obtained in studies of "cultures at a distance" studied through the Internet? Are participants "informants"? Or is something new and different taking place?
3. What special considerations should be in place for obtaining informed consent with vulnerable populations?

Chapter Four

Transparency and Deception in Anthropological Ethics

The oft-cited rendering of the Hippocratic oath, "first do no harm," can be rephrased for this chapter on ethics and transparency as "first, do not lie." "Thou shalt not lie" is one of the Ten Commandments on which a Christian and all moral systems, and lying, secrecy, and deception, are based and are topics of significance that have been addressed in social science–research ethics.

It is expected that anthropologists and social scientists will practice openness and disclosure in their relations with research participants. This key feature of ethical discourse and practice is a recognized cross-disciplinary standard. The current AAA code of ethics says that "anthropological researchers must be open about the purpose(s), potential impacts, and source(s) of support with funders, colleagues, persons studied or providing information, and with relevant parties affected by the research" (American Anthropological Association 2009, III. Research).

However, unlike other codes in the social sciences, the topic of secrecy in the AAA anthropology codes has been a subject one author has argued is more akin to an obsession (Lucas 2009). This unique emphasis on secrecy is worthy of examination and analysis as there is no parallel in any other social-science discipline's ethical discourse or codes. And it is noteworthy that secrecy is not a major feature of the codes of the allied subdisciplines of anthropology, physical anthropology, or archaeology. It amounts to an almost prima facie case of the politics of ethics rather than the overriding values of right and wrong conduct inherent in other codes of ethics.

The political history of secrecy needs some examination. We must, of course, begin with Franz Boas's 1919 letter of outrage railing against anthropologists' alleged use of the profession as a cover for espionage in Central

America for the Office of Naval Intelligence in World War I. Typical of such allegations, we know more about the accuser than the accused. The protest was registered, Boas was censured as the messenger two weeks later, he retreated, and the issue of covert research was not raised again in the discipline until the Vietnam War. For anthropology, the matter of secrecy appeared as more objectionable than the espionage, leaving open the question about whether the criticism would have been neutralized had the anthropologists been open about their work for government intelligence.

Secrecy was vigorously opposed in the Vietnam-era principles of professional responsibility but was not mentioned in the 1998 code where once-anathema government research was addressed: "Whenever possible anthropologists should disseminate their findings to the scientific and scholarly community" (American Anthropological Association 1998, B.4). I have written that since "secret research is never intended to be made public [or] disseminated and because it may involve deception, and since it is likely to be contracted by defense and intelligence agencies in governments, it is not anthropological research but intelligence gathering" (Fluehr-Lobban 2003b, 230). Anthropologists consulting with the State Department, armed forces, war colleges, and defense and intelligence seminars have not been subjected to negative critical comment, and such engagement is more approved in the current era where it might be believed that more enlightened approaches to foreign policy are engendered through anthropological information and analysis. As Price has argued, increased secrecy is not the more "intelligent" road to pursue in engaging in new relationships with the defense and intelligence agencies and national security (American Anthropological Association 2007).

Allegations of deception carried out in social-science research have been numerous enough to be treated in a separate chapter and have been damaging enough to destroy careers and reputations. Moreover, suspicion and presumption often cloud the picture, making the truth difficult to discern. The case against deception can be as fundamental as the religious commandment "Thou shall not lie" to my own mother's admonition that telling a lie is a wrong that will always haunt you and, moreover, you will always be found out. Philosophers have argued that the only justification for deception is when you are aware of being deceived and agree to it, such as a magician's trick (Gert 1988, 127). "Deceiving always needs some excuse or justification in order to be justified." For the purpose of research ethics, the questions may be raised, What is the effect of lying? Does it contribute to or result in harm? "Deceiving always needs some excuse or justification in order not to be morally wrong" (Gert 2004, 41).

By its very nature and the stigma attached to deception, it is impossible to know when and how anthropologists have deceived their "informants" or us the consumers of their ethnographies. While allegations are greater in number, actual cases documenting deception in research are few. The best-known cases lie outside of anthropology and are more widely known for the greater good of the public interest. Once such case was the demonstration of systematic generation and use of fraudulent data relating to the IQs of lower-class and minority students by Cyril Burt in the United Kingdom, whose "scientific proof" of white superiority through intelligence testing was "demonstrated" through a nearly perfect distribution of points on a bell curve. Burt's "normal" curve of intelligence mirrored perfectly Britain's class structure, with lower-class persons having lower IQs and professional classes having the highest. Further, the numbers he reported in two scientific journals were exactly the same, although the surveys were separated in time by thirty years (Fluehr-Lobban 2006a, 152). Nonetheless, Cyril Burt was knighted for his work and is known to history as Sir Cyril Burt.

In some minds the Central Intelligence Agency (CIA) symbolizes the very definition of deception. Part of the CIA's mission includes clandestine operations, but in recent decades the CIA has been engaging in greater public disclosure. Nonetheless, they have extensive protocols about ethics and an overarching responsibility to their Code of Conduct (1982) regulating the behavior of government employees. I do not choose to be naïve here as some public historic clandestine operations, such as the failed Bay of Pigs invasion of Cuba in the 1960s, are still available for public review and criticism.

Anthropologist Rob Johnston has conducted an ethnographic study of the CIA from an insider's perspective, and his work is a candid assessment of the impact of the reports that intelligence workers produce, especially after 9/11 (2005). He found among those at the Agency a great desire to find better and more ethical ways to do their intelligence work about which they are passionate. Moreover, since the failures of intelligence highlighted by 9/11, there is a humility that now combines with a demand to do better, and part of doing better is defined in ethical terms. Johnston is critical of the remnant past culture of supporting "confirming reports" that do not challenge conventional views or policies over "discomfirmatory evidence" (a term that only the CIA could have invented) that reflect unwelcome but truthful reality. Selected chapters in his study include "Ethnography of Analysis" and "Ethnocentric Bias." The book stresses the fundamental conflict between the competing "goods" of secrecy, necessary for many operations, and openness, necessary for public legitimacy.

In an article in *Philosophy* on the justification of deception in social-science research, Steve Clarke (1999) argues that deception is incompatible with informed consent in that it involves the unlikely rational choice of the use of deception by the "subjects." Even if the deception in research is significant, the question is often raised, Do the ends justify the means? Or, in the acknowledgment that deception is taking place in research, it is best to keep the deception honest, so to speak, in a manner that is open and transparent. This is said while keeping in mind that lots of little deceptions go on in social-science research that for the most part go unrecognized and unacknowledged.

SECRECY AND CONFIDENTIALITY CONFUSED: TRANSPARENCY, AN AMERICAN INVENTION

Secrecy includes acts conducted without the knowledge of others. Secrecy is synonymous with confidentiality, things "spoken or written in confidence, in secret, intimacy" (*American Heritage Dictionary* 1985). Confidentiality refers to acts in confidence.

Transparency by the dictionary definition refers to "light transferred as through a glass; also, open, frank, candid as a man's transparent intentions." As a matter of ethics it is a rather new concept in American public political-ethical discourse, and it is one that has been translated across languages and cultures, particularly with the spread of American-aid dollars and political culture. I first heard the Arabic term *shafifiyya* in Sudan—"transparency" used in the sense of looking through glass and seeing through it. That it had entered Arabic vocabulary surprised me but spoke to the penetration of the concept and of aid culture even into places where there are no diplomatic relations between our countries. There is hardly a protocol on ethics, especially in government and politics, that does not contain wording on transparency.

OPENNESS AND FULL DISCLOSURE IS THE STANDARD

Disclosure of the nature and intent of research is an accepted standard in biomedical research, and avoidance of any deception is preferred in most social-science research and is required by the code of ethics of the American Sociological Association (1999).

Trust building is essential for the primary anthropological method of participant observation in initiating research and in its continuation in subsequent work. Conversations about informed consent that are characterized by full disclosure and openness are the best way to build trusting relationships between researchers and their participants.

But what are the implications for openness and disclosure when an anthropologist contracts to carry out proprietary research, and when is the line crossed in the "avoidance of deception" in contracted research? Is there a different ethical standard regarding openness when the anthropologist works for a private contractor—governmental or nongovernmental—and the findings are not for public or general scholarly dissemination?

Anthropological ethics may be compromised by national-security mandates that conflict with standards of fully informed consent of participants in research. This was a central factor in the Human Terrain System controversy. A new Ph.D. anthropologist considering proprietary contract research or employment with U.S. security and intelligence communities needs to inquire about any limitations to openness and disclosure as a condition for the work. Although deception is to be avoided or is specifically rejected, there are cases where it can be justified.

SECRET RESEARCH, PAST AND PRESENT

In the debates surrounding the 1998 proposed changes to the AAA code, the language on "classified research"—much debated over the decades under the rubric of "secret" or "proprietary" research—remained ambiguous, perhaps intentionally so. By 2007, as the heat of the wars in Iraq and Afghanistan was intensifying, the old issue reemerged largely due to the activism of anthropologists like Terrence Turner, whose resolution at the AAA meeting in 2007 demanded that the old language on secret research from the 1971 code be restored verbatim. That wording was explicit—"no secret or clandestine research" is acceptable for anthropologists, and engaging in such research is unethical (Fluehr-Lobban 1991).

As the issue was revisited, again in the context of war, there was an acknowledgment that the language of 1971 is inadequate to present-day complexities of engagement. The issue of secret research had evolved to alternative conceptions, such as transparency, openness, and disclosure, even used by agencies well known for their secrecy, such as the CIA. Moreover, government-classified documents can be accessed by scholars or journalists, while truly top-secret documents are intelligence research rather than anthropology. Certain exceptions of the secrecy ban were acknowledged, including anthropologists' respect for "secret societies" in ethnographic research and a case that I raised involving the need for secrecy when anthropologists are documenting cases of human-rights abuses and where the identities of the victims need to be protected for their safety and security. In such cases maintaining secrecy in the identity of the rape victim, for example, is the preferred ethical choice, adhering to the principle of the "first responsibility to the people studied" over, in this example, a Western demand for legal documentation of the crime of rape.

With the completed and scheduled withdrawals from Iraq and Afghanistan, the immediacy of the debates over anthropology engaging with the military faded, perhaps to be viewed by students and professionals in the rearview mirror hoping that there are lessons learned and insights gained. A new field of "military anthropology" opened in the wake of these debates and controversies that has been generated by a new group of applied anthropologists working with the military and intelligence communities in a variety of capacities (McFate 2005; Rubinstein, Fosher, and Fujimura 2012).

Government-Classified Research and Corporate Secret Research

Secrecy surrounds many aspects of national security and, after 9/11, homeland security. It is a nontransparency that Americans now expect and accept drawing on, in some cases, well-founded fears of insecurity. Secrecy may not be discernible in defense "compartmented projects" where anthropological knowledge "products" are only as segments of projects, and the whole picture and major mission may not be visible or knowable. The engaged anthropologist providing subject-matter expertise (SME) may not know the direct or indirect impact of their engagement. In such situations where exists a potential to misunderstand or miscalculate the effects of anthropological engagement, it is best to avoid them *both* because of nontransparency and possible, but unknowable, harm.

Biodefense research, along with a host of other types of research, is secret, stemming from national-security priorities and also protection of intellectual-property rights (Resnik 2006). Much medical and scientific research is also kept secret to preserve its cutting edge and to avoid competitive research bodies from benefiting or stealing the research findings. However, often this research is university based and their IRBs may be asked to exempt it from review due to its "secret" national-security focus. This presents serious challenges to the usual openness and sharing environments of a university community and also to academic freedom. Universities are increasingly reluctant to sign on or to sponsor classified research.

Transparency in international research may not be sufficient where America's image has been damaged and trust undermined. Many anthropologists, myself included, report being thought of as spies irrespective of their transparent presentation of self, of their research objectives and methods, and of funding sources. The years ahead may find anthropologists increasingly selecting countries "friendly" to Americans or conducting research among internationals based in the United States or the West.

"Classified" information is that which is only available to those who have "clearance" bestowed by a governmental agency and process. Persons who participate in research that is classified agree to be bound by the rules of nondisclosure and nontransparency. It is derived from legislation passed by Congress in 1917. Normally extensive background checks are carried out on government researchers who acquire classified status. Part of the practice of closed forums where sensitive subjects are discussed—Chatham House Rules—often prevail. These rules, originated at the British think tank Chatham House, request that participants maintain anonymity in attribution of comments and presentations while leaving open the choice of quoting or referencing the remarks.

In some cases—probably judged to be exceptions—the use of deception might be justified because of the greater benefit from the research that may result by not informing participants of the goals and possible uses of that research. The 2009 AAA principles admonish anthropologists to be transparent and open about their research. However, there is less clear consensus about deception among other social and behavioral scientists, especially psychologists who regularly employ and sanction deception as a methodological tool. Deception in anthropology generally has not been explored but mostly condemned, as with Boas's "anthropologists as spies" letter he wrote the nation in 1919 and the Darkness in El Dorado controversy that erupted in 2000 when it was alleged that Napoleon Chagnon's acknowledged use of deception in his research among the Yanomami cause harm (Chagnon 1968; Fluehr-Lobban 2000c).

As with a great deal that has been discussed in this book, it is the balancing of risks and benefits, of competitive values of openness and secrecy, of moral-ethical reasoning and choices, of scientific freedom and constraint of research with humans, of drawing away from absolutes in evaluating rights and wrongs, and of learning as much about a research project as possible before joining it that all lead to better ethical conduct of research. A key consideration is how to advance scientific research without compromising human participants.

Deception and the Yanomamö Case

Controversial anthropologist Napoleon Chagnon is the author of *Yanomamö: The Fierce People* (1968), which is easily one of the most, if not the most, studied work by an anthropologist in American postsecondary education. The popularity of this work and the accompanying films that documented an Indiana Jones–like figure in ethnography is the necessary background to the controversy that ensued after the publication of *Darkness in El Dorado: How Scientists and Journalists Devastated the Amazon* (Tierney 2000). The fallout from the controversy continued into the twenty-first century but was for a time overwhelmed by the anthropology and national-security concerns that emerged after September 11, 2001, though it revived briefly with the publication of Chagnon's memoir (2013).

In his ethnography Chagnon openly described the deception he used in order to gather data about Yanomamö kinship, a subject that is kept secret and is a taboo topic among the people. Indeed, the people gave him false information when the subject was initially probed in 1964 (1968; 1983). Chagnon justified lying and the use of methods normally viewed as unethical, such as deceit and bribery, to obtain the data he needed for the genetic research his coinvestigator James Neel desired and for Chagnon's own hypotheses about male dominance, kinship, and homicide. He was apparently not interested in the Yanomamö construction of their own kinship, normally a part of an ethnographic study, but seemed determined to get the accurate biosocial data that the research project demanded. Because the Yanomamö refuse to speak the names of their dead they could or would not talk to Chagnon about their deceased relatives. They invented names for their dead relations —"Fart Breath," "Eagle Shit"—and he wrote, "As I became more proficient in the language and more skilled at detecting fabrications, my informants became better at deception (1983, 21). In frustration, Chagnon resorted to multiple forms of deception. The following is taken from the third edition of his ethnography, *The Yanomamö: The Fierce People*:

> They quickly grasped what I was up to and that I was determined to learn everyone's "true name," which amounted to an invasion of their system of prestige and etiquette, if not a flagrant violation of it. They reacted to this in a brilliant and devastating manner. They invented false names for everybody in the village and systematically learned them, freely revealing to me the "true" identities of everyone." (1983, 19)

Chagnon continued researching the Yanomamö until 1995, having received grants in the 1970s and 1980s from the Wenner-Gren Foundation for Anthropological Research, the National Science Foundation, the National Institute for Mental Health in 1974 through 1978, and the Guggenheim Foundation (Fluehr-Lobban 2003a, 91). The part that ethical considerations may have played in the initial or continued funding by these sponsors, or in its subsequent review of findings, is not known. Although the AAA code was in existence for Chagnon's subsequent research, it is fair to say that many sponsors of research then did not require an ethical component before their review of research proposals. It is possible that Chagnon's growing notoriety inoculated him from such review before a university IRB.

With the 2000 publication of *Darkness in El Dorado* a furor erupted over the allegations of misconduct, including the incendiary language comparing the Neel-Chagnon research to Nazi-era human biological experimentation, written in a memorandum sent by Terrence Turner and Leslie Sponsel to the AAA, which recalled that the Nuremburg Trials served as the basis for the generation of all professional ethical codes after the end of the Second World War. This constituted the first volley in the war of words and resolutions that ensued as the AAA struggled to find a clear course through the growing publicity and controversy based on ethical matters. A task force in the AAA was formed and issued its first report in 2001, the *El Dorado Interim Report*, with a *Final Report of the Task Force on El Dorado* released in 2002. Significantly, the final report did not make any significant finding of ethical-standards violations by Chagnon or any other American anthropologist but faulted Tierney for violating journalistic ethics. Rather, the task force called on anthropologists to seize this opportunity to consider the ethics of the anthropological enterprise, the plight of the Yanomami and other indigenous peoples, and to use this case to reflect on the ways they conduct research (American Anthropological Association 2002, preface). The AAA believes, the preface added, "that the greatest value of this report is not to find fault or to defend the past actions of specific anthropologists but to provide opportunities . . . to consider the ethics of the anthropological enterprise" (Fluehr-Lobban 2003a, 88). Nonetheless, Chagnon supporters pressed for the report to be rescinded, and in 2005 the AAA membership voted 846 to 338 to do so, responding to growing criticism that judgment had been passed using the Tierney book as its major source of information and that the book's content had not stood up to close scrutiny. Tierney has since gone on record that he had abandoned complete objectivity in his book and had become, instead, an advocate for the Yanomami (Eakin 2013).

In 2013 Chagnon published his memoir, stimulating another round of discussion of his work, motives, and ethics, from which emerged a reflective and insightful article by Emily Eakin (2013). Eakin correctly noted that the reflexive, postmodern turn in anthropology that was part of the reaction to the book took place with the disappearance of the world's indigenous peoples, anthropology's historic subjects. In this context, there was a shift toward activism on behalf of those studied as an ethical-moral imperative connected to the global human-rights movement. Thus, the paradigm shifted from "the Yanomami are violent and not in need of protection" to "the Yanomami are nonviolent and in need of protection" (ibid.). In the 1990s Chagnon created the Fundafaci Foundation, ostensibly to protect the Yanomamö, but it was linked with gold-mining interests and involved collaboration with the highest political-economic interests of Venezuelan president Perez to create a "biosphere" around Yanomami lands, akin to a human zoo, where gold was mined and possibly resulted in greater harm to the Yanomamö than had Chagnon's original deception. Chagnon's motive was summed up in his own words when the project ended in 1993: "I got a year's worth of data. It was worth it for that reason" (ibid).

Chagnon's blunt and, for cultural relativists, offensive, use of language to describe the Yanomami has also been a factor. In one quotation, as he attempted to humanize the Yanomami to his critics, he wrote, "The Indians get dirty, smell bad, use drugs, belch after they eat, covet and sometimes steal each other's women, fornicate, and make war. They are normal human beings, reason enough for them to deserve care and attention" (Eakin 2013).

He is also well known for his confrontational style when responding to questions of his use of language. At a talk he gave in the early 1970s at my home institution of Rhode Island College, Chagnon replied to a criticism I raised of his description of the fecundity of the Yanomamö as "breeding like rabbits": "Well, they don't breed like celery." A young anthropologist, I was then stung by his retort, but I can see more clearly now that it may have been a defensive response to growing criticism of his writing as sociobiology, which critics associated with race and gender bias.

When Yąnomami indigenous activist Davi Kopenawa asked members of the AAA Task Force if anthropologists were fighting among themselves because of the book, he was told yes. He responded:

> So, Chagnon made money using the name of the Yąnomami. He sold his book. Lizot too. I want to know how much they are making each month. How much does any anthropologist earn? And how much is Patrick [Tierney] making? Patrick must be happy. This is a lot of money. They may be fighting, but they are happy. They fight, and this makes them happy. (Eakin 2013)

AAA president Jane Hill, who presided during the years of the El Dorado Task Force, was quietly critical of Tierney's book but nevertheless sided with continuing anthropologists' access to Latin American indigenous peoples. Referring to Tierney's book as "just a piece of sleaze," she said that the AAA had to act or else anthropologists' ability to work in indigenous South America "was put seriously at risk" and silence on the part of the AAA would have been interpreted as either assent or cowardice. "Whether we're doing the right thing will have to be judged by posterity." As if to confirm this admission of misjudgment on the part of the AAA, in 2012 Chagnon was elected to the National Academy of sciences (ibid.).

This case involving ethics was the most serious until the controversy over anthropologists and the Human Terrain System erupted in 2007. It is an excellent case for discussion of ethics "then and now" (the title of an essay I wrote in 2004) and for consideration of multiple broader issues. Recalling chapter 2's discussion of primary harm—to the people studied—and secondary harm to the anthropologist, it is clear that for the public discussion of these events the secondary harm to the reputation of the anthropologist overrode the primary harm to the people.

Secondly, the question of advocacy is illustrative. Tierney eventually admitted that he had changed from an observer to an advocate, at which point he had retreated from objective journalism (Eakin 2013), revealing the subjective course that is followed when journalists or anthropologists become advocates. As appealing as advocacy is in terms of both morality and ethics for the anthropologist, who it may be said naturally allies with the people studied, when there is a shift to a position of advocacy it changes the nature of the research and the science being conducted. It is, perhaps, best to make conscious decisions about advocacy as separate acts as a citizen or human-rights activist but not to confuse these with research objectives and findings.

Finally, the "Mengele-Nazi era" criticism levied at Chagnon and his supporter's accusation that he was being subject to a witch hunt pitted anthropologist against anthropologist, made the whole thing unseemly. But this has been all too frequent in American anthropology's history. George Lucas described the discussion surrounding the Human Terrain System as a ritualistic "litany of shame," illustrating the discipline's pattern of blaming and shaming, which needs to be addressed, recognized, and hopefully eradicated as future cases inevitably arise. Eakin described the whole episode as a "ritual cleansing" of the discipline, and this observation can also be profitably discussed.

It is perhaps a result of the withdrawal of any grievance model or procedure from the anthropological codes of ethics that has precipitated this behavior of publicly airing collegial disputes that can be disguised as fundamentally about ethics when they are actually about other grievances.

I encourage students and their teachers to study and consider this case as illustrating (1) the concepts of primary and secondary harm introduced in this book, (2) the blaming and shaming too common in anthropology, (3) advocacy as a choice, not a responsibility, and (4) the effect of the use of crude language to casually and disrespectfully describe the people studied.

Philosophical Perspectives: Bernard Gert on Secrecy

Dartmouth College philosopher Bernard Gert and I enjoyed a professional relationship of mutual exchange and respect for nearly a quarter-century until 2009, just three years prior to his passing in 2012.[1] I quote extensively here from a personal communication to a series of questions I'd raised with him in 2009 as the matter of secrecy was again being brought to the fore in the debates over the potential military and intelligence applications of anthropology. He wrote,

> Secrecy is an interesting concept. Over twenty years ago, I reviewed Sissela Bok's book *Secrets: On the Ethics of Concealment and Revelation.* If my memory is correct, she seemed to hold that secrecy is like deception in that it always needs to be justified—that is, unless one has an adequate justification for keeping what you are doing secret, then doing so is immoral. The 1998 AAA code of ethics [for which Gert had been an outside consultant] did not view secrecy and deception in the same way; it encouraged making one's research public, but, as the following quote shows, it explicitly forbids deception. "Anthropological researchers bear responsibility for the integrity and reputation of their discipline, of scholarship, and of science. Thus, anthropological researchers are subject to the general moral rules of scientific and scholarly conduct: they should not deceive or knowingly misrepresent [i.e., fabricate evidence, falsify, plagiarize] or attempt to prevent reporting of misconduct or obstruct the scientific/scholarly research of others." (Code of Ethics

of the American Anthropological Association, Approved June 1998, III. Research B. Responsibility to scholarship and science: Paragraph 2)

Deceiving is violating a moral rule, and so it needs justification. If information has significant practical use in preventing serious harm, then, depending on the other features of the situation, many would hold that it is justified to deceive. For anthropologists, this means that research that involves deceiving is not allowed simply in order to get a publication, but research that involves deceiving may be allowed if this information can only be obtained by deceiving and may prevent serious harm to those who are being deceived. Deceiving people in one group to prevent harm to those in another group is more difficult to justify, unless the first group is planning to harm others. That a group is planning to harm others is what justifies deception of criminals and violent gangs by undercover police.

Some anthropologists might view deceiving, or even harming, the people being studied as justified if the research aids national security, while others might claim that national security does not override the primary responsibility of anthropologists to the people they study. But unless the people being studied are planning to harm others, so that anthropologists can claim that they are justified in the same way that undercover police are justified, it does not seem that national security can justify deceiving or harming the people being studied. Secrecy is different; it does not need to be justified unless it involves deceiving or significantly increasing the probability that the people being studied will be harmed. But then it is the deception, or increasing the risk of harm, not the secrecy, that needs justification.

In fact, sometimes we regard secrecy as good. For example, physicians and lawyers are required to keep what their patients tell them secret; although when we approve of secrecy, we usually give it a different name, for example, confidentiality. Secrecy is not prohibited by a general moral rule, and, hence, unless secrecy is prohibited by some duty imposed by their profession, members of that profession, for example, anthropologists, may decide on their own whether to keep their research secret from the general public. The question that should be considered by anthropologists, most of whom depend on the people they study trusting them, is: whether the trust of the people they study requires that all anthropological research be made public unless there is an adequate justification for keeping it secret. If they decide no, then there should be no general rule prohibiting secrecy. If they decide yes, then they must decide what morally relevant features of the situation they think provides an adequate justification for keeping their research secret.

Reflecting on Gert's thoughts on deception and secrecy, I see that he argues that the use of deception in research requires justification, which is mainly justified as a harm reducer or ameliorator. He uses the example of undercover police, presumably working to reduce harmful trafficking in drugs or prostitution, but his example is rendered instantly complex as to whether their work targets drug lords or street sellers, or in prostitution pimps, johns, or trafficked women from poor countries.

The anthropological community could have benefitted from Gert's view of secrecy—that it is not an unmitigated evil and does not need to be justified unless it causes harm. Secrecy is the intention not to share information and is the opposite of transparency. The historical preoccupation with secret research, originally articulated in 1971 and revived in 2007, is unique to anthropology. The condemnation of secret research was presumably deployed as key to an improved ethics; however, it was not articulated as a harm reducer but as a moral imperative. Anthropologists differ, Gert correctly notes, over the use of national security as a justification for the use of deception in research, but he adds that consistent with the history of anthropological ethics this is only the case if the people studied are planning to harm others. What comes to mind are covert studies of extremists and terrorists, whether an extremist Christian planning to bomb a clinic where abortions are performed or an extremist Muslim with explosives hidden in shoes or underwear, where public harm could result. Or in the case of an anthropologist studying violent racist organizations who learns of planned attacks on targeted racial groups, breaking a promise of secrecy is justified, as in not doing so harm would likely result to innocent persons.

Gert reminds us that secrecy can be a good thing, as between a doctor and patient or lawyer and client, where it helps define the relationship. Thus, anthropologists can decide whether to keep their research secret or not when there is adequate justification for keeping it secret, such as the promise not to divulge information about secret societies or requests I have received from Sudanese litigants who do not want the details of their cases to be written about or published. Gert asks if the trust relationship between the anthropologist and the people studied requires public dissemination or demands secrecy. If there is no such requirement, then there is no general rule regarding secrecy. If the answer is yes, then what moral imperatives constitute a justification for keeping the research secret?

Cases of Possible Justified Use of Deception

Anthropologist Nancy Scheper-Hughes's use of deception in documenting international organ trafficking provides an excellent opportunity to explore the issue. She studied the darker side of organ transplants in response to a demand for "fresh organs" where networks of organized crime—what she calls the "body mafia"—mobilizes organ buyers, itinerant kidney hunters, outlaw surgeons, medical technicians, makeshift transplant units, and clandestine labs (Scheper-Hughes 2009). The profitable trade and trafficking of human body parts flows from poor to rich nations and persons, where the value of an Indian kidney was put at $1,000, a Filipino kidney $1,300, and a Romanian kidney $2,700! At the point of distribution a Turkish seller can command $10,000 to $30,000 for the sale of a kidney, a price driven by market forces of international supply and demand.

To date Scheper-Hughes related that only kidneys, bone marrow, and liver lobes can be harvested for transplant). Trafficking occurs in some of the world's major cities—London, New York, Tokyo, Istanbul, Tel Aviv, Mumbai, Johannesburg, and Manila. The trafficking and trace preys on two vulnerable populations: the desperately sick and the desperately poor. Scheper-Hughes founded the human rights group Organs Watch, for which her team posed as customers to interview dozens of kidney buyers and sellers. She writes, "Though I am not proud to reveal it, I posed during fieldwork in Turkey in February 2002 as a buyer desperately seeking a kidney for a family member in order to meet sellers at a "Russian suitcase market" in a run-down, immigrant section of Istanbul" (2009, 180). She admits that Organs Watch "blends genres and transgresses longstanding distinctions [between] anthropology, political journalism, scientific reporting, moral philosophy, and human-rights advocacy." She goes on to ask,

> How does one investigate covert and criminal behavior as an anthropologist? To whom does one owe divided loyalties? In traveling incognito, as I did when investigating allegations of illegal organs and tissues harvesting at the Argentine asylum, Montes de Oca, for the profoundly mentally retarded, I had only Laud Humphreys [Tearoom Trade study, 1970] and his highly questionable, later roundly condemned, observational study of impersonal sex in public bathrooms as a shaky reference point. But how else, except in disguise, could one learn of the hidden reality of an invisible population? How can the mute and the profoundly mentally retarded possibly speak for themselves? What alternative methods of investigation are appropriate? This kind of work requires a certain militancy as well as a continuous and relentless form of self-criticism and a constant rethinking of anthropological (as well as medical) ethics and practice. (Scheper-Hughes 2009, 180).

Scheper-Hughes argues that the case for organ trafficking requires going "beyond bioethics"—the traditional empathy is for the sick organ recipient and not for the donor, living and brain dead, whose suffering is hidden from the public. If the source and associated suffering were known, potential recipients might opt out of procedures. Live donation remains risky, and whereas bioethical law in the United States and Europe follows contract law, like surrogacy, it is subject to choice, but choice is a questionable fact among such vulnerable populations. The usual organ-recipient lists include infants and persons over seventy years of age under a system of "presumed consent," such as organ donation on driver's licenses in which all citizens are potential donors at brain death. This practice is widespread in Europe, where organ transplant is seen as a general social good in which no one is included or excluded based on the ability to pay (ibid., 192). She sees her research as essentially one of social justice and human rights and concludes with a "radical ethical challenge" in which the body is viewed as a gift that should not be sold or bought.

When Is Deception Necessary to the Research-Project Design and Execution?

Deception is closely related to the consent process, and its use needs to be justified. Studies that use deception as a research tool present special problems as to what is meaningful consent for the researcher and for the review board. Some questions that can fruitfully be raised to engage discussion of the pros and cons of the use of deception in research follow.

1. Is the use of deception justified in the research design? What is the rationale for using this technique?
2. Are nondeceptive methods feasible? If so, why are these not used?
3. Will the deception be expected to cause physical pain or psychological distress?
4. Will the deception be fully explained to the participant as early as possible?
5. Will the participant be informally or formally reconsented as to the true nature of the study?
6. Is the explanation of the true nature of the study accurate and complete?
7. Is the explanation of the true nature of the study expected to cause any level of psychological distress or social embarrassment to the participant? (extracted from Social and Behavioral Sciences Working Group on Human Research 2003)

Examples of Hypothetical Studies Using Deception

Case #1

An anthropologist has been employed to study the acceptance of a new hair-care product that is targeting "new markets" in a Latino community. The product has advertised the promised result of added "shine" and "brilliance" to hair, but its models thus far have been white, and the company wants to hire a Latino to gain cultural authenticity and its entry to nonwhite Hispanic markets. The anthropologist, though classed as white on college records, is phenotypically of ambiguous race and successfully poses as a Latino in order to enhance appeal to the marketers and to the employers. The justification is that race has little to do with effective performance on the job, thus a "little white lie" that the anthropologist is half-Cuban (on the mother's side, thus answering questions about the surname) is justified for the sake of the greater good of getting the job.

What do you think? Is the deception by the anthropologist-applicant justified for the sake of employing an anthropologist, many of whom remain unemployed or underemployed despite earning their Ph.D.s? What would you do? Are there alternative forms of disclosure that would be both more truthful and transparent and not involve deception?

Reflection: Since it is best to not lie or deceive, the anthropologist should have been truthful about his/her ethnic/racial background when applying for the job. It is unlikely that being Latino or "appearing" Latino is a requirement for the job, and the anthropologist could have emphasized his/her academic preparation for the job as a cultural specialist. Emphasizing a command of culture over appearance in the job interview would be both more effective and more truthful. Deception in this case is not called for.

Case #2

An anthropologist has been contacted to be a part of a team investigating human-rights abuses in an African country. The anthropologist happens to be a native of that country and is a desirable member of the team for her cultural and linguistic knowledge. However, some members of her family were victims of these abuses, and disclosure of her true identity would compromise the execution of research, as sampling responses to questions by the abusers as well as victims is part of the research design. Thus, the research designers decided that the anthropologist's identity would be altered, her name would be changed, and her profile would be kept low, even though for the majority of respondents her national-cultural affiliation would be an asset to the study.

Reflection: The use of deception in this research may be justified for the "greater good" of carrying out research that might end in the documentation of human-rights, which could lead to favorable humanitarian outcomes, such as bolstering cases for asylum seekers who had fled from a totalitarian regime. However, contact with victims by researchers from outside the country could place the respondents in greater danger. Whether the outcome is perceived as positive or negative, it is nonetheless based in the factor of deception. Is the risk worth the possible benefit? What would you do?

There is an acknowledged type of research where deception is necessary to its design and validity. These are more common in psychological research and market research. A low degree of deception might consist of the researcher offering only limited knowledge about the subject of the research so that the participant will respond naturally. A high degree of deception might consist of the researcher actually lying about the purpose of the study or about the reason for participation in the study. Humphreys's tearoom trade in the 1960s, the Tuskegee syphilis study in the 1940s, and Milgram's obedience study (where participants were deceived into believing they were administering electric shocks to subjects) are among the few recognized examples of unethical use of deception. In order to justify the intentional use of deception, researchers must demonstrate that the deception is both necessary to the validity of the study and valuable to the scientific community. The American Sociological Association requires that researchers debrief participants who have been deceived, allowing the researcher to assess any concerns the participants might have. The goal of the debriefing is to correct the inherently unethical nature of the deception by being honest about the study and to correct any problems or misunderstandings. But debriefing may result in negative feelings of anger or embarrassment and may have the unintended consequence of mistrust of both the researcher and of research itself. As such, there is a potential disincentive on the part of the researcher to debrief (wikis.lib.ncsu.edu/index.php/Deception_in_Social_Research).

SECRECY AND THE HUMAN TERRAIN SYSTEM

A key factor in much of the opposition to the Human Terrain System (HTS) was that it became part of U.S. intelligence and is thus by definition not fully transparent. The original intent of the HTS program was cultural advising, but it evolved into an intelligence function. The ethical problem of its mandatory secrecy was part of both of the reports on the HTS issued by the AAA Commission on the Engagement of Anthropology with the U.S. Security and Intelligence Communities (CEAUSSIC). In response to the controversy centering on ethics and the lack of any meetings with HTS personnel by the full CEAUSSIC commissions on which I served, I accepted an invitation to write a chapter in a book on HTS edited by Montgomery McFate, the most public face and controversial figure for the program in anthropology. I was provided with contact information for current and past anthropologists and social scientists working as part of Human Terrain Teams (HTTs) and interviewed eight of them for the article, which I coauthored with philosopher George Lucas, who had written extensively about the debates in anthropology (Lucas and Fluehr-Lobban forthcoming; Lucas 2009). The issue of secrecy and the inherent problem or possible violation of ethics that secrecy represents was directly addressed by the respondents.

The fact that HTS was intended as a nonclassified, open program but then became closed and classified ultimately explains the attitude of organized anthropology and its opposition by the AAA. However, the program was condemned before it was investigated by the AAA. In my interviews one HTS respondent opined that secrecy is easier than the messier option of openness and disclosure. That is a correct and instructive observation.

One of the respondents was keen to point out that secrecy was practiced in HTTs for the protection of local contacts in Iraq and Afghanistan and that strong measures were taken to protect the identities of sources for the purpose of harm prevention. The respondent argued that the main objective is the information and not the source. It was further argued that trust and mutual respect are the greatest harm reducers in military engagement in the war zones of Iraq and Afghanistan.

Another team member mentioned that the only justifications for secrecy in military engagement are troop movements and personnel matters. However, when the HTS changed its charge to being classified it reneged on the original nonclassified nature of the program. This was a disappointment to the former HTS personnel I interviewed, as the original idea had been for culturally based research to be shared inside and outside the defense and intelligence communities. The military may well have viewed the ethics debate in the HTS program as an academic problem and not a practical one, one of the respondents opined.

By 2009 and 2010, when the HTS became more militarized, away from their original model of providing cultural advice, there were few further attempts to further engage the social sciences in strategies for fighting the wars in Afghanistan and Iraq. Taking a balanced view, it can be said that for anthropologists who opposed the HTS this was good news, while for others who saw the harm-reducing potential of the HTS it was an unfortunate but cautionary lesson.

Anthropological Research in Countries with Chronic Militarism

As a member of both AAA commissions on the engagement of anthropology with military and intelligence agencies, I have reflected on the matter of my working in a research environment in Sudan where chronic militarism and repression of free speech can compromise openness and transparency. Over the course of four decades of research, from 1970 to 2009, except for a brief period of democracy between military rulers, a state of emergency has prevailed in that region, and my responses, adaptations, and responsibilities as a researcher have been shaped by them.

1. For all these years, the "state of emergency" has meant lack of full freedom of movement and expression for citizens–research participants.
2. I knowingly and willingly accept the potential restrictions on my freedom to transparently observe events and meet with individuals in the

society. I have repeatedly been *granted* visas from successive military governments, which process is by no means automatic.

3. I am open about my research project, its sponsors, and intended outcome(s); increasingly my work is translated into Arabic and subjected to local scrutiny and debate.

4. I am transparent and do not use deception with anyone; if deception would be required in order to meet an individual or observe an event, I avoid those situations.

5. I take advantage of my outsider status and language skills to listen to informal complaints and information from individuals, information not available in the public domain. This means overhearing conversations in public places.

6. In the field I may observe, but never participate in, public demonstrations or protests against the lack of freedoms in the military regimes. I do, of course, write about these.

7. I strive to be objective in my public interviews and commentaries, despite a desire to have me take political stands on a variety of issues.

8. I accept the reality of the general lack of freedoms of speech and open assembly and the potential harm it represents for the participants who choose to collaborate in my research. Thus, although my participants may not be free to speak, I exercise a personal freedom of speech and movement to the degree possible.

9. Access to vulnerable populations, such as IDP camp residents, is granted by a government humanitarian agency where human-rights victims are a particular concern.

10. Outside of Sudan I freely criticize, on the public record, the lack of freedoms, denial of human rights, etc., for citizens of Sudan. I am frequently an expert witness in political-asylum cases where the conditions of chronic militarism are at issue.

11. Openness and negotiation of the known risks and benefits of research with informed individuals within an otherwise restricted environment has been my modus operandi.

The institutional review board (IRB) of my home institution asked me to respond in person to a number of questions they had regarding the safety and well-being of the research participants in my study of Shari'a, and I just remind the reader that the main intent of my IRB was to protect the Sudanese in my study assuming that I had the knowledge and agency to take care of my own well-being, although almost every colleague and acquaintance cautioned me to be careful before departing for Sudan.

The protocols were for scheduled interviews. Consent for my observation of public behavior was viewed as unnecessary. In spite of this, I asked myself whether it was my obligation in that environment to inform random people of my knowledge of Arabic since the IRB was concerned about any potential harm coming to Sudanese participants. Was it a low-grade form of deception to disguise my knowledge of Arabic when the average citizen assumes—quite correctly—that foreigners, especially Westerners, do not know the language? As a matter of personal choice I decided on transparency and frequently joined public conversations to let people know I understood public discourse. This decision was reinforced by the almost uniformly positive reaction of strangers to the use of Sudanese colloquial Arabic from nearly every ethnic and class background. An interview I gave in Arabic with my husband, Richard, was repeatedly rebroadcast during the Muslim and national holidays, giving us some notoriety, whereby people recognized us as Arabic-speaking Americans. Thus, the issue of transparency regarding my ability to overhear and assess everyday conversations, for example, on buses and in the market, dissolved to a natural practice of ethical conduct.

TRANSPARENCY AND INTERNET RESEARCH

If you browse the Internet for discussion of the ethics of Internet research, you will discover that (1) European social scientists are ahead of North Americans in discussing and debating the subject and 2) the rules for Internet research are generally the same as for other types of research, revealing the truth of the maxim that in matters of ethics, research is research and there are neither exceptions for anthropologists nor for Internet researchers. The basic principles of honesty, to tell the truth about the nature of the study and to not lie or misrepresent your research, are fundamentals that are known to in-country and international fieldworkers and to the new world of Internet research.

The federal principles enunciated in *The Belmont Report* include the principles of (1) autonomy, (2) beneficence, and (3) justice, which are all applicable and are to be balanced for their relevance in Internet research. Assessing both the probability and magnitude of any harm that might result from research is advised. The possibility of the National Institutes of Health's issuing a Certificate of Confidentiality—regardless of funding source—that will protect research findings from any forced disclosure exists for high-priority research.

Internet research is also broached in chapter 2's discussion of informed consent, and to add a bit more complexity to this emerging arena of social-science research I mention a few additional concerns regarding transparency. Some of the problems with Internet research that the federal Office of Human Research Participants (OHRP) has identified are (1) the difficulty of determining the adult status of participants, (2) the difficulty of determining "personhood" in the virtual world, and (3) the potential for re-identifying by the use of social-networking persons who have been "de-identified." Also, a phenomenon of "data scraping," whereby data is extracted from social-networking profiles, provides identifying information for individuals who are assumed to be anonymous. Beyond these, blogs, quotations, and IP addresses compromise anonymity. It is hardly a surprise that Internet-research ethics is something of a moving target, so researchers are encouraged to keep up to date with changing technologies and ethical issues.

The AAA's new code of ethics, designed as an educational device, advises abandoning research that requires deception. Once lying and deception have become an established part of the methodology, they will overwhelm the research. It is a mistake to presume that research occurs in a vacuum or that the people studied are passive and take little notice of our methods.

QUESTIONS FOR DISCUSSION

1. Can deception in research be justified? If yes, what are sufficient justifications for deception?
2. If deception is necessary to get the data, should the study be abandoned?
3. What old and new ethical challenges are raised by Internet research? What are some novel strategies for the ethical conduct of research?

Chapter Five

Moral and Ethical Anthropology

Average people across cultures do not need to read a book on morality in philosophy or religion, or a chapter in a book on anthropology and ethics, to know how to act morally and to understand the difference between right and wrong. Indeed, when I first began to write about ethics and anthropology in the 1980s, when there were few texts to read, I often relied on my own gut reactions to a dilemma before overthinking a case. After years of writing about ethics, I still do this.

Ethics and morality on the surface may appear to be identical or so similar that distinctions between them are slight and the terms interchangeable. Morality is more often discussed in religion or philosophy, although anthropology has a great deal to contribute to its discussion across cultures, time, and space. In *A Companion to Moral Anthropology* Didier Fassin argues that the distinction between morality and ethics is far from universally understood or accepted by philosophers, nor, as a logical extension, by anthropologists (2012, 6). Moreover, ethics and morality are often confused in everyday life and language, and this confusion has been transferred to discourse in anthropology. Morality as a culturally defined set of ideals and rules is more ambiguous than is ethics, normally discussed as specific professional responsibilities. Philosopher Bernard Gert has defined morality as "an informal public system applying to all rational persons, governing behavior that affects others, and has the lessening of evil or harm to others as its goal" (2004). Philosopher John Rawls, who wrote the 1971 classic work *A Theory of Justice*, established the "equality principle"—a universal moral sense that humans equate with fairness. Public systems of fairness or justice are disclosed, understood, and explained through a mind experiment devised by Rawls whereby a "veil of ignorance" is imagined in which all are impartially positioned as moral agents to determine what is right, fair, and just. The anticipated commonality of morality and justice are derived from a shared public conception of justice—for example, that it is right to view all humans as equals and therefore is wrong to discriminate on the basis of race, gender, or class. Rawls's theory has had such intellectual power that he was awarded the National Humanities Medal in 1999 for his contribution to reviving democratic discourse of a generation. When you read the simplicity of Rawls's core ideas of fairness and justice being foundational to morality, it is easy to recall that many a child's first protest is often "It's not fair!"

Ethical codes are often statements of conduct that reflect informal public systems of disciplines and professions that are usually not enforced, such as the anthropology codes. Codes are enforced if they are tied to licensing standards and grievance models. Since anthropology abandoned its grievance model in 1998, a system with a recognized authority to determine what counts as morally acceptable or unacceptable professional behavior has not been established, and many would argue that it should not be. Indeed, one of the few recent cases where a grievance model was invoked was in an effort to sanction an anthropologist associated with the *Darkness in El Dorado* controversy. The recently established principles of professional ethical practice were drafted and approved without any specific reference to moral behavior (American Anthropological Association 2009). Anthropologists have tended to view morality as more subject to cultural relativism than as a universal in human culture. Moreover, differences in core values and in religious beliefs mean morality is viewed in fundamentally different terms—for example, the divergent views in America over the "right to life" and the "right to choose" devolve to moral positions on abortion or termination of a pregnancy.

So, what do anthropologists think morality is? Anthropologist Didier Fassin writes that moral action is what is viewed as good, right, just, or altruistic (2012, 5). He adds that moral anthropology is a form of empirical inquiry investigating how social agents articulate and negotiate moral claims in local ethnographic contexts. Another simpler rendering might be that a moral anthropology is one that seeks to use the discipline to make the world a better place; but just what constitutes that better place is subject to debate.

Moral values likely evolved out of human group social life and psychology emphasizing in-group and out-group perspectives, ideas of right and wrong that were adaptive to human survival. In contemporary life morality is associated with activities based on a collective shared worldview and cooperation as to what is virtuous living. Morality can have relativist and nonuniversal expression in nationalism and patriotism where one nation's projected good is another's evil. Insurgencies and counterinsurgencies are examples, as were pro- and anticolonial struggles in Africa, or the Global War on Terror, where the moral and immoral, right and wrong, are shaded by culture, religion, and history of conflict.

A model used by anthropologists and derived from French sociologist Emile Durkheim views morality as the set of values and norms that determine what people as agents are supposed to do and not to do, colloquially referred to as the list of do's and don'ts. Anthropologists who favor a postmodern analysis, associated mainly with the writings of Michel Foucault, view ethics as the subjective work produced by people who as cultural agents decide how to conduct themselves in their inquiry about what a good life is (Fassin 2012, 7). Fassin questions what could or should be a "moral anthropology" (ibid., 14).

Before Foucault became synonymous with postmodern theory, an American anthropologist-philosopher couple interrogated the "quest for moral understanding in anthropology and ethics," reversing the order of words in their pioneering book (Edel and Edel 1959). Their work includes chapters on "The Mark of the Moral," noting that there are no extant definitions of "the moral" in anthropology, although there are many in philosophy. This is probably due to anthropology's cultural relativism and historic lack of moral judgment of cultural practices. The Edels conjured a spectrum of "ethics wide and narrow," denoting universal and relative values and the diverse range of cultural-moral differences in anthropology as contrasted with the historic quest for universals in philosophy. They explored moral feelings and cultural sanctions as expressions of right and wrong. They decried the historical view that so-called primitives have no morals to a post–World War II Western world of increased moral complexity: "Human problems are becoming more complex and have to be confronted directly as moral" (2000). They were among the first to use the term *metaethics* as the linguistic science of ethics. Ultimately they call for anthropology to study morality and for philosophy not to study morality in isolation from culture.

Lynn Meskell and Peter Pels argue that rather than seeing ethics as rights and wrongs of anthropological researchers, it should be the responsibilities to "those from whom they distinguish themselves as experts and in which they argue that responsibility in front of their peers. This principle embeds ethics in anthropological practice" (2005, 3). Their edited work *Embedding Ethics* is an argument to view ethical practice as part of everyday anthropological or archaeological practice, never separated from them. Meskell writes that "ethics is essentially a theory of social relations," a fundamental part of human interaction (ibid., 126).

British philosophers and anthropologists are exploring greater collaboration and the common questions both disciplines share about agency, the psychology of moral judgment, the interpretation of individual and collective values, and normative conceptions of reason, authority, relativity, pluralism, and objectivity (King's College and Churchill College 2012).

Carlo Caduff (2011) offers the valuable insight that the subject of ethics in anthropology often causes discomfort, often of a moral cast. If questions are raised about research methods, there is a tendency to assume that this is because some wrongdoing has taken place. This automatic response can still be the case as ethics is not discussed enough in educational settings as a regular and normal part of all anthropological teaching and discussions. It is still a special subject, either left to the end of the course or is a subject that elicits a certain ill ease. The challenge of a moral anthropology, or an "anthropology of ethics," as Caduff prefers to call it, is to bring general anthropology into a productive relationship with the ethics of anthropology. The discomfort often felt with discussions of ethics is actually a valuable heuristic device that can profitably be used to improve ethics education in anthropology. Other European anthropologists have added their voice to the call for an explicit anthropology of moralities, using traditional ethnographic methods, noting that discussion of morality in the field reflects more the ideas and views of the social scientists than of the people they study (Zigon 2007).

BERNARD GERT ON THE MORAL RULES FOR PROFESSIONALS

The following is a personal communication Bernard Gert made to me in 2009, three years prior to his passing.

> Members of particular professions may have duties that they are morally re-
> quired to perform as professionals, but they are not exempt from any of the
> moral rules that apply to all normal adults. These moral rules are universal and
> apply to everyone but are not absolute—that is, they have exceptions. It is
> important to realize that when presented with different views of morality one
> is not required to choose between moral absolutism—the view that all equally
> informed impartial rational persons will always agree on the correct answer to
> every moral question—and moral relativism—the view that equally informed
> impartial rational persons need not agree on the correct answer to any moral
> question. These extreme views are exciting, but after examination they are not
> very plausible. For example, all equally informed impartial rational persons
> agree it is not acceptable to deceive people or harm them in order to advance
> one's career, but they may disagree on some important controversial moral
> questions, such as abortion or the treatment of animals and the growing public
> acceptance of same-sex marriage.
>
> Most moral disagreements involve disagreements about the facts, includ-
> ing the probabilities of various alternative courses of action. Everyone agrees
> that death, pain, disability, loss of freedom, and loss of pleasure are harms, and
> all rational persons seek to avoid these harms unless they have a reason not to.
> Even though rational people, within limits, rank these harms differently, my
> experience on a hospital ethics committee was that when people agreed on the
> facts, including agreement about the probability of harms from various treat-
> ment options, there was almost no disagreement about what should be done.

But even when there is complete agreement on the facts, there can still be disagreements. These disagreements fall into four general categories:

1. Rational people disagree about who is impartially protected by the moral rules. Many hold that nonhuman animals are not protected as much as human beings; some hold that fetuses are not protected at all or not protected as much as babies, children, and adults. That is why the question of abortion and the treatment of animals are such controversial matters.
2. Rational people disagree in their rankings of the various harms or evils. For example, rational patients rank death and pain differently. Some patients with terminal illnesses prefer painful treatment to be stopped because they rank constant pain as worse than an earlier death; others with the same terminal illnesses prefer painful aggressive treatment because they rank an earlier death as worse than constant pain. Both decisions are rational, and in most cases doctors are required to abide by the patient's decision.
3. Rational people disagree in their estimates of what will be the consequences of everyone knowing that a certain kind of violation of a moral rule is allowed and the consequences of everyone knowing that it is not allowed. When there is no way to determine which estimates are correct, the disagreement is an ideological one that depends on one's view of human nature. This ideological dispute is why there is disagreement about whether white lies are morally justified.
4. Rational people disagree in the interpretation of the rules—for example, whether dyeing one's hair counts as deception or whether abiding by a patient's refusal of life-prolonging treatment by turning off his ventilator counts as killing.

Realizing that on controversial issues there is usually not a unique correct answer can result in far more civil and fruitful discussion of these controversial issues. If each side to a dispute regards the other as morally depraved or obtuse, they are not likely to work together to try to work out a compromise that will best meet the goals of both sides. If people on both sides think that any compromise involves a loss of moral integrity, they will not be inclined to compromise.

The duties that members of a profession impose on themselves are parallel to the moral requirements that are imposed on everyone by the moral rules—that is, violating a duty needs justification. This means that professions must be very careful in imposing duties on members of the professions—that is, duties that go beyond what is required by the general moral rules—because by imposing these duties they are restricting the freedom of the members of their profession. Before imposing a prohibition on secrecy, it is important to investigate whether secrecy itself—that is, not making one's research publicly available—is responsible for a loss of trust in anthropologists. The question for anthropologists is whether imposing a duty on anthropologists to make their research publicly available will enhance the ability of anthropologists to do anthropological research. Or since I think that negative formulations are generally clearer than positive ones, the question for anthropologists is whether failing to impose a duty on anthropologists to make their research publicly available will hinder the ability of anthropologists to do anthropological research. Anthropologists are more qualified to make that judgment than I am. But one does not need to be an anthropologist to know that deceiving is morally prohibited unless it can be justified—that is, unless the circumstances in which one is violating the rule against deception is of a kind that one would be willing for everyone to know that they can violate that rule in the same circumstances. It is important to realize that deceiving includes more than lying. Just as doctors deceive when they do not tell patients the risks of a treatment when they are asking for the patient's consent to an operation or procedure, so anthropologists deceive when they do not tell the people they study the risks to them of the research the anthropologist is planning to do. That is why informed consent is now incorporated into the anthropologists' code of ethics.

I have done a lot of work in medical ethics, but I realize that those in the medical profession—doctors, nurses, and other health professionals—know far more about their profession than I do. Without consultation with those in the profession, I would never claim that the medical profession ought to impose duties on its members that require them to do more than is required by the moral rules that apply to all human beings. However, I am clear that those in the medical profession are not exempt from any of the general moral rules and that they are allowed to violate them only in those circumstances when they would be willing for everyone to know that they can violate them in the same circumstances. Similarly, anthropologists know far more about their profession than I do, so I would never claim that anthropology ought to impose duties on its members that require them to do more than is required by the moral rules that apply to all human beings. However, I am clear that anthropologists are not exempt from any of the general moral rules and that they are allowed to violate them only in those circumstances when they would be willing for everyone to know that they can violate them in the same circumstances. Thinking that one is exempt from the moral requirements that apply to everyone is a failure to acknowledge the impartiality that morality requires and exemplifies a kind of arrogance that anthropologists, perhaps more than most, should realize is unacceptable.

From Gert's remarks about morality in philosophy the impact on ethical codes is clear in the trends toward acceptance of greater agency for the people studied; the increasing recognition that the stakeholders need to be at the table, so to speak, when ethical norms, rules, and enforcement are discussed; and an understanding that the use of deception under any circumstances must always be justified.

MORAL ANTHROPOLOGY AND DOING NO HARM

As noted in chapter 2, philosophers recognize a definition of morality as actions having the effect of lessening of evil or harm and establishing justice

(Gert 2004; Rawls 1971). In this respect, the injunction to do no harm can be considered to be both moral as well as ethical. Avoiding or lessening harm is considered here as a key element in a moral anthropology.

"Do no harm" is both a moral statement as well as a succinct expression of professional ethical guidance. Anthropology evokes, and is uniquely capable of addressing, human moral and ethical dilemmas. Avoidance of harm as an example of an overriding moral evocative is likewise the moral cornerstone of every professional code of ethics irrespective of discipline or field of work. It may be assumed that rational, moral humans understand what it means to do no harm, but when its presumed intent is applied to professional ethics it may not be so clear (Fluehr-Lobban 2008c). As discussed in chapter 2, avoidance or amelioration of harm as a moral imperative would concentrate on harm to the most vulnerable segments of the population: women, children, the aged, indigenous peoples, targeted ethnic minorities, and other vulnerable people. The application of specialized cultural knowledge that anthropologists possess is an obvious priority for informing decision making involved with harm reduction.

But for whom, and for which intended moral purposes, is anthropological knowledge deployed? Such questions have been raised for all manner of government and nongovernment organizations that have been called to account for their actions and their use of anthropological information. What agenda(s) does a religiously based organization like Save the Children have or a secular nongovernmental organization (NGO) like Amnesty International? Or where and how is there moral accountability in the powerful global economic institutions of the World Bank or the International Monetary Fund? Or what about the United States Agency for International Development (US/AID) or the U.S. military? Anthropologists are employed or carry out contract work in all of these government and nongovernment agencies. Could it be asserted, for example, that the only moral and ethical engagement for anthropologists operating in zones of extreme poverty, chronic conflict, and humanitarian crisis, working with or for missions whose intent is to reduce, ameliorate, or prevent harm or further harm? When this has been raised as a moral imperative, critics have countered that anthropology is not in the business of international or domestic social work.

The complexity of interpreting harm in a variety of culturally relative contexts is still in the early stages of discussion by anthropologists, led by moral concerns with universal human rights. Up for debate is an entire spectrum of existing harmful human practices—from culturally legitimated homicide to domestic and family violence to forms of body mutilation, such as female circumcision, and more. A line of distinction has been drawn between anthropologists who see human-rights advocacy as a moral and professional responsibility (Turner's and Graham's chapters of Goodale 2009) and those who see such advocacy as a moral choice but not an ethical obligation

(Fluehr-Lobban's and Cowan's chapters of Goodale 2009). At this point in the discussion, the ambiguity between professional obligation and personal choice is not viewed as a case of moral right and wrong but a matter of reasonable persons—who happen to be anthropologists—disagreeing. Anthropologists have asserted, but not debated sufficiently, "good" and "bad" cultural practices. Moreover, they have generally been wary of recommendations as to the appropriate interventions that might be advocated or applied. By contrast, human-rights advocacy groups have made clear moral choices about these cultural practices, such as the Western feminist campaigns against female circumcision, a practice they have unilaterally labeled *female genital mutilation* (FGM), a term anthropologists, myself included, generally do not use.

MORAL CHOICES

Human-Rights Advocacy by Anthropologists: A Branch of Moral Anthropology

The distinction between primary harm to the people studied and secondary harm to discipline professionals can be interpreted as a moral imperative. Indeed, the "primary responsibility to the people studied," first enunciated in the AAA's 1971 principles of professional responsibility (PPR), was viewed as a moral injunction to anthropologists at the time of the Vietnam War (American Anthropological Association 1971).

In the discussions that led up to the drafting of the present AAA code of ethics, published in 1998, I suggested the language that "anthropologists may choose to move beyond disseminating research results to a position of advocacy but that making this choice is not an ethical responsibility" (American Anthropological Association 1998, III.C.2). I continue to hold this view, but I might add that advocacy can be a moral responsibility that anthropologists choose in today's national and international environment of research. Advocacy is, of course, subject to an anthropologist's views regarding a particular issue. It is therefore personal and subjective. In human-rights discourse, as elsewhere, there can be a range of views that are oppositional, such as the debates over "choice" or "right to life" in the U.S. discourse over abortion. Both sides of this bitter debate argue from fundamental moral, human-rights perspectives opposing the rights of the woman-mother with those of the unborn. Thus, advocacy might be best employed as a personal choice that anthropologists may exercise in their lives as citizens of their respective nations or states or as citizens of the world. But when they use their anthropological knowledge and expertise to influence policy or affect the course of events in the lives of individuals or groups whom they study, is this a professional or moral responsibility? I argue that it is the latter and not the former.

It is noteworthy that not all human-rights groups—or those describing themselves as human-rights groups—are equal. International human-rights movements have broad, highly differentiated moral and political agendas. Many anthropologists would find themselves in broad agreement with advocacy groups such as Amnesty International or Human Rights Watch. Indeed, such groups have gained both high international credibility and legitimacy and are often seen as needed suprastate watchdog groups for violations of human rights in criticized states that have not responded to other international pressure. But others have explicit religious agendas in addition to their humanitarian ones, such as the Catholic Church's Save the Children or Franklin Graham's Samaritan's Purse. For example, various human-rights groups were not unanimous in their use of the term *genocide* to describe the conflict in Darfur, and it might be argued that the politics of genocide made the human-rights response more complicated as a result.

Universal Human-Rights Standards, Anthropology, and Cultural Relativism

In some West African societies clitoridectomy (cutting the tip of the clitoris) is performed on infant females, much the same way that infant males are circumcised—often without anesthesia—in American hospitals. Is the harm less when the circumcised is an infant male in the United States or an infant female in West Africa as compared to an older child or a pubescent girl? It is clinically demonstrated that "lighter" forms of circumcision result in less physical harm, while the extreme form of female circumcision, infibulation (excision of the labia and clitoris and closing the vaginal opening until marriage), causes both physical and emotional harm. However, an indigenous ethnographer who conducted extensive interviews with circumcised and infibulated Sudanese women provided narratives that minimize the extent of the lifelong harm and suffering (Abdel Halim 2006). Moreover, why should an anthropologist bear any ethical responsibility for what the people they study do to their own? Gruenbaum examines the limits of cultural relativism, citing extreme examples of slavery or genocide that nonetheless can have their cultural justifications (2001, 30). She argues that ethical judgment need not be suspended, no matter how satisfying it is to pass judgment, and that right and wrong are subject to diverse cross-cultural interpretations. Although moral universals are satisfying to assert, logical arguments cannot easily dislodge beliefs and practices rooted in culture, faith, or any other belief system. The most important thing—and, I would add, perhaps the more ethical approach for all concerned with the issue of female circumcision—is to be informed, to keep up to date of changing practice and law, and to act according to one's conscience on that basis and not on the imagined horrors of a harmful cultural practice.

MORAL CHOICES: CHRONIC CONFLICT ZONES AND
HUMANITARIAN CRISES; SUDAN

The nation of Sudan has been plagued by war, chronic conflict, and ethnic cleansing over the decades. Twenty-two years of civil war resulted in the separation of the country into North and South Sudan in 2011. The region's politics have received much international attention, but little reflection has been given the complexities of anthropologists engaging and researching in a context defined by the region's chronic conflict and resulting humanitarian crises. This is not a hypothetical case but one with a real, mostly unexamined, history involving opportunities as well as pitfalls for ethical engagement by anthropologists for research or contract employment with a host of potential employers, from defense and intelligence to humanitarian aid organizations.

One dilemma faced by the anthropologist is to decide if and how to engage with a country that has become notorious for human-rights violations. Which options might be selected or declined among the multiple opportunities for applied-anthropological employment with US/AID, a host of NGOs operating in the country, and governmental or nongovernmental funding of academic research? My research trips to Sudan were often met with the moral question, "Professor, can't you do something about Darfur?" "Oh, are you going to Sudan to help deliver food to those poor people?" At times or in certain circumstances there are conditions that are so morally and ethically complex that they can have a paralytic effect on an "expert" anthropologist, or can at least cause temporary paralysis. Despite provoking an intense moral urge to "do something," these are circumstances where it may be better to do nothing, or to engage minimally. In my experience, Sudan is such a case.

Anthropological research is always a challenge, and ethical decision making is rarely simple or straightforward. If it is thought to be simple, then it may be better to have a second look. But considering the range of ethically conscious employment or research in a divided nation, wracked by civil war and chronic conflict, which have been especially deadly and socially devastating over recent decades, the complexity of those choices can be challenging both to the researcher and the oversight bodies. Sudan has had conflicts described as "Arab and Muslim" against "African and Christian/animist"— as "Arab" and Janjaweed (devils on horseback) against "blacks" of Darfur. This is a nation where the United States and key allies alleged genocide in a dangerous war of words that not only failed the test of critical international intervention in such cases but probably intensified suffering as Western humanitarian aid groups were denied access. In my view, the world's most serious moral charge of genocide became a cheapened idea where any mass killing or death could be characterized as such and could well have been deployed to distract attention from contemporaneous events in Iraq, Afghanistan, and Palestine. The deaths in Kenya after its troubled elections in 2008 became a "genocide," as did the suffering of masses in Zimbabwe under a corrupt dictator.

During the years of the Darfur conflict as Sudan was accused of carrying out genocide, French NGO Zoe's Ark kidnapped a number of Fur and Za-ghawa children along the Sudan-Chad border, wrapped bloodied bandages around their limbs and heads, and claimed they were orphans they had saved. The children were being taken to France for adoption when their "interven-tion" was stopped. The children's parents protested that they were not or-phans, and Chadian authorities arrested and tried the humanitarians for inter-national kidnapping. Adding to the moral complexity, Sudan's head of state, Omer al-Bashir, was issued a warrant for arrest for crimes against humanity by the International Criminal Court (ICC) in 2009 of which neither the coun-try of the accused nor many of its accusers, including the United States, are signatories. On matters of international politics and morality, it has been noted that a majority of the recent ICC arrest warrants or indictments for thirty persons have mainly been Africans. It is highly improbable that war crimes and human-rights abuses are concentrated solely in Africa. Moreover, on the moral question of the death penalty, the United States has been criti-cized for being the only major Western democracy that still carries out exe-cutions, and the racial and class bias of the application of the death penalty has been repeatedly noted.

In Darfur Western humanitarian-aid organizations predominate and rely on local translators and social scientists—including anthropologists—to as-sist them. Increasingly, the Western researcher him- or herself becomes a subject of suspicion in this complex environment, and the trust on which the anthropologist relies is no longer a given. Where is the right and the wrong, the moral and immoral, the ethical and unethical in all of this for the anthro-pologist to support or deny support, to defend or critique, to engage or refrain from engagement? For nearly two decades anthropologists and other re-searchers effectively boycotted work in Sudan. However, when the first of a series of peace accords was signed in 2005, I returned, with a handful of others, first in 2005, funded by two European university grants through the European Union, and subsequently in 2007 through 2009, this time funded by the U.S. Institute of Peace.

This return added more complexity to the ethical, moral, and professional questions I faced regarding continued research in Sudan. As Sudan's prob-lems erupted across the world media, I as a cultural expert was presented with multiple opportunities for professional engagement. As a founder and twice past president of the Sudan Studies Association, I was received as a country expert whose commentaries, in private and public, were scrutinized. Attempting to retain the objectivity of the social scientist, I found myself invited to go on the record with the print and electronic media. I found myself in awkward public contexts where I was asked to express in Arabic nuanced differences between Islam and Islamism, between Muslim and Christian political opponents to the regime, and the attitude of the United States and the West to Islam and Islamist movements. This terrain of moral as well as political complexity consisted of multiple government armed forces, residents and their overseers of camps of internally displaced persons (IDPs), and innumerable international and indigenous humanitarian-intervention agents, including both indigenous and Western anthropologists hired to facilitate and improve program implementation. Negotiating this terrain was always challenging, but it was also stimulating of a continuous assessment of ethical choices and possible outcomes. The process was one of balancing ethics and morality, considering both the right thing to do professionally as an anthropologist and personally as a human being. It is easier to rely on the fundamentals in these day-to-day choices: avoid or reduce harm; discuss or obtain formal consent; be transparent about the research goals and funding; do not lie; be collaborative, and try to find a way to give back to those who provide information. I have often remarked while in the field, somewhat sardonically, that "a bad day in the field is still better than a good day doing committee work at home."

Applications of a Moral Anthropology: Female Circumcision and Granting Asylum to Immigrants

I have described my personal evolution from a position of cultural relativism on female circumcision to one of engagement using my knowledge of the practice to assist female asylum seekers in the United States. Asylum for victims of female circumcision was recognized in 1996 with the landmark case of Fauziya Kasinga, a woman from Togo who successfully argued that her removal by the Immigration and Naturalization Service would violate her human rights and the rights of her little girl. Critical to the success of this case and the others that followed suit in both the United States and Canada was the antirelativist argument that the harmful cultural tradition of female circumcision presented such a threat to the well-being of the asylum seekers that their cases were upheld. Moreover, some attorneys argued that the use of the cultural defense for harmful practices like female circumcision is offensive to law, morality, and justice.

The discussions of female circumcision in international and Western human-rights contexts brought me to the realization that there was a moral agenda larger than myself, larger than Western culture, the culture of northern Sudan, or the tenets of relativism of the discipline of anthropology. I decided to join colleagues from other disciplines and cultures in speaking out against the harmful cultural practice of female circumcision (Fluehr-Lobban 1995). The sense of paralysis that I described was largely attributable to my anthropological training grounded in cultural relativism. While I would not hesitate to criticize breast implants or other surgical modifications of the female body, I withheld judgment from a conditioned relativist reflex. A double standard, that Western cultural harms could be critiqued but non-Western ones were left untouched, had crept into my thinking. This contradiction needed correction, so my taking a stand, egged on by a strong moral sense of what was right, was to offer my services as an expert witness in support of circumcised immigrant women seeking asylum in the United States who feared that their daughters would be circumcised if they were forcibly returned to their home countries, usually in Africa.

Beyond these cultural and moral considerations is the legal environment in the United States and elsewhere. Fauziya Kasinga's winning political asylum in the United States was a turning point. Prior to this decision, articles had appeared in American law journals arguing for the United States to follow the examples of France and Canada and "legally protect" women and girls at risk by criminalizing female circumcision and by extending political asylum. Authors also argued against the cultural relativist or traditionalist justification for female circumcision. Typical customary cultural arguments in defense of female circumcision include the assertions that (1) it is a deeply rooted practice, (2) it prevents promiscuity and promotes cleanliness and aesthetics, and (3) it enhances fertility. Defenders of the practice, female and male, African and Western, inevitably invoke cultural relativism and ethnocentrism. Opponents argue that while the morality and values of a person are certainly shaped by the culture and history of a given society, this does not negate the philosophical theory that human rights, defined as the rights to which one is entitled simply by virtue of being human, are universal by definition. So, although human behavior is necessarily culturally relative, human rights are universal entitlements that are grounded in cross-culturally recognized moral values. Moreover, moral philosophers and legal practitioners have argued that any use of relativist arguments as a defense of or excuse for violence, injustice, or other social ills is unacceptable.

As an expert witness I have been asked to testify to the grave danger into which a woman, or an underage daughter, from Sudan, Sierra Leone, Burkina Faso would be placed if forcibly returned to her native country where female circumcision is required for the girl or woman about to be married. I make my argument based on the facts described by the asylum seeker in her affidavit and create my own affidavit in which I describe the overall cultural context in which the operation would be required. The threat of harm or personal disfigurement is central to the success of such cases and the eventual awarding of asylum. Thus far, I have not had a single case of this type denied and have heard informally from lawyers and judges that they view such harmful cultural practices as immoral as well as a violation of human rights.

MORAL ISSUES IN BIOLOGICAL RESEARCH AMONG
INDIGENOUS AND VULNERABLE PEOPLES

The Human Genome Project (HGP) resulted in great scientific advance for anthropology in that it resolved several long-standing questions of human origins and racial formation. But, as might be expected with any massive research enterprise, it raised new questions even as it solved old ones. It has been confirmed, for example, that humanity originated in Africa with all of its species present in the genomic DNA record and with the dispersal of humans out of Africa taking place about one hundred thousand years ago. This resulted in the spread of humans across the old-world continents and social groups of Asia and Europe, as well as Africa. With the diversity of humans, *race* developed as an example of natural selection in skin tones, hair forms, and other outward physical characteristics as humans adapted to climatic conditions and solar-radiation exposure in the locales in which they settled and reproduced (Fluehr-Lobban 2006b, 35–39). The HGP confirmed what archaeology and linguistics had long suggested—*Homo sapiens* migrated into the New World across the land bridge of the Bering Strait, with their relatively late arrival some ten to fifteen thousand years ago. The scientific information challenged existing hypotheses and common views. I was a beneficiary of the National Geographic Genomic Project that collected global samples of humans, and which in the United States focused some research on Indian populations as theoretically "pure" and thus of high scientific value. Since I taught "Anthropology of Race and Racism" on an annual basis for students in Rhode Island, usually of diverse cultural-racial backgrounds, I appealed to University of Pennsylvania genetic researchers associated with the HGP to sample the members of the class. We swabbed our cheek cells, sent in our samples, and analyzed the results of each sample's mitochondrial DNA (inherited through the mother's line), which proved to be as perplexing as had been predicted, given the genetic diversity of the human species, especially the hybrid populations of the New World. Thus a dark-skinned Haitian student was surprised to find his MtDNA to be primarily from Northeastern Europe; a phenotypic white student had primarily American Indian Haplogroup; and an African American was pleased to find his genetic roots in east Africa. What was surprising were the reactions of many white students to *not* having deep ancestral roots somewhere outside of Europe. It was a fascinating pedagogical exercise for which I remain grateful to this day.

But, since the research grant targeted Indian populations, the reactions to genetic research have been quite different. Among indigenous people and their agents a new general tone has been set that research must benefit tribal people; it needs to represent a balance of tribal sovereignty and research ethics; and it shifts the balance of power and agency from the researcher to the researched. Indigenous peoples across the globe have complained about the extraction of their blood samples for genetic studies and the uses to which these have been put without the informed consent of the indigenous blood donors. The ownership and control of biological samples now legally regarded as property is a foreign, strange, and even distasteful idea to indigenous peoples who nonetheless have had to respond to this novel demand for their collaboration in research.

Ownership of Blood Samples and Trust Issues in Research with Vulnerable People

The moral question of the ownership of one's own DNA requires more attention. In the case of Henrietta Lacks—whose DNA was widely used in modern medicine—discussion of ethics has been on lack of informed consent, whereas the moral question of the ownership of human tissue is unresolved.

The Moral Suasion of an Apology

The United States did not apologize for their ill treatment of Native Americans until 2009 under the Obama administration, and indicative of the political courage and will to do so, the apology was tucked into page forty-five of the sixty-seven-page Defense Appropriations Act of 2010, Section 8113, "Apology to the Native Peoples of the United States." It states, "The U.S. acting through Congress apologizes on behalf of the people of the U.S. to all Native Peoples for the many instances of violence, maltreatment, and neglect by citizens of the U.S." The apology makes it clear that it in no way admits any liability or "authorizes or supports any claim against the U.S.; or serves as a settlement of any claim against the U.S." Although the apology urges the president of the United States to acknowledge the wrongs committed as a way to bring healing to the land, since the enactment of the Defense Appropriations Act of 2010 the office of the president has not publicly acknowledged the apology. One might ask what the value of a largely unknown apology is. In only two other cases has the United States offered apologies: to Japanese-Americans for their World War II internment and to native Hawaiians for the overthrow of the Hawaiian kingdom (McKinnon 2009).

Also in 2009, nearly 150 years after the passage of the Thirteenth Amendment ending slavery, the U.S. Senate unanimously passed a resolution apologizing for slavery, following a similar apology made by the House of Representatives in 2008, both failing to deal with any entitlement to reparations or compensation for enslavement. These were also not front-page news, although the wording included the legacies of enslavement for African Americans, noting that they "continue to suffer from the consequences of slavery and Jim Crow—long after both systems were formally abolished—

through enormous damage and loss, both tangible and intangible, including the loss of human dignity and liberty, the frustration of careers and professional lives, and the long-term loss of income and opportunity." Many commentators argued that the apology is hollow without the mention of reparations, while others see these two national apologies as a part of the moral agenda of America's first black president.

Virtually alone among the Pacific nations that have conquered territories occupied by indigenous peoples, the nation of Australia has expressed "regret" for its government policy of removing Aboriginal children from their families and placing them for adoption in white families. On the first national Australian Sorry Day over a million signatures were written in Sorry Books, and in 2000 an Official Document of Reconciliation was drafted. These official regrets and sorries are mentioned to underscore the ethical-moral challenge put to nations struggling to apologize for historical wrongdoing. As for land law in Australia, Aboriginal peoples have populated the continent for fifty thousand years, but land rights have been adjudicated only since the arrival of Europeans and their laws. It was not until 1978 that the first Australian Aboriginal–owned land, a jointly managed national park, Kakadu, was established in the Northern Territory, beginning the Aboriginalization of land through national parks that continued, such that thirty had been established by 1995. The moral healing that such apologies might mean—as the Australians have attempted with their Sorry Day—can only be imagined as there are few other comparable cases to study. But all humans know that a sincere apology opens a door to new or renewed human relations.

Indigenous Peoples' Postcolonial Assertion of Sovereignty over Research as a Moral Imperative

It is a legacy of colonialism and occupation of the lands of indigenous people that their ideas are often overlooked and undervalued. Resistance and fight back by indigenous peoples have evolved to push back in the realm of research whereby "tribal" sovereignty has come to prevail over any absolute freedom and autonomy in anthropological and other research, including, importantly, medical and biological research.[1] Indeed national codes of ethics outside of the West are difficult to find and study. This is especially true in Canada, the United States, and Australia where activism by native peoples has been strongest and most effective.

The detailed regulation outlined below, with clearly stated protections for tribal members, is indicative of a bitter and painful past, well known to any researcher who takes the time to study the history of U.S. government–Indian relations and of outsider, nontribal researchers who seek to study American Indians today. This control over research stands as a sovereignty over what little remains after conquest, as an asserted agency mindful of past harm, and as a contemporary moral imperative.

American Indian tribal research review boards have become the new standard in conducting research among American Indians. The Oglala Sioux tribal review board (TRB) emphasizes the "exercise of our sovereignty." The board states its power to "approve or disapprove as well as monitor" grant proposals and research protocols. The American Indian Law Center drafted a Model Tribal Research Code in response to complaints from some Indian tribes about ethical misconduct by researchers (1999). These complaints protested (1) participation in research they did not understand, (2) participation in research being linked to the retention of the right to health services, (3) researchers not respecting human dignity or confidentiality, (4) research emphasizing Indian "pure" genetic strains over their personhood, (5) researchers having profited from research and having not hired Indians, (6) Indian researchers having been treated as "informants" and not colleagues, (7) researchers having sought and published sensitive religious and cultural information, in some cases destroying its efficacy by publication, (8) researchers having published false information, (9) researchers having published and profited from cultural knowledge "owned" by the tribe, (10) researchers having sensationalized Indian tribal, community, family, and individual problems despite negative impact on Indian communities, and (11) researchers having broken their promises to share results or give communities the opportunity to participate in the formulation of recommendations in final reports, despite promises of collaboration (American Indian Law Center Model Tribal Research Code 1999). Given this extensive list of complaints, it is understandable that American Indians have asserted their right of control over research among them as a basic right of their sovereignty.

Since some of the foregoing complaints constitute violations of recognized standards of research conduct, while others violate common courtesy and respect for human dignity, the argument for tribal regulation that supersedes federal and state regulation has strengthened to the point that it has become a new standard. The standard model details protocols for tribal oversight that may require the researcher to sign a contract including the researcher's sponsoring institution with terms of enforcement detailed. Other items may include fees for service based on the estimate of the administrative cost to the tribe of review and tribal approval for research. The requirement of permission to conduct research is to be obtained from the TRB, with the provision that research permits or licenses can be withdrawn, work stopped, and the researcher expelled and/or fined for misconduct or violations of the rules and standards of research. Moreover, the tribe retains the right to file a formal complaint with the researcher's funding institution, its IRB, and notification of professional association and peer researchers. Protocols for the postresearch phase empowers the tribe to ask the state to enforce a tribal court order restricting further researcher access (ibid.).

Indigenous anthropologists outside of the United States are often university contract workers hired by international NGOs whose local knowledge and linguistic skills are valued. They may also have a personal commitment to human rights, peace, and nation building in their countries, but their work rarely attracts scholarly attention. Partnership between Western anthropologists and indigenous anthropologists is becoming more common, but equality and full agency between the partners may be asymmetrical. Setting the agenda for research and collaborative work may also be driven by asymmetrical funding or by the agendas of powerful international funding bodies or NGOs. Collaborative publication is a high form of ethical engagement.

Morality and the Ethics Codes: "Good Anthropologist/Bad Anthropologist," Then and Now

Although the focus on the history of ethics is usually on that of the largest professional group, the American Anthropological Association, the first code of ethics in the United States was generated by the Society for Applied Anthropology (SfAA) in 1949, in the postwar, post–European Holocaust awakening of the need for greater scientific responsibility and with the publication of the United Nations' Universal Declaration of Human Rights in 1948. Article 27(1) of the declaration ensures that all humans have the "right to participate in the cultural life of communities and to share in scientific advancement and its benefits." This began a moral quest whose practical program was the beginning of mandatory review of medical research, with echoes of Josef Mengele, the Nazi medical experimenter, that later was extended to social and behavioral-science research years later. Still, it took the deep moral questioning of the Vietnam War for the American Anthropological Association to offer its first professional code of ethics, the PPR, in 1971. It was brought forth out of a crisis of moral-political controversy over alleged clandestine counterinsurgency research carried out by anthropologists in Thailand, relating to the broader war in Southeast Asia. A grievance model for sanctioning anthropologists was adopted but never used in this or any other case relating to ethical malpractice involving the people studied. Indeed, the grievance model was dropped in 1998, as it had only been solicited in cases involving alleged plagiarism or conflicts between university colleagues over tenure and promotion matters.

The specter of labeling anthropologists as "good" or "bad" may be the danger from which the AAA backed away at the time. The AAA's overhaul of anthropological ethics between 1995 and 1998 was spawned by former chair of the Committee on Ethics Janet Levy who observed that the grievance model in place from 1971 had not been used for its intended purpose of investigating and sanctioning unethical behavior by anthropologists but only for disputes between colleagues. The lack of applying the grievance model to cases of alleged wrongdoing led the review commission to choose an education model for a revised code. Interestingly, during the Human Terrain System controversy there were calls for the return of the grievance model in the national anthropology meetings, as if to have a mechanism to punish alleged wrongdoers, although there was no mass move to return to this, as there seemed little point in drumming someone out of the corps when there is no licensing of anthropologists.

The most severe test of the old grievance model and the new education mandate came with the controversies surrounding allegations of wrongdoing by anthropologist Napoleon Chagnon and geneticist James Neel for their decades of research among the Yąnomami, treated at length in chapter 4. Primary harm to the Yąnomami people had been alleged not only by journalist Patrick Tierney but also by anthropologist Terence Turner and others who had fieldwork experience among the Yąnomami. Harm was especially perceived to have come from Chagnon's characterization of the Yąnomamö as "the fierce people" in his best-selling ethnography. The case ended being more about the secondary harm done to the anthropologist than the concerns over primary harm affecting the people studied.

MILITARY ANTHROPOLOGY AND MORAL COMPLEXITY

As there is no military anthropology as a recognized section in the AAA or any other anthropology association, military anthropology is a potential future subfield. It was first proposed in 2012 in *Practicing Military Anthropology*, a volume edited by Rubinstein, Fosher, and Fujimura. Kerry Fosher writes that the AAA code of ethics is not very helpful in navigating a career outside of the academy (96). She sees military anthropology as a branch of public anthropology. She recounts an episode that occurred at the 2007 AAA meeting in reaction to a session she and Brian Selmeski had organized, "The Empire Speaks Back: U.S. Military and Intelligence Organizations' Perspectives on Engagement with Anthropology." The day after the session there was a public comment made at the business meeting that all those on the panel should be considered "war criminals." Out of this provocation, no doubt causing moral perplexity as well as insult, came *Practicing Military Anthropology*, in which those accused began with the premise that most of the negative reaction to military anthropologists was based on supposition rather than empirical investigation. Indeed the Human Terrain System was judged and found guilty before it had been objectively investigated. The Society for Applied Anthropology had a more muted response, calling for a careful evaluation of data and warning about a rush to judgment, while noting the contributions to understanding that have come from anthropologists embedding in industry, government, and medical and retail establishments (Rylko-Bauer 2008).

David Price and others have asserted that when anthropology is tied to the military it is "weaponized" (Price 2011). He argues that anthropological knowledge is weaponized when linked to the American war machine as "soft power"—or cultural knowledge. That war machine is seen as an essentially undifferentiated entity, placing on an equal moral footing applications of anthropology that might take place on the battlefield or through various forms of aid facilitated by the military, whether the aid is to human beings or to build infrastructure. Thus linked to the war machine by extension, a military anthropology is unethical and possibly immoral—except for perhaps military education. Price considers the Human Terrain System concept to be a "militarized form of anthropology" (29). It was this view that pushed the ethics envelope within the AAA and the two commissions to investigate the engagement of anthropology with military and intelligence communities. This latest round of ethics discourse mainly focused on the HTS and not a host of other matters—like what a military anthropology might look like—that might have been profitably discussed in a less volatile and hostile environment.

Price argues that it is war in the United States that has given anthropology its ethics, an assertion that generally meshes with anthropological and American history—although America's longest war, waged against American Indians, did not evoke a conscience or consciousness about ethics in the newborn discipline of anthropology in the late nineteenth century. Price's work and those of other critics of military engagement asks whether military anthropology is moral. Those who have criticized military engagement as unethical or possibly immoral neglect to consider that anthropologists working for or with the military in theater are bound by codes of ethics other than those lacking enforcement, like the AAA code, including the Uniform Code of Military Justice and the Guidelines for Professional Practice that require HTS personnel to "seek to mitigate harm whenever possible." Anthropologists advising U.S. peacekeeping missions, or drafting "do not bomb" protocols in conflict zones (as my husband has done for both South Sudan and Libya), can hardly be accused of acting in an immoral way. Like everything else in ethics, regardless of discipline or issue, it is the context and the content of the actions that is determinative.

IS THE HTS AN IMMORAL PROGRAM?

In the Human Terrain System controversy, the allegation that this was a continuation of secret research and constructed for immoral purposes

(González 2009) was as "inherently unethical" (Gusterson quoted in Jaschik 2009). The vast majority of complaints about the HTS program came from outside the program itself, primarily from members of the community of academic rather than practicing anthropologists as ethics became the major vehicle for condemning the program (Lucas and Fluehr-Lobban forthcoming). Some critics suggested that the information gathered about local populations might be used to deliberately harm them, by compromising professional values of relations of openness and trust and enabling the occupation of one country by another (Network of Concerned Anthropologists n.d.). Price refers to HTT training's "Heart of Darkness" in one of his chapter titles and describes Montgomery McFate, the most public anthropologist working for the HTS, as "Working for Robots."

The emerging field of military anthropology would take issue with this view, and this perspective should be interrogated and incorporated, not isolated, in general anthropological discourse. Anthropologists as citizens certainly can and have taken stands on moral questions, but they need to be careful about labeling certain applications of anthropology "immoral." The allegation of immorality for the HTS program, for its presumed harm-inducing rather than harm-reducing mission and the impossibility of obtaining informed consent, led to an assumption that the participating social scientists were behaving immorally as well as unethically.

"So confusing did the [HTS] debate become," Lucas writes,

> that it was sometimes the case that even knowledgeable participants sometimes could not distinguish what specific practices were being denounced, nor determine to what degree it might be inherently wrong for social scientists to collaborate or serve as employees with the government or military in any sense. Were other practices that fell under this large umbrella—such as teaching military students, compiling cultural data and information for their orientation to new cultures before deployment, or carrying out anthropological ethnographic studies of military cultures themselves—all properly subject to professional disapprobation? At one point, an anthropologist engaged in the seemingly innocent and scientifically significant exploration of indigenous archaeological sites and repatriation of Native American ancestral remains (in part to assure faithful compliance with the terms of the Native American Repatriation Act of 1990) discovered on federal land found herself and her work sharply denounced by colleagues as unethical and unprofessional, simply because her employer was the U.S. Army Post at Fort Drum. (Lucas and Fluehr-Lobban forthcoming)

The practice of military anthropology is introduced in the first work on the subject that seeks to demonstrate that academic anthropologists within this broadly defined subfield are not secretly engaging in "espionage and clandestine research" and neither are they betraying the confidence and risking the welfare of those they research (Rubinstein, Fosher, and Fujimura

2012). Although reliable data and concrete evidence concerning the HTS program were admittedly difficult to come by in the early years, details published in the *New York Times* and the *Washington Post* were reliable, attempting to offer balanced and fact-based assessments of the impact of the program (Rhode 2007; Gezari 2009; Cohen 2009). But these reports were denounced by critics as inaccurate and one-sided or dismissed as part of an "orchestrated campaign" and "ongoing uncritical fawning coverage of the program uniformly presented by the American media" (Price 2011, 96). Thus, Montgomery McFate, the most public figure associated with the program, had her name added to anthropology's litany of shame. During this latest chapter, the additional allegation of immoral behavior to this engagement created the potential for this view to be a gloss for all engagement with the military.

The depth of moral feeling about war and its multiple harms inflicted on populations anthropologists study is evident in this current controversy and in the past. Also present is anthropology's historic assistance to America at war, whether with its own indigenous peoples or its foreign enemies. Antiwar activism is best waged in the public domain of citizen engagement, and whether one favors or opposes a war with which the United States or any country is engaged, directed cultural advice, intended as harm reducing and provided by anthropology or anthropologists, can be seen as taking place in a neutral zone of useful applied anthropology. Comparable (and equally impassioned) debates in the United Kingdom over academics'—including anthropologists'—general refusal to work with British antiradicalization research initiatives have been fleshed out, along with much of the American debate, in the pages of *Anthropology Today* (the journal of the Royal Institute of Anthropology).

Anthropologists know that war is a part of state formation and states and that it is always about politics. When ethics and morality are brought into this mix, their entwining becomes irretrievably political. Absolutist moralist judgments about military anthropology as right or wrong in what is likely to become a legitimate subfield of the profession of anthropology are premature and, as yet, lacking in balance and wisdom.

Immorality in the Field

The codes of ethics and committees on ethics have not dealt with immorality, and there are few agreed-upon cases of immorality in research, such as the Tuskegee experiments of the progression of syphilis among African American prisoners—perhaps a reason why prisoners are considered a vulnerable research population to this day. It is best that codes of ethics do not delve into the realm of morality, as these values are both culturally relative and subject to other belief systems, such as in religion. But for a chapter on moral anthropology in a book on anthropology and ethics it is useful to offer a case that most anthropologists, and likely impartial human beings, would agree is one of immoral acts in the field. Once again attention is drawn to the *Darkness in El Dorado* controversy, this time through Brazilian filmmaker José Padilha's *Secrets of the Tribe*, which premiered at the Sundance Festival in Park City, Utah, on January 22, 2010.[2] The film is an HBO and BBC production focusing on elements of the controversy through a series of interviews that relate the story from multiple perspectives. It explores several allegations in Tierney's book and, to some degree, presents evidence that supports rights-abuse allegations, including sexual abuse. Acts that are immoral as well as those that might be considered immoral are documented, including exploitative sexual relationships engaged in, in the field, by French anthropologist Jacques Lizot (a member of the original 1968 interdisciplinary research team studying the Yanomami). The film alleges that access to trade goods and medical care were exchanged for sexual acts, including some reported cases of pedophilia. The sexualized nature of Lizot's research as reflected in his dictionaries, and as reflected in Yanomami accounts, recount the "known secret" of Lizot's pedophilia and the varied responses to this by the Yanomami themselves, a Salesian missionary, American anthropologists, and commentators in France. Also, the marriage of American anthropologist Kenneth Goode to a Yanomami girl—an appropriate age for the culture of the studied but not the anthropologist—raised questions of propriety and ethics at the least and a possible case of immorality. The allegations levied against Napoleon Chagnon, while often summarized as unethical, have not generally been characterized as immoral.

AAA's Actions Questioned

In a turn revealing the often-personal aspect of ethics discourse, in 2011 historian Alice Dreger wrote an article in *Human Nature* reviewing the *Darkness* controversy, concluding that something of a witch hunt had taken place. Subsequently, the charge was reiterated in *Human Nature*, the Evolutionary Anthropology Society's newly formed online publication, by biological anthropologists Jane Lancaster and Raymond Hames (the latter resigning from the AAA task force investigating Tierney's allegations). They wrote that "Alice Dreger . . . documents the extent to which the AAA broke their own bylaws, relied on a sensationalistic work judged by most experts to be without empirical foundation in its major claims, and ignored rules of fair play in their persecution of two scientists [Neel and Chagnon]" (Lancaster and Hames 2011). Their article followed a December 2010 meeting of the American Anthropology Association in which a panel discussion was held to reexamine *Darkness* that, "like a meeting held ten years earlier, dissolved into rancorous debate, with arguments spilling into the hallways" (ibid.), only this time most of the criticism was leveled at the AAA, not Chagnon. Dreger summarizes the many flaws and false statements Tierney made in *Darkness* but holds the AAA more accountable for using the flawed book as a roadmap for its investigation in its investigative task force (Dreger 2011, 13–15). Dreger refers to the quote from Jane Hill, then AAA president, that even if the task force were flawed, it performed the important work of "preserving the ability of anthropologists to continue to work in South America." Noting that the AAA had not responded to charges the Brazilian Anthropological Association had raised about the representation of the Yanomami twelve years before the Tierney book was even published. In a letter addressed to the AAA Committee on Ethics in 1988, the association wrote that "harm was being done to the Yanomami due to the circulation in the local press of articles from U.S. newspapers focusing on Chagnon's view of the violent and homicidal nature of the Yanomami (Fluehr-Lobban 2003c, 103). This letter went unanswered by the AAA.

Leslie Sponsel, who with Terrence Turner had coauthored the memorandum to the AAA warning of a looming controversy after the publication of *Darkness*, countered that Dreger is a partisan of Chagnon and that the AAA task force investigating the allegations made in *Darkness in El Dorado* had concluded that "Chagnon's representation of the Yanomami as fierce people" conveyed a false image that was damaging to them. He lamented that the focus remains on the anthropologists and not the conditions of the Yanomami, underscoring my view that secondary harm to the anthropologist became the primary harmful consideration in this case that has dragged on for over a decade. Napoleon Chagnon has not appeared at an AAA meeting since the controversy erupted in 2000, and according to Dreger he was never invited to the AAA to respond. William Irons, Dreger's colleague at Northwestern University and Chagnon's friend, had been Chagnon's major defender until the Lancaster and Hames article.

Is Secret-Clandestine Research Both Unethical and Immoral?

Secrecy, like so much else in ethics, is a matter of judgment, context, and the overriding principles of harm prevention or avoidance and consent. There can be no absolutist approach to secrecy or confidentiality for that matter, as the latter should itself be negotiated. Confidentiality is not a default button to be automatically selected. The question of whether an information provider wishes to be identified or remain anonymous is up to the researcher and the informant to determine through the use of a form or in a specific conversation detailing these options.

Documented cases of anthropologists conducting clandestine research are rare, although more are alleged. The cases of 1960s Camelot counterinsurgency research in South America involved Latin American anthropologists, and the anthropologists involved in comparable research in Vietnam were not named, nor were they subjected to the AAA grievance procedure when it was in effect after 1971. It is important to remind students of this era that during the First World War Franz Boas was censured by the Anthropology Society of Washington for his public protest in a letter to *The Nation* that anthropologists had used their research as a cover for their activities as spies and that Boas was not uncensored until 2004 (Silverstein 2004). The AAA's first PPR in 1971 was clear about "no secret research" and repeated Franz Boas's 1919 warning to anthropologists working for any government for the potential damage done to science and to relations in the fieldwork site. Although in 1971 the drafters of the PPR did not state explicitly that secret research is immoral, nevertheless the long-term and widely accepted disapproval of secret or clandestine research approaches a de facto statement of moral behavior in anthropology. In this era of Facebook, Google searches, the general lack of privacy of one's credit card and financial information, and Wikileaks in the political arena, it appears anachronistic to keep beating the drum about no secret research. If we speak about intelligence gathering, that is another matter, acknowledged as *not* research but, well, intelligence work.

Philosopher George Lucas (2009) has critiqued American anthropology's preoccupation with secrecy, which, he charges, approximates for them a sacred language. He argues that there is an American obsession with secrecy and clandestine research when, in fact, the case for the actual use of these is weak in the real, not imagined, history of American anthropology. Secrecy has been defended when deployed in the interests of the people studied where revealing their secrets would likely result in harm to their well-being or cultural heritage. The classic example offered is that of secret societies found in many cultures whose secrets must be respected and protected, as well as secret or confidential information confided to researchers with explicit admonitions not to be revealed. In consultation with research participants, I have made decisions over decades of studying Islamic family law of when to reveal and when to conceal cases. I have used anonymity as a default position in recording cases that I personally observed in court where obtaining consent was not possible given the decorum of an Islamic court setting. However, in some instances I could discuss and obtain consent with the litigants, and for appeals and High Court cases these are part of the public record.

Moral Complexity of Anthropologists in World War II Internment Camps

The United States has admitted wrongdoing to the approximately one hundred thousand Japanese-Americans who were interned in War Relocation camps in 1942 as a security precaution because their loyalty was questioned during America's war with Japan. The internment ended with a 1944 unanimous Supreme Court decision declaring that U.S. citizens, regardless of cultural descent, could not be detained without cause. Moreover, the 1983 commission to study the relocation and internment of Japanese-Americans recommended $20,000 be made in reparations to each identified Japanese-American who had been a victim of the policy. On December 7, 1991, the fiftieth anniversary of the attack on Pearl Harbor, President George H. W. Bush issued another formal apology.

The experiences and perspectives of indigenous anthropologists are rarely incorporated into discourses of ethics. Peter Suzuki, a Japanese-American anthropologist who spent part of his adolescence in a WWII internment camp, has raised his voice in protest of the role of anthropologists who carried out research and alleged espionage in the camps during the years of the war. He related that he started his research on camp anthropologists solely out of curiosity as a former internee and was not out to undo anyone.

Peter Suzuki was born in Seattle in 1928 and was interned at Camp Harmony, Puyallup, Washington, and later at Minidoka Relocation Camp in Jerome County, Idaho. At age fifteen he left Minidoka alone under the War Relocation Authority's (WRA) relocation program and moved to a Michigan town in order to attend a normal high school. His oldest brother was a volunteer in the 442nd Regimental Combat Team fighting in Italy and France and returned with a Bronze Star and a Purple Heart. Another brother fought against the Japanese in the Pacific and returned with a Silver Star and two Purple Hearts. Despite this clear patriotism, Suzuki and his family were interned along with thousands of other Japanese-Americans. After the war, in 1945, his parents and twin sister left Minidoka for Connecticut for work as domestics. Suzuki went on to earn his A.B. and M.A. degrees from Columbia University and his Ph.D. in anthropology from Leiden University in 1955. In a 2006 presentation at the AAA meetings in San Jose, he described "the unethical activities" of a number of named anthropologists. These anthropologists had passed information about internees on to the FBI (Suzuki 1981; 2009). Any Japanese-American suspected of disloyalty was considered a candidate for further segregation, according to Suzuki's firsthand reports (1986).

Collaborative Research: Partnership; a Moral Methodology That Results in Better Research

The new anthropology journal *Collaborative Anthropologies*, launched by Luke Eric Lassiter, reflects the growing interest in collaboration both as a method and mode of analysis.

Despite their self-image or protestations to the contrary, researchers are powerful people, relatively speaking, from wealthier classes and nations. Although many work in non-Western countries and comparative research or in a variety of NGOs, they do not usually see themselves in this light. It can at least be acknowledged that they are perceived as powerful individuals representing powerful and wealthy institutions, governmental or nongovernmental. Even such relatively powerful individuals may not make a moral practice of anthropology a priority. The term *subject*—as in human subjects—is a profound statement of hierarchy in the research relationship, yet it remains a major descriptor of the person(s) studied, as in the federal mandatory regulation "Research with Human Subjects." Collaborative, participatory research models are beginning to displace the old paradigm of conducting research *on subjects* (who are still typically called *informants*). This decisive shift parallels and reflects national and global changes following decolonization; the end of the Cold War, with its politicized discourse on human rights; the search for international standards of human rights, irrespective of nation or culture; and the many reflections on these relationships in post–9/11 America and elsewhere.

Thus, *research with, rather than on, peoples* takes the discourse on ethics, research, and practice into new directions that may be described as moral. The moral connection in the shift from "do no harm" to "do some good" is obvious. However, the bonus in terms of enhanced research outcomes when individuals or a community are organically involved with the design, execution, analysis, and outcomes of research—including copublication of findings with the anthropologist—has increasingly been demonstrated using collaborative methods.

A collaborative model of research involves the people studied in an active way—as individuals or as a group—with a vested interest in participating in the study. Jointly directed and jointly authored projects begin to replace the older model of research "from above"—planned, executed, and published by the anthropologist alone. Community or individual involvement in the progress of research, thus designed, becomes a condition for its success, not simply a fortuitous by-product of work with communities. Collaborative Anthropology, now a recognized trend with a journal of the same name, recognizes that not only is collaborative research more ethically conscious, it also results in better research results.

A PUBLIC MORAL SYSTEM FOR ANTHROPOLOGY

The idea of a *public moral system for anthropology* would argue for the ideal of a universal morality recognized by all rational anthropologists. Although informal, such a system still can refer to the general public moral system for morally acceptable behavior. However, even an informal public moral system for anthropology, which should be accepted by all anthropologists, would likely be challenged by some anthropological relativists as imperfectly universal for enunciating a set of ethical standards. Absolute cultural relativism has been questioned by many anthropologists (Shweder 1990; Fluehr-Lobban 1995).

Any potential public moral system for anthropology would be an informal one where, within limits, anthropologists can be said to agree or disagree with each other on what behavior counts as morally acceptable professional behavior. This means that, except for mandatory review by IRBs, each anthropologist determines for him- or herself what moral behavior is. Thus, any public moral system in anthropology exists mostly as a self-imposed, self-regulated set of ideas of ethics.

The closest things to a universal philosophical, moral, and ethical norm are the "avoid or do harm" and informed-consent principles, which are core principles in nearly all codes of professional ethics. A public moral system in anthropology would elaborate on these with exploration of the cultural and moral foundations and illustrations of doing the right thing, making a good or correct moral decision. When these principles are integrated into anthropological research they constitute processes of moral engagement with research participants.

CONCLUSION

Anthropology as the study of humanity in all of time and space has such breadth, depth, and complexity that discussions of ethics and morality within its scope can be daunting. Nonetheless, ethics, and by extension morality, is central to our work, our discipline, and our legitimacy as a profession. Lucas has observed that anthropology's moral narrative has been a "strange reflective" without critical substance apart from its "litany of shame" (Lucas 2009). Its major organizations have acted more like professional organizations (protecting the anthropologist) rather than crafting a disciplinary narrative. Lucas further remarks that if this distorted focus continues, it will have "decided negative consequences for the moral self-consciousness of the discipline" (ibid., 89). As anthropology has made its stock and trade from the study of the other, it is well advised to listen to the diverse voices of its own as well as voices from outside the boundaries of the profession.

QUESTIONS FOR DISCUSSION

1. Is moral anthropology an accepted branch of the discipline of anthropology, or does it belong to action or activist anthropology in the humanitarian tradition and not in the scientific scope of anthropology?

2. Discuss the complexity of moral choices that anthropologists may need to make in the course of research or the practice of the profession.
3. What special considerations, prompted by morality, are incumbent on researchers working with vulnerable populations?
4. Explore both philosophical and anthropological perspectives on universal human rights and cultural relativism.

Chapter Six

Institutional Review Boards, Anthropology, and Ethics

Institutional review boards were established in 1974 by the National Research Act under Title 45 of the Code of Federal Regulations. They grew out of notorious cases of the abuse of human subjects in medical experimentation under the Nazi regime during World War II and the American Tuskegee experiments involving African American subjects in syphilis experiments. Institutional review boards—or IRBs—are established for independent ethical review for biomedical and behavioral science research. Using a balance of risk-benefit analysis the goal is to protect humans involved in research from physical and psychological harm. Research projects are subjected to either full or expedited review or are judged to be exempt from review due to low or minimal risk.

At one point ethnography was exempted from review, but no longer—perhaps due to increasing agency by anthropologists in IRBs—and the only exempted research involves (1) research in an educational setting involving normal educational practice, (2) research on educational testing, (3) research involving programs for public benefit, and (4) taste and food-quality surveys and research.

IRBs must be constituted of at least five members, balanced by gender, professions, scientists, and the public or communities, and they must meet regularly and review research proposals by institution members including students in educational institutions if their research projects involve humans. Reference is made to the supra-institutional documents regarding ethical research, *The Belmont Report* and the federal guidelines. IRB protocols involve submission of a research proposal with a detailed account of the plan for the ethical engagement including, most significantly, the plan for obtaining informed consent—written, oral (expressed), individual, or group—and a request for full or exempted review, with justification if requesting exemption from review.

Anthropologists had a history of resistance in the early years of IRBs, mainly due to the requirement for the submission of informed-consent forms that many anthropologists saw as inappropriate in the trust-building relationships that cultural anthropologists develop with their "informants." On the IRB side, there may have been an initial lack of understanding and appreciation for the long-term and personal relationships that ethnographic research often requires. Anthropologists are unlikely to use one-off surveys or questionnaires where human contact is limited and instead value the subjective research-self in relation to observed-other.

IRB review and approval of research above the undergraduate level is required of anthropologists and other researchers in the biomedical and social sciences. Although ethnographic research has been historically considered exempt from review—as being of minimal risk—all research proposals should be considered and reflected on as to their potential risks as well as benefits to those studied. It is this balance of risk and benefit that has driven and continues to drive research regulation.

The IRB cannot assume that all ethnographic research involves no more than minimal risk. Reflective anthropologists know this fact, but some may fear or resent having to undergo the required process of review. When the history of federal regulation is reviewed—drawn from harmful, exploitative, and unethical studies such as the Tuskegee experiments (or those conducted on the mentally deficient without informed consent)—the importance of public, collegial, and other stakeholder review of the potential risks and possible benefits to research participants is a civic and professional responsibility. The IRB ought not be viewed as an obstacle to research freedom but an opportunity to reflect on responsibility in research, allowing the student or professional to engage with this history and her or his own research project. The IRB process has been subjected to some mystification as not understanding the nature of anthropological research, or simplification as something "you have to get through," possibly as a result of inadequate ethics education and candid, sustained discussion of ethics in research methods courses. Ethics education—including understanding and appreciating the IRB opportunity—has been consistently identified as a need in overall anthropology education and the preparation of anthropological professionals, applied and traditionally academic. Still, the IRB process retains a lingering image of non-applicability to anthropological research and an unnecessary bureaucratic stumbling block to the initiation of research. This view is not necessarily limited to anthropologists or their students but also may be prevalent among other disciplines as the sheer volume of work that institutional review boards must undertake often requires filling out multiple online forms and responding to queries raised by board members.

With the goal of conducting ethically conscious research, the student or researcher—at every stage of a professional life—can always profit by reflecting on the issues and concerns of institutional review of their research goals, procedures, and likely outcomes.

TYPICAL IRB PROTOCOL

While institutions must be guided by the Federal Guidelines for Research with Human Subjects, institutions are nonetheless capable of drawing up their own protocols within this framework. For example, when I chaired my home institution's IRB we changed the name from the Committee on Research with Human Subjects to the Committee on Research with Human Participants. Changing our reference to people studied in the protocols from *subjects* to *participants* emphasized the value of nonhierarchical, participatory methods. Thus, a typical research protocol would likely include the following (drawn from the Rhode Island College IRB website):

Application for New Projects

1. *Name and contact information* of the researcher; the name of the responsible investigator (supervising professor or institutional official)
2. *Funding sources*, existing or submitted
3. *Type of research*, previously collected or current; public benefit, educational
4. *Project information* (description of research goals, methods/procedures, impacts on those studied, consent process; materials used for research; incentives or compensation)
5. *Risks and benefits*: (a) any tangible benefits during or after the research; potential conflicts of interest (b) risks (use of deception; procedures that request or require ingestion of food, liquids; procedures considered sensitive or embarrassing; data collection of illegal activities; procedures considered physically or psychologically stressful; medical data protected by federal law; discuss with parts privacy protection; risks to participant's physical, emotional, or psychological well-being, self-esteem, reputation, personal relationships, effects on employment)
6. *Informed consent*: for those under eighteen years of age; limitations to giving full informed consent: mental illness, dementia, etc.; vulnerable populations or those potentially coerced from authority; pregnant women; use of audio or visual recording, must include specific consent from participants; use of non-English consent or other materials; waiver of documentation of consent (must be justified) and any changes to informed consent procedures
7. (Optional) *Request for collaborative review* for multisite research involving other IRBs

8. (Optional) *International projects*: identify countries; do they have IRBs? Discuss role of collaborating institutions; describe local context and how this affects perceptions about the study
9. *Clear statement of responsibility* by the researcher responding to above

Ethnographic research is now widely used in the other social sciences and in the fields of education, management, and business and in public-health research, among other fields. Participant observation in public places as well as controlled settings—such as classrooms or special focus associations, as well as a host of organizational settings—has been recognized as a powerful method for disclosing the "native" point of view, giving visibility and voice to the people studied directly rather than through the filter of the researcher. The ability to continue to use these tools of ethnography and their protection and development is important to the future of IRB protocols and ethnographic research, including participant observation.

DEFINITION OF *ETHNOGRAPHY* FOR PURPOSES OF IRB REVIEW

It may be surprising that there is no standard definition of ethnography, although the term is widely understood. Elizabeth Campbell and Luke Eric Lassiter offer this: "Ethnography is often described as both a fieldwork method and an approach to writing. As fieldwork, ethnography usually involves participating in the lives of others, observing and documenting people and events, taking detailed field notes, conducting interviews, and the like. As an approach to writing, ethnography asks us to organize, interpret, and inscribe this collected (and, as many argue, constructed) information as text" (Campbell and Lassiter, forthcoming, chapter 2). The key here is the anthropologist's construction of knowledge through the lived experience of others, which is a great intellectual leap of faith. Readers of ethnography rely on the honesty and integrity of ethnographers and their ability to be objective reporters, not an easy task under any circumstances. As a research method that is dependent on relations with human others, ethnography is at the heart of IRB regulation of anthropological research.

I coauthored a "Working Definition of Ethnographic Research" with Patricia Marshall in 2004 as the AAA was grappling with mandatory federal review of anthropological research. We wrote:

> Ethnography is scientific research based upon systematic methods and data collection. It emphasizes the study of communities in the international and domestic arenas that may involve short- or long-term relationships with research participants and employs multiple methods including: unobtrusive observation, participant observation, structured and unstructured interviewing, and focused discussions with individuals and community members.

> Ethnographic analysis is inductive and builds upon the perspectives of the people studied. Because of its complexity, variable contexts, and duration, ethnographic research is not automatically exempt from IRB review, although researchers may request such exemption. IRBs cannot presume that all ethnographic research involves no more than minimal risk. Most often ethnographic research is not exempt. (Fluehr-Lobban and Marshall 2001)

At the 2003 cross-disciplinary conference at the Belmont Center (where I was the only anthropologist in attendance) a special session on ethnography was held at which relations with IRBs was discussed and a working definition of ethnography was drafted:

> Ethnography is the study of communities in the international and domestic arenas that embraces multiple methods, including but not limited to observation, participant observation living within the community over relatively long periods of time, structured and unstructured interviews, and focus groups with community members. These methods may be unknown, underappreciated, or undervalued by IRB members. (Social and Behavioral Sciences Working Group on Human Research 2003)

Further, IRBs cannot assume that all ethnographic research involves no more than minimal risk. It is incumbent on researchers proposing to conduct ethnographic research to provide the IRB with sufficient information on the following:

1. What are the temporal, physical, and social boundaries of the study? What constitutes public places for observation? What are culturally appropriate privacy issues?
2. How is the researcher gaining access to the community or country?
3. What review board(s), other than the IRB, is/are relevant to the study—for example, tribal review boards, national review boards?
4. What are the terms of engagement with the research community? How might research methods be changed toward a more equal power relationship between researcher and people studied? Are there benefits from the research to the community?
5. What is the process of informed consent, recognizing that written consent forms in English may be inappropriate? Issues of effective consent that might be addressed by the IRB include:

    a. Individual, group or community consent?
    b. How will each be obtained?
    c. How will the researcher document and verify group and/or community consent?

It is possible that these forms of consent may take place in the form of a conversation, or town meeting where the researcher may explain the purpose(s), potential impact(s), and source(s) of funding through a process of open dialogue and negotiation with the people studied. It was noted that the required elements of disclosure may not apply or be sufficient.

Further, individual, group, or community consent may need to be layered or approved in phases from initial entry through the conduct of research to its actual outcomes. Thus, an approach that is flexible and appreciates the dynamic process of consent may be appropriate. This may involve building in a process of monitoring ethnographic research over a period of time as specified by the IRB.

As an early recognition of the multiple issues that Internet research raises, this second Belmont Conference in 2003 (the first having established the federal guidelines) recognized that virtual ethnographies of communities in the United States and internationally may begin to substitute for the "real" social and behavioral arenas studied. Privacy, anonymity, informed consent, and the potential for risk or harm are just a few of the issues that come immediately to mind.

This historic conference and its substantive consideration of ethnography and its complexities constitute one of the best treatments of ethnography for the purposes of IRB review.

LINGERING LIMITATIONS OF FEDERAL GUIDELINES IN ANTHROPOLOGICAL RESEARCH

Understandably, U.S. federal guidelines focus more heavily on domestic research, and the major focus of ethics remains with America's dominance in biomedical research. Lingering weakness in the key areas of harm, informed consent, and vulnerable populations outside of the historic categories of pregnant women and fetuses, prisoners, and the mentally challenged clearly only have marginal relevance to most anthropological research. Likewise, international research is mentioned as an arena outside of the United States, but its complexity and relevance remains unexplored for the considerable involvement of biomedical researchers as well as social and behavioral sciences researchers. This is clearly an area where anthropologists could be of assistance to the process and progress of federal regulation.

However, in recent years there has been progress within the federal Office of Human Research Protection (OHRP) in international research for their recommendations for obtaining consent that "honors local custom," including assessment of (1) potential risk/benefit, (2) language sensitivity, (3) who is/are effective community spokesperson(s), (4) cultural sensitivity, (5) justification for the use of the population for study, (6) evidence of an in-country ethics body equivalent or IRB, (7) any potential coercion, and (8) evidence of paternalism.

Another weakness in the federal guidelines is its greater emphasis on individual rights and responsibilities over the collective social environments in which anthropologists engage as researchers and with their participants in groups and communities. This may be the result of the strength of the larger and more influential research environment generated in psychology where research with individuals is more prevalent.

It is strongly recommended that the anthropological researcher work constructively with the relevant IRB(s) regulating research goals, methods, and domestic or international environment of research, assessing its potential risks as a means of self-reflection and monitoring that is key to a continuous consideration of ethics that is fundamental to the anthropological enterprise.

ETHICAL QUESTIONS: DILEMMAS INHERENT IN SELF-MONITORING

Anthropologists often work alone in research environments that are isolated from the security and familiarity of home, in a language that is not their mother tongue, and for long periods of time. Close personal engagement with those studied is often discussed in terms of trust building that is essential to good ethnography. But the self-monitoring of ethics that is also a part of the research method of long-term participant observation and other forms of research is as yet insufficiently explored. IRBs may conduct a thorough and penetrating review of research that results in detailed protocols for the conduct of research (such as that constructed for my research in Sudan from 2007 to 2009 by my IRB, as discussed in chapter 3), but the implementation of the protocol is left to the researcher. There may be requests for interim reports, but the monitoring of the day-to-day interactions with research participants is left to the personal integrity and level of consciousness about ethics of the researcher. I present this as a dilemma without having a solution to it. The best that I can do is reflect on my own challenging experience in Sudan.

My IRB presented me with an elaborate protocol that emphasized the protection from harm of Sudanese who might be at risk for collaborating with me, an American researcher in a country whose president had an arrest warrant from the ICC for crimes against humanity. Beyond this, I was subjected to U.S. sanctions against Sudan that prohibited bringing any electronic equipment into the country, my hiring Sudanese for any purpose other than a taxi driver, or having contact with or interviewing any official of the pariah government. I met these conditions using gifts and reciprocal exchanges in lieu of any payments for equipment or services, and I have never paid information providers, and in the culture of hospitality prevalent in Sudan it would have been insulting to suggest this. However, when I was presented with the unanticipated opportunity to conduct research in camps of internally displaced and had no means of contacting my IRB, I depended on full openness and disclosure with the persons who agreed to speak with me and my graduate-student assistant. As it turned out, camp residents were keen to speak out and use any opportunity to be heard by foreign, seemingly powerful researchers. Placed in a position of generation of new protocols as well as the usual self-monitoring of respectful engagement or partnership with information providers, the best that I can do is to share the experience and use the case as one for education.

Ultimately, the dilemma inherent in self-monitoring in ethnographic research is best treated in ethics education where reflexive anthropology may be best put to use. Training in how to self-monitor through personal diaries, interaction and discussion of ethics with local colleagues, maintaining contact with the IRB or professional colleagues at home, and developing a presence of mind that thinks "ethics first, research second" can all be recommended.

CODES: DEBATES ABOUT THEIR EFFICACY

Codes are not necessary to conducting ethical research or to preventing the conduct of unethical research. There may be something reassuring to professional associations about having codes of ethics, and no self-respecting professional association would hang out their shingle, so to speak, without a code of ethics. Apart from the Hippocratic oath for physicians (the first being the American Medical Association's in 1847), there were few professional codes of ethics before World War II. It is unknown how much, if at all, anthropological codes of ethics are consulted in advance of or at any stage of research. Anecdotal history suggests that the codes are often consulted in their breach or quoted to make an argument about something else. After some concerted effort, ethics education is improving in undergraduate and graduate anthropology courses and is included more in general anthropology textbooks and is monitored by the AAA's Committee on Ethics.

Peter Pels has argued that there is an inherent tension in anthropological codes of ethics with Western ethics discourse and with the epistemology of anthropology as the study of the other (1999). This *duplexity* (his term) creates an unintentional double standard in professional practice, a discourse for the West and another for the Rest (of the world). However, in the legalistic and litigious United States, elimination of codes of ethics is unlikely to be a banner raised. Instead the application and use of codes is debated, not their inherent worth. Noting in 1994 that codes are not uniform in their most basic ethical stands, Pels observed that "it might be that one code says the interests of the research participants should be paramount (U.S. AAA and British ASA codes) while another says that the prime responsibility is towards 'science' (as in the Dutch code for sociologists and anthropologists)" (1999, 9).

As discussed in this book, diverse and evolving views persist regarding the efficacy of codes of ethics, their interpretation, and their use. Professional codes in the United States have been driven by federal regulation of research and the Common Rule, while the AAA history is also one that reflects journalistic coverage of anthropology and American wars and politics. There has been a grudging acceptance by anthropologists of federal and institutional regulation of research, the institutional review boards to which anthropologist researchers must apply and receive approval for their research proposal.

Charles Bosk notes a "chorus of complaints" from anthropologists to IRB protocols who are critical of the board's lack of full appreciation of what ethnography entails and how it does not fall easily into the existing IRB protocols (2007). There is a failure of both complexity and reflexivity on the question of ethnographic ethics, including "ethics creep" emanating from the IRB to the anthropologist's research mission and design. This is beyond the bounds of the IRB, Bosk argues. It seems there is certainly much room for negotiation between anthropologists and ethnographers and the IRB.

Canadian sociologist Kevin Haggerty also references ethics creep in the regulation of social-science research (2004). He also complains of IRB overregulation, especially with somewhat mechanical concepts of harm (any act that "might cause serious or lasting harm to a participant"). He argues that for social science harm is less than medical harm (primary and secondary harm?) and argues further that journalists are able to do what anthropologists are constrained from doing in terms of informed consent. IRBs are cautious and conservative and universities and university lawyers are driving the process, he argues.

Rena Lederman asks with whom might ethnographers find common cause—journalists, for example (2007)? She asks what the real effects of disciplinary boundaries are among the social sciences regarding ethics. Anthropological research is not psychology, but it shares a great deal in common with sociology. Greater collaboration and coordination among the social sciences and with other professions—such as journalism, social work, or human biologists, just to name a few examples—can provide profitable conversations for the ethics work ahead.

USING THE NEWEST CODE: GUIDING PRINCIPLES FOR ANTHROPOLOGISTS

I suggested the following principles for using, discussing, and debating the new AAA code of ethics for anthropological work (2009b, 9):

1. Anthropologists in all of their actions must ensure that, to the greatest extent possible, their research [does] not cause or result in harm to the people they study, either directly as individual field researchers or remotely as part of teams conducting action or policy-related research. They must be particularly sensitive to power differentials between researcher and researched and to potential harm to specific vulnerable populations. They must also understand the limits of their ability to anticipate, prevent, reduce, or ameliorate harm.

2. Anthropologists must actively understand and update their practice regarding current standards of informed consent in research affecting humans, including the practical applications of conducting research—direct or remote—with openness, disclosure, and dissemination of results in appropriate channels of communication.

3. Anthropologists work in transparent environments. If a project or contracted research is not subject to public review, the anthropologist must weigh the consequences of its inherent value as science and be aware that the work may, in fact, cross a line into intelligence work rather than anthropological research conducted with openness, disclosure, and dissemination of results. In rare circumstances where transparency might result in harm to the people affected by research, such as the protection of a sacred archaeological site, anthropologists should follow a process of independent consultation with colleagues. A collegial conversation with an independent body of colleagues, such as the Friends of the Committee on Ethics, could assist the anthropologist in determining if the cost of a lack of transparency is justified by the benefit of preventing harm.

4. Anthropologists must understand the agenda(s), fundamental mission, and financial sponsorship of their research or application of anthropological knowledge. This applies equally to employment or contractual work with nongovernmental as well as governmental agencies. If they cannot know these basic facts, they should avoid the work as nontransparent or "secret."

5. Anthropologists as professionals must exercise integrity in their work. Unethical conduct results in harm to the profession as well as to the people affected by research. Harm to the profession of anthropology is secondary to harm caused to research populations, but it is nonetheless a harm. While advocacy is a personal choice and not a professional responsibility, monitoring the effects—positive, neutral, and negative—of research, or contracted work, upon the people studied by anthropologists is a professional duty that enhances both the integrity of the professional as well as the profession.

There are compelling reasons for an educational model for the AAA code of ethics.

The core underlying assumption that the code of ethics is *meant to be studied* is reaffirmed. While there is greater presentation of ethics in general anthropology and more texts focusing on ethics education, nonetheless the deeper rooting of ethics education in professional undergraduate and graduate education has yet to be achieved. The educational model shifts the responsibility for ethical conduct to the individual anthropologist and encourages a process of active consultation because it is not a legalistic statement of do's and don'ts. An educational code of ethics is *meant to be discussed.* The Friends of the Committee on Ethics was established as an informal, consultative body that will respond to questions brought to it for nonbinding, collegial advice on ethical dilemmas.

A code of ethics that is publicly studied and discussed underscores a professional *responsibility of public education.* Shared information focuses on discussion of issues and avoids the negative energy that results from a focus on individuals accused of misconduct. Public education about ethics also serves to highlight best practices in current anthropological research. Over time proactive ethics education could produce a public moral system for anthropology that is generally accepted and likewise studied.

Finally, an educational code of ethics requires simple language and an accessible design that is *meant to be used* constructively by professionals. The best codes are composed in clear, succinct language where principles prevail and exceptions to the rules are few and are justified. A usable code is one that can be readily accessed by an anthropologist seeking advice from a professional association where guidance for ethical decision making is offered and, if the dilemma or information sought is not provided, a process of consultation with colleagues is available.

Ethics education is active, not passive, and a code of ethics that is designed to be educational promotes its study, discussion, and use by anthropologists in an ever more complex environment of research, application of cultural knowledge, and contemporary professionalism.

CHALLENGES OF WORKING WITH AND FOR IRBs

Campus or other institutional review boards tend not to have high profiles, and neither is their important work well understood in their communities. There can be confusion and misinformation in the institutional culture about the rights and obligations of researchers, perhaps reflecting some knowledge of publicized negative cases, such as those involving journalists who have gone to prison to protect the confidentiality of sources. There is also the sheer workload carried by the IRB responsible for reviewing of all research carried out under the auspices and supervision of the university. In one case brought to my attention a student researcher with sensitive data involving a visible, vulnerable population and with IRB approval was told by an administrator that her tapes "can be turned over to the press without her or her participants' consent." She rejected this and sought affirmation and support from the IRB in her refusal, while the grants-administration office provided further clarification about the relationship of confidentiality between researcher and people researched, despite any public interest in the project on the part of the press. This resolved the matter but revealed an inadequate knowledge base about research in administrative circles.

PROTOCOLS REGARDING THE REVIEW OF COURSE-BASED STUDENT RESEARCH

With the often limited institutional support by way of offloading or compensating IRB chairs or members, it is impossible for an IRB to monitor or review all research that takes place on campus. Of special concern are the large numbers of student researchers who are mobilized within social- and behavioral-sciences classes to learn about research methods by conducting class-based research, especially at the postgraduate level. Master's-degree research may not be reviewed by IRBs; however, all doctoral students are required to have their research approved by the IRB. This creates confusion and a hierarchy of research priority such that institution-wide policies need to be developed that are consistent, clear, and broadly disseminated. In this potential void of preprofessional research conducted by students are federal guidelines including new protocols regarding course- and program-based undergraduate and graduate student research to be discussed and recommendations made. I would argue that included in protocols involving student research should be consideration of how best to achieve the goal of increasing awareness and the development of an institutional culture that centers ethics education as a part of instruction in the social and behavioral sciences as well as biomedical research.

IRBs can identify practices that should not be supported as part of compliance or in addition to federal guidelines. For example, federal guidelines have been silent about the use of what are called "subject pools," groups that may be subject to coercion as volunteers giving full and informed consent to participate in research. For example, in some university psychology departments students have been required to participate in department or faculty research, or in other cases research is conducted with students in classroom settings where participation may be thought to be a course requirement. Ideally, discussion of these cases as they arise could lead to a campus-wide dialogue about the dynamics of coercion in research, involving differential power relations, significant amounts of research funding, or majority-minority issues, among others.

Challenges in Reviewing Protocols

It can be challenging for an IRB to operate with a full committee, including all of the federally required members, including student representation, an off-campus medically trained professional, as well as an off-campus representative. Moreover, IRBs may not be adequately supported by the institution. They can be attached to offices of grants administration with largely voluntary participation of its members and a chair who serves with minimal compensation or offload. The committee is often loaded down with electronic "paperwork" that must be reviewed by all members and archived when decisions are made. Coordination of the college calendar of faculty research committees with the IRB can be problematic and is left to the good will and hard work of all parties. Waiting periods can delay the onset of research.

Developing and sustaining a culture of collegiality among equals can be a challenge, as the IRB reviews and questions colleagues' research methods or those of their students. It can be a challenge as to how to avoid placing colleagues or students on the defensive while undergoing IRB review. My experience has been that conversations among the IRB, the researcher, and her sponsoring professor make all the difference. Of course, the IRB does have the force of law behind it, and that coercive power needs to be acknowledged and used responsibly.

Additionally, healthy cross-disciplinary dialogue is needed within institutions, and not just within professional circles, in order to foster a culture that not only is cognizant of compliance rules regarding research with humans but also cultivates an ongoing conversation and institutional culture whereby certain methods are acknowledged as questionable—for example, use of students in personal research—while others are recognized as best practices—for example, innovations such as students developing and using a declaration of participants' rights instead of a more traditional informed-consent form. In the end it is the conversations that count in ethical decision making and practice.

A CASE OF ALLEGED IRB OVERREACH REGARDING STUDENT RESEARCH IN THE FIELD

A case of student research in Tunisia was related to me by anthropologist Lawrence Michelak who, as director of a research center in Tunis from 2006 to 2009, worked with a study-abroad program that required each student write a paper based on local research working with a specialist. Michelak served as an adviser to the program and in this capacity worked with a student researching traditional herbal medicine. The student's research proposal was reviewed and approved by the academic division of the center as well designed and presenting no human-subjects problems. The student also wanted to use the research toward her senior thesis at her home university, which required approval from an IRB. The student communicated with the IRB, described her project, and asked for approval. The IRB replied that they were not going to meet for several weeks and that apparently the student would be leaving Tunisia before the IRB could review the project. The IRB realized that the center had approved her project and that she was going to conduct it. However, since the rules of the IRB did not allow retroactive permission for research, she could not use the research toward her senior thesis. The delay was over permission to conduct interviews with local herbalists who would in any case not have been named in the research paper. It might be argued that the student should have gotten the approval before she left the campus, but the choice of topic was based on the student's experience in Tunisia, which could not have been anticipated. Professor Michelak believed that approval by a full IRB was not needed. What was needed was a waiver, which should have been given by a responsible person within the IRB authorized to do this. A waiver is appropriate if the informants are anonymous, no identities are revealed, the topic is not sensitive, such that there might be repercussions for the informants, and there are no vulnerable populations involved. In this case, all the IRB did was obstruct scholarship.

Other instances of IRB overreach have included IRBs requiring that even for simple projects the anthropologist read a long statement to each interviewee and then have the interviewee sign a paper indicating informed consent for an interview, even when the research might have only involved visiting a public place and chatting with people.

Professor Michelak opined:

> Human-subjects approval all too often presents a problem for anthropologists. It can be a nightmare, especially since many grant agencies require IRB approval before a funded project can have a disbursement and before the research can begin. For some reason that I don't understand, IRBs for social-science approval often include medical people, who are the people whose ethical transgressions (such as the Tuskegee syphilis study) made IRBs necessary in the first place. Medical people tend to apply an inappropriate scientific model and make social scientists jump through innumerable irrelevant hoops before they can do even the most innocuous research. (personal communication, January 5, 2012)

This challenge—related as an informal complaint to me and published with the consent of Professor Michelak—is illustrative of some of the frustration that anthropologists have historically expressed and continue to experience in some IRBs. Parity between biomedical and social-science research is generally a misleading road to follow, even for the most conscientious IRB members. The stakes are higher in biomedical research, their funders are often powerful research agencies, and their research results can have significant repercussions on human well-being. Social-science research tends to have less impact on human well-being and is more reflective and even subjective. In short, the stakes are not so high, but they should also not be minimized as was the case with the historical treatment of ethnographic research as exempt from review.

A Model Approach

Canadian social-science researchers developed a concise, thorough, and state-of-the-art declaration at the Ethics Rupture Summit in October 2012, comprising researchers from Australia, Brazil, Canada, Italy, New Zealand, the United Kingdom, and the United States, all of whom committed to enhancing ethical research practice and to supporting innovative alternatives to the regulation of research ethics that might achieve this end. With their permission I reprint their declaration:[1]

The signatories of the New Brunswick Declaration declared their commitment:

1. *To seek to promote respect for the right to freedom and expression*;
2. *To affirm that the practice of research should respect persons and collectivities and privilege the possibility of benefit over risk.* We champion constructive relationships among research participants, researchers, funders, publishers, research institutions, research-ethics regulators, and the wider community that aim to develop better understandings of ethical principles and practices;
3. *To believe researchers must be held to professional standards of competence, integrity, and trust,* which include expectations that they will act reflexively and responsibly when new ethical challenges arise before, during, and long after the completion of research projects. Standards should be based on professional codes of ethical practice relevant to the research, drawn from the full diversity of professional associations to which those who study human experience belong, which include the arts and humanities [and] behavioural, health, and social sciences;
4. *To encourage a variety of means of furthering ethical conduct involving a broad range of parties* such as participant communities, academic journals, professional associations, state and nonstate funding agencies, academic departments and institutions, national regulators, and oversight ethics committees;
5. *To encourage regulators and administrators to nurture a regulatory culture that grants researchers the same level of respect that researchers should offer research participants;*
6. *To seek to promote the social reproduction of ethical communities of practice.* Effective ethics education works in socially embedded settings and from the ground up: it depends on strong mentoring, experiential learning, and nurturance when engaging students and novice researchers with ethics in research settings;

7. *To be committed to ongoing critical analysis of new and revised ethics regulations and regimes* by: highlighting exemplary and innovative research-ethics review processes; identifying tensions and contradictions among various elements of research-ethics governance; and seeing that every venue devoted to discussing proposed ethics guidelines includes critical analysis and research about research-ethics governance; and
8. *To work together to bring new experience, insights, and expertise to bear on these principles, goals, and mechanisms.*

(Ethics Rupture 2012)

WHAT'S IN A NAME?

At Rhode Island College, at my initiative, the name of the IRB was changed from the Committee on Human Subjects in Research to the Committee on Human Participants in Research. The name change was initiated in the early 1990s and signaled a difference in outlook and emphasis from committee members—many from the social and behavioral sciences—that "subjects" are people on whom research is conducted, while "participants" are people with whom one works when conducting research. Emerging social- and behavioral-science models of participatory research—especially stemming from feminist, sociological, anthropological, and some psychological domains—have strongly influenced this change in outlook from human subject to participant. For the committee members, *subject* conveyed a hierarchical relationship between researcher and researched where the consent process may not be free of the power relations implied. *Participant* conveyed more openness in the consent process, less potentially coercive voluntarism, and a more active role for the people researched (Fluehr-Lobban 2003e).

A participant-centered approach for IRBs reflects a trend away from a "subjects" model, which implies a hierarchy between researcher and persons studied. Although "human subjects" is still the language of many codes and federal regulations, a shift toward a participation model is already in evidence in the codes and guidelines of many professional associations and can be anticipated to eventually replace the original referent for those whom social scientists study.

DISCUSSION QUESTIONS

1. Why have anthropologists tended to resist IRBs and their protocols for ethnographic research?
2. Are codes of ethics and IRBs the best way to monitor and regulate anthropological research?

3. What are, or would be, model approaches for anthropologists' review and approval of their research proposals and conduct of research?

Chapter Seven

Framing Future Debates: Collaborative Anthropology as Twenty-First-Century Anthropology

Ethically conscious anthropologists can only use the past and present as guides to planning for ethical engagement in the near and distant future. Anthropologists in the postcolonial, postmodern, and post-9/11 world can expect "the field" to be a far more complicated prospect than it has been for previous generations. The assumption, from another era, that anthropological researchers can go anywhere and do anything is simply no longer operative. Researchers must carefully investigate contemporary conditions (not relying on outdated reports) affecting the country and social group that is projected to be studied. They need to develop alternative plans and build these into their research proposals. They need to be cognizant of the core ethical principles of avoiding, or trying to ensure, that their research results in no harm and that they have thought about and planned the best ways to obtain informed consent. Informed consent is to be obtained from those individuals, groups, and communities potentially affected by their research using ways and means of negotiated agency by members of the studied population including their participation and/or collaboration in the conduct of research at all stages. This active, preresearch preparation of the groundwork for the study translates not only into better ethical engagement but also better research results and field relationships that can be sustained for decades.

WHO IS AN ANTHROPOLOGIST?

In the most generous sense, an anthropologist is a person "doing" anthropology. "Anthropology is what anthropology does" provides a broad tent under which those who study humans, past and present, in their full complexity—physical and biological, cultural, historical, and linguistic—are anthropologists. In the past informal questioning about who an archaeologist was arose to exclude so-called pot hunters from "proper" scientific archaeology. More recently, the effort to define who an anthropologist is arose in the controversy over the Human Terrain System in the suggested exclusion of trained anthropologists (some with a master's degree) from being considered "real" anthropologists because of disagreement with the professional role they were playing. Otherwise, it is a mark of the openness of the field that anyone with a postgraduate degree in anthropology in the United States is capable of being called an anthropologist. Needless to say, this is quite different from the professions of law and medicine where credentialing is essential to professional practice.

Consulting anthropology's default website, the American Anthropological Association, it is found that rather than defining who is an anthropologist the AAA defines what anthropology is and how anthropologists are employed in the United States. "Anthropology is the study of humans, past and present. To understand the full sweep and complexity of cultures across all of human history, anthropology draws and builds upon knowledge from the social and biological sciences as well as the humanities and physical sciences" (www.aaanet.org/about/WhatisAnthropology.cfm). This broad sweep was well characterized by anthropologist Alfred L. Kroeber (1876–1960), who said that "anthropology is the most scientific of the humanities and the most humanistic of the sciences." Added to this definition of domain is the AAA add-on that "a central concern of anthropologists is the application of knowledge to the solution of human problems." And for American anthropology the purview of anthropology embraces four areas of study: sociocultural anthropology, biological/physical anthropology, archaeology, and linguistics. The intellectual potency of this broad field embraces all of humanity in all of time and space. Anthropologists often integrate the perspectives of several of these areas into their research, teaching, and professional loves, thus reiterating the strength of the Boasian four-field approach that distinguishes American anthropology. European forms of anthropology—and those in their former colonies where anthropology diffused during colonial times—separate social anthropology from archaeology, which is often considered as a branch of history, physical anthropology, often a branch of human biology, and linguistics, its own science often separate from anthropology. The holism of American anthropology remains formally intact, but increasing specialization of knowledge and practice is having centrifugal pressures on the old-time anthropology.

Most practically and realistically the AAA definition of anthropology describes the types of employment that anthropologists acquire. "Anthropologists are employed in a number of different sectors, from colleges and universities to government agencies, NGOs, business, and health and human services. . . . Anthropologists contribute significantly to interdisciplinary fields such as international studies and ethnic and gender studies, and outside the university anthropologists work in government agencies, private businesses, community organizations, museums, independent research institutes, service organizations, the media, and others work for agencies such as UNESCO, the World Health Organization (WHO) and the World Bank. More than half of all anthropologists work in organizations outside of the university" (www.aaanet.org/about/WhatisAnthropology.cfm).

The second-largest professional association, the Society for Applied Anthropology (SfAA), states its objective to be "the promotion of interdisciplinary scientific investigation of the principles controlling the relations of human beings to one another and the encouragement of the wide application of these principles to practical problems" (www.sfaa.net/sfaagoal.html). It is explicit about the identification of M.A.s and Ph.D.s in anthropology as "professional anthropologists who will be employed outside of academic positions in the upcoming decade" (ibid.) Moreover, "the occupation of 'anthropologist' should be promoted as a satisfying, rewarding, and professional role whether as an independent consultant, an employee of public agencies, corporations, [or] nonprofit organizations, or as a university faculty member or administrator" (ibid.).

In the United Kingdom the Royal Anthropological Institute effectively answers the "what is anthropology?" query through a description of what anthropology is not, viewed through misconceptions about the profession. On their website they write that, counter to popular views, anthropology is not just "bones and fossils," and neither do anthropologists exclusively study "tribal" peoples in "remote" areas who are perceived to be "exotic." The engaging website adds a summary quotation by famous anthropologist Ruth Benedict: "The purpose of anthropology is to make the world safe for difference" (www.discoveranthropology.org.uk/).

FUTURE DIRECTIONS IN ANTHROPOLOGY AND ETHICS

The old anthropology of the bygone colonial era and that of American study of American Indians also decisively ended the era of absolute freedom of research for an anthropologist to go anywhere and research any subject using any methods. Archaeology is undergoing fundamental paradigmatic transformation as decolonization impacts old ways and assumptions of Western control of the world heritage. Ownership of cultural heritage and property, argued in print and in courts of law, has witnessed a postcolonial agency on the part of the heritage bearers. Meskell and Pels write that "our ethical responsibility in the contemporary world is that of helping archaeology to move beyond the paradigm of dead subjects toward a new vision of lived histories" (2005, 146). By "lived histories" the authors point to the developing intellectual and emotional connections between past and present that the descendants of the bygone civilizations and cultures archaeologists study that are now part of the research environment.

The post-9/11 era has also fundamentally changed the international environment of anthropological research from all vantage points—those of researchers and of those researched. With the United States having the largest number of anthropologists and the greatest number of professional programs, American anthropology is unchallenged globally at the present moment in time. With this overarching reality in mind, and with advances of the field in many areas of research and applications, comes professional responsibility in ethics to the domestic and international communities that are affected by anthropological research. American anthropology has not assumed this international mantle of responsibility, and the AAA acts primarily as a national organization, although it has many international members and many of the world's anthropologists were either trained in the United States or have some professional experience in the country.

The world anthropologists study—what used to be called the "Third World" in the context of the Cold War's East/Soviet Union—West/United States rivalry, with "the rest" being the Third World—continues in its path of decolonization, intellectually and practically. Voices from these regions are increasingly being raised and heard. The dominance of American anthropology will only end with the demise of U.S. economic and political dominance. Signs of this future are already evident in headlines pointing to the rise of China and Africa as regions for investment of economic and human capital. Anthropology will inevitably follow these trends. And new ethical challenges will arise surrounding every issue raised in this book and some that cannot be anticipated at this moment.

But as the "past is present" mantra prevails in ethics, understanding and appreciation of the complexity of the principles discussed in this book will offer the anthropologist of the future the tools with which to grapple with new ethical dilemmas. The unprecedented effects of Internet and global communication is a new context for anthropology and ethical consideration and reflection that European anthropologists are addressing but Americans have not appreciated fully as yet. Greater agency on the part of those who have historically been the "subjects" of anthropological research is a decisive trend, already evident in the regulation and control of research by indigenous peoples in North America and Australia. It is critical to recall that this assertion of control is often a result of negative experiences or misconduct by researchers who have been granted access to indigenous societies. It is likewise imperative that the anthropologist always remembers that she or he is a guest of the people studied and that access is always *granted* to the anthropologist and is never to be assumed. This is a foundation of thinking about ethics in anthropology and postresearch gratitude that can be expressed in a variety of ways of continuing engagement with the communities anthropologists study.

It can be anticipated that research access is not likely to expand greatly under present models of research that may be less than fully ethically conscious. The balance in terms of engagement is shifting toward the regulatory institutions of the nations and people studied. The qualified (linguistically and culturally), sincere, and well-prepared researcher who approaches the government and local institution—including local hierarchies and grass roots–desired contacts—with respect and integrity will more often be successful. Any hint of arrogance or superiority on the part of the researcher—whether by virtue of personal behavior, funding, prestigious association, or some other perceived advantage—will be noticed and be ultimately detrimental to the trust building and long-term relationships essential to rich ethnography and analysis. This is, of course, both common sense and common courtesy in all human relationships. But the othering of peoples whom anthropologists study affects all who have been exposed to Western ideas regarding "primitive" or "exotic" peoples, or have been affected by new stereotypes of whole groups of peoples, such as Arabs and Muslims.

Harm Prevention/Amelioration: Doing Some Good; the Mind, Heart, and Gut Tests

Having just said that behavior in the field is very much like that at home where mutual respect and an acceptance of the equality of humans are at base what we call common courtesy and upright behavior, I would add to this common-sense approach what I call the "mind, heart, and gut tests." If your mind tells you that your behavior or course of action is right (and not wrong), and if your heart does not disagree, and if your "gut feeling" is that you are doing the right thing, then probably you are doing the right thing. For decision making about what is right and wrong in ethics (and in life), if the proposed action does not pass all three tests—those of the mind, heart, and gut—each of which is experienced in three different organs and centers of being human and making choices, then the decision should not get a full pass.

Try some exercises—taken from personal or hypothetical examples and discussed with friends or in class—and put to the three-organ test the proposed research subject, such as a study of drug sales using minority youth as couriers, or a study of domestic violence and the relationship of complaints or arrests to immigrant status, or a study of victims of domestic violence in countries with weak laws or consciousness protecting them. The conversations that you have will be the most important part of deciding what to do. Always consult with peers, supervisors, and knowledgeable outsiders when ethical questions or dilemmas arise.

INFORMED CONSENT, COMPLIANCE, AND CONSIDERATION OF OTHERS

Informed consent and the injunction to do no harm are the twin engines essential to the ethical conduct of research. Recall how recently language on each of these core ideas has come into anthropology codes of ethics, only since 1998, and approach these giants of ethics with a humility that comes from a historical lack of experience and debate in anthropology.

Informed consent, cooked down to its essence, means that you describe and seek in advance of the beginning of research the approval and consent of those whom you are seeking to study. This means having conversations with individuals, groups, or communities of people who are to become your research participants. This discussion can and should be a normal and natural part of establishing the relationship and should ideally be conducted in the first language of the participants, as ethical norms for social science may not be well understood in the general population. *Participants* can be a meaningful word with value added, as these individuals can also become your research collaborators as well.

Transparency Is Honesty in Practice

So much of ethics is about the fundamentals of good and upright conduct and respect for those whom we study. Bernard Gert summarized the core of transparency by paraphrasing one of the ten commandments: Tell the truth, and do not lie. This is good advice for living one's life and is good advice for conducting research. Being honest and open, and practicing full disclosure about the goals and intent of your research, its methods, and funding sources is just about the best way to get started in social research. The conversation easily leads to discussion of ways and means of potential collaboration and opens the door to novel methods of research that are devised and implemented in the research partnership between the researcher and persons being studied. These initial frank conversations are often the first of what become years or decades of collaboration and form the basis of what are called "long-term relationships of trust" that anthropologists are capable of building. The research partnership often elides into a sincere friendship based on mutual respect. A research relationship that is built on or relies on deception cannot have this outcome. There are cases where the line between researcher and participant blurs and high forms of collaborative work result, such as coauthoring texts analyzing findings or initiating social-action projects that benefit the communities in which research took place.

What I am describing may be an ideal, and the accounts of misconduct by researchers related in this book can be seen as cautionary tales in regard to ideal ethical and moral relationships with the people we study.

COLLABORATIVE ANTHROPOLOGY AS TWENTY-FIRST-CENTURY ANTHROPOLOGY

For many years I have argued that collaborative research is "ethically conscious" research.[1] Moreover, not only is collaborative research ethical and thus morally preferable to historical models of research, but it is also better research because of its methodology emphasizing multiple, polyphonic perspectives leaving a richer heritage of ethnography to subsequent generations of ethically conscious researchers.

Collaborative research involves the people studied in an active way, as individuals or groups having vested interests in the project through their participation in research design, execution, publication, and outcomes potentially related to community or individual improvement of well-being. Collaborative studies can potentially inform or affect social policy. Often jointly directed and jointly authored projects replace the older, more hierarchical model of research planned, executed, and published by the anthropologist alone. Community or individual collaboration in research—with partnership incorporated in every phase of research—becomes a condition for its success, not simply a fortuitous by-product of work with communities. This newer model of research presumes, for the most part, a literate, socially conscious set of partners who not only participate in research but also read and critique drafts of publishable results. However, literacy among research participants is not essential to its viability or success, as openness and mutual exchange of research ideas and outcomes can be communicated without the ability to read or sign informed-consent forms.

Collaborative research stands in dramatic contrast to historical models of Boasian anthropology—with its general emphasis on "informants," "ethnographic subjects," and a central objective of data collection—and it contrasts sharply with European social anthropological methods' linkages to colonialism and latter-day postmodernism. Uniquely, the subfields of applied anthropology in the United States and development anthropology in Europe have recognized and embraced the value of collaboration in research as it is necessarily attached to applications of anthropology to institutions and agencies—

governmental and nongovernmental—whose mission is to promote the well-being of humans. It is this mission of research designed to promote human well-being that has led critics to view collaborative research as advocacy, confusing anthropology with social work (Gross and Plattner 2002). Others view collaborative research through the lens of the same history of anthropological research and would argue that the approach reflects an increasing decolonization of the discipline.

Neglected by the Euro-American dominance of the discipline and profession of anthropology are the numerous examples of practice by indigenous anthropologists, many trained in the Euro-American "classical" tradition but who are active as collaborative anthropologists in environments where of necessity researcher and researched are cocitizens with shared heritage and common futures. Anthropological practitioners in Africa, Asia, and Latin America approach research with a greater emphasis on national priorities where practical outcomes favoring improvement of societal well-being replace older colonial and neocolonial models. Examples of collaborative projects reflect national interests, such as the status and rights of native peoples to land and resources; conflict resolution and the condition of internal displacement of peoples; or public health, family planning, and the well-being of women and children. Ahfad University for Women in Sudan has mobilized an interdisciplinary research group of social scientists, including key roles played by local anthropologists, who design and carry out research focused on women as peace builders designed to assist with the development of policy initiatives. This research is grounded in models of feminist, collaborative research and is part of a long-term project called the Building Peace through Diversity Series. The funding of such projects may be external—in this case Oxfam, the Netherlands—but the research and publications outcomes are decidedly local (Badri, Jamal, and Martin 2005). Indigenous anthropologists are also employed providing vital cultural and linguistic links between humanitarian-aid organizations and vulnerable local communities, as is currently the case in Darfur.

In the twenty-first-century, postcolonial, "emerging-markets" global context, collaboration is the key to the sustainability of anthropological fieldwork and research, and perhaps for anthropology as a discipline. Voluntary, informed, negotiated, open, and reciprocal research, based in locating a common ground of mutual interest and benefit between researcher and research populations, is increasingly supplanting the individual, self-generated, and externally funded research of previous generations. The unequal-partners-in-research model, with its top-down approach and hierarchy between researcher and subject, is shifting substantially toward greater equity in the research relationship. This is not necessarily a result of moral or political motives but is emerging as an increasing imperative for garnering research permission and conduct research between the traditionally unequal researcher and re-searched.

FEMINIST PIONEERS IN COLLABORATIVE RESEARCH MODELS

A debt of acknowledgment and thanks must be paid to second-wave feminist methodology and epistemology for the novel approaches in research methods and outcomes generated by collaborative anthropology. Feminist methodology employs inductive strategies to elicit voices, narratives, and perspectives of the historically suppressed collective voice of women in the West and elsewhere. Indeed, feminist research and collaborative anthropology offer multiple areas of mutually reinforcing approaches. The weakness of Western feminism has been its Euro-American centrism, and thus a feminist anthropology had an opportunity to step into this ethnographic vacuum. Collaborative anthropology benefits from the dual strengths of an infused feminism for its non-Western research and the transformation of the research relationship that it represents. A majority of American anthropologists are women, and this demographic transformation is also a factor in the increasing use of feminine, more-collaborative models of research that are gradually displacing older, hierarchical—"masculinist"—research models.

Central to a feminist approach to research is its egalitarian, nonhierarchical methodology that tends to view its "informants"—who were often women like the researcher—more as "participants" with whom the researcher engages in mutual exchange and sustained trust-building conversations. This groundwork of trust and mutual confidence can readily evolve into long-term, trusting relationships where research codesign, execution, and publication embrace both community-based as well as theoretical interests. The latter result is both desirable and potentially transformative. For years I have collaborated with the Rhode Island Coalition against Domestic Violence in which we discussed research and approaches to non-Western cultural ideas and practice of violence against women in order to offer more appropriate interventions. Since 2011 the coalition has explicitly requested more theory so as to develop strategies that address the root causes of the social-historical roots of patriarchy and violence against women. Novel approaches are guaranteed to result. Feminist sociologist and ethnographer of Inuit women Janet M. Billson for years has practiced a collaborative method of data collection and analysis, where it is standard procedure that her collaborators read and approve the final drafts of published works, including both ethnographic monographs and more summary and analytical books (Billson and Reis 2007). Coresearching, cotheorizing, and ultimately coauthoring works based on mature, collaborative anthropology methods are destined to result.

FROM "SUBJECTS AND INFORMANTS" TO
"PARTICIPANTS AND COLLABORATORS"

If a central goal of collaborative research is to work *for* as well as *with* research communities, and to develop reciprocal relationships where projects are initiated, discussed, reviewed, and evaluated through a process of continuous consultation and collaboration, *then* the language of the research relationship needs to evolve and change. At the core of collaborative research is informed consent in the broadest meaning and application of the concept. I have written elsewhere about the resistance among anthropologists to informed consent (Fluehr-Lobban 1994; 2003a), in part due to the perceived nonapplicability for the social sciences of biomedical models of research where the concept originated. Although widely adopted by the social sciences, anthropology lagged behind and did not adopt language on informed consent until the AAA published its 1998 code of ethics. This was perhaps due to a tendency toward anthropological exceptionalism—that anthropology-fieldwork ethics are unique—or from a latent paternalism/maternalism among anthropologists suggesting that the researcher knows what is best for the research population. The obvious lack of agency afforded the research population implied in the above was less of an issue in adopting the informed-consent doctrines than the necessity of anthropologists to comply with federal guidelines regarding informed consent. Critical discussion of mechanical forms of applying informed consent in biomedical research, especially as used in research among vulnerable, non-Western populations, justifies some of the reservations by anthropologists that consent is a one-way street where forms are used more to protect the researcher than the human participants. The powerful alternative of collaboration in research is embedded in reciprocal informed consent.

Reciprocal informed consent challenges the problematic historic models of informed consent that are based in unilateral, signed forms designed more to protect the right of the researcher than the researched. Such forms have reflected a one-way strategy empowering the right to conduct the research, in a formulaic way promising confidentiality and anonymity (usually without asking the informant if she or he desires this) and self-defining the project as involving "minimal risk." This language suits the federal regulators more than the interests of the researched and appears designed to meet the concerns of the members of institutional review boards over those of the research population. A signed form, or an informed conversation, using reciprocal informed consent would establish the mutual interests, rights, responsibilities, and potential joint outcomes of the research. Confidentiality and anonymity, for example, would be negotiated as desirable, or unnecessary, if a joint publication results. "Risk," if it exists at all, would be neutralized, as an issue as the mutual right to withdraw from the research would be negotiated, together with the mutual responsibility to design, conduct, and publish the research. It is self-evident that reciprocal informed consent presupposes an environment of openness; mutually informed agreements as to the conditions, timetable, and expected outcomes of research; and dynamic, sustained conversations about all phases of the research project.

This spirit of informed consent is reflected in the terminology that defines the nature of the research relationship. In traditional and still-extant models, the researcher is powerful and in charge, whereas the subject is structurally acted on and is relatively or absolutely powerless. Traditional hierarchical models emphasize the agency of the researcher and the passivity of the research population. Indeed, federal regulation of research is monitored by mandatory university and institutional Human-Subjects Committees, dreaded by graduate students and some anthropologists where requisite approval is often met with the relief of a successful rite of passage or dodged bullet. Unfortunately, the IRBs, structured and composed by institutions, are often driven by a narrow view of informed consent as obtained mechanically through a signed form. This reinforces the coercive, one-way-street notion of the researcher informing the subject of the terms of research. Standard language of a form may include the "right" of the subject to withdraw from the project at any time or the fact that the subject's identity is absolutely protected, a right often *not* sought by the researched, either the relatively vulnerable or more empowered.

The standard anthropological reference to information providers as "informants" has not been subjected to much debate. The term *informant* conjures notions of a special, proprietary relationship between researcher and researched, akin to spying and devoid of the covenantal relationship that some admire in the anthropological fieldwork experience (argued by Murray Wax, and reflected in the 1998 AAA code of ethics, A.5). A terminological and thus ideological shift from *informant* to *collaborator* or *participant* may be under way, spearheaded by such journals as *Collaborative Anthropologies*. However, the fundamental paradigmatic change in research methods and analysis that is represented by this shift is fundamental and radical and is therefore not to be seen as easy or inevitable. The process of change is both moral and political.

BETTER ETHICS, BETTER RESEARCH

The practical applications of collaborative research are not difficult to imagine, and if realized as a twenty-first-century standard of research practice, it can be transformational. New centers offer services to assist agencies and contractors with collaborative initiatives in complex multicultural, cross-cultural communities, especially in the field of public-health research. Such initiatives have filled a void left by a general failure of the discipline and profession of anthropology to adequately train the latest generation of anthropologists either in theoretical or professional ethics—in all of its present complexity—or in the alternative of collaborative anthropology.

Collaborative research may become a decisive trend for American and global anthropology in the twenty-first century. This historic shift results from the feminization of anthropology, from decolonizing theories as well as methods, and from a growing recognition that collaborative-research methods result in not only more ethical research but better, more reliable research results. The benefits of collaboration in terms of social-scientific reliability and authenticity of voice are already evident, but the benefit of developing better theory from collaborative research can only be imagined.

CONCLUDING REMARKS

This book is dedicated to anthropology students and their teachers in the hope that it will be used as a tool for exploration, discussion, and, most importantly, debate about the conduct of research and all work as anthropologists in an ethically conscious manner. The phrase *ethically conscious* has been used throughout this book without expressing what it means, or might mean. I first heard the phrase in conversation with an early collaborator in ethics, David Hakken, and I liked what it conveyed and used it as a subtitle for the second edition of my edited work *Ethics and the Profession of Anthropology*, originally subtitled *Dialogue for a New Era* (1991) and then *Dialogue for Ethically Conscious Practice* in the second, substantially revised, edition (2003b). First, the phrase *ethically conscious* suggests, even admonishes, the researcher to think about ethics as a regular, normative part of the practice of anthropology. *Conscious* also invites the anthropologist to reflect on ethics in the day-to-day practice of anthropology. This book is subtitled *Ideas and Practice*, meant to evoke a conscious reflection about ethics, agency, transparency, and collaboration. These are all accessible ideas that rely on easily understood principles of professional conduct, as well as fundamental human ways of being and acting in reciprocal relations of respect and mutual interest.

There is really no substitute for the important conversations about ethics that anthropologists engage in—whether in formal classroom settings or informal discussion of real or hypothetical dilemmas faced in research. There is no statute of limitations in ethics discourse—as we have seen in the rehashing of old conflicts about ethics—nor is there any necessary superiority of age or experience when we enter into ethics dialogue as equal moral agents. Ad hominem attacks on personalities and allegations of misconduct are generally a waste of time, but critical analysis of anthropological practice—from best to worst examples uncovered in personal narratives that anthropologists provide—is worthwhile, as cases are the best pedagogical tools. I have tried to frame a personal narrative in this book using ethically conscious reflection in writing about my years of research experiences in Sudan.

Talking about ethics is the first step toward ethically conscious research. It used to be that the subject of ethics was only mentioned in the breach. Some anthropologists that I approached to contribute to the first volume of collected essays I edited on ethics—only a few decades ago in the early 1990s—were fearful of participating in such a project. While this primal fear no longer exists, we are still not entirely comfortable as a profession in talking to one another objectively, constructively, and compassionately about ethics. It is a regrettable feature of the history of ethics in anthropology that so much of its debate has been generated by controversy and public disagreement among colleagues, often about subjects other than ethics but using ethics as the battleground for these conflicts. This unfortunate context is evident in both of the most recent controversies—*Darkness in El Dorado* and the Human Terrain System. I lament this truth every time I write about it, but by now I accept it as the predictable pattern it has become, although I can readily imagine other, better ways to conduct anthropological discussions of ethics. In future dialogue about ethics and anthropology, issues and practice must be the focus and not individuals. The future of the discipline and anthropologists' ability to continue to conduct research in communities that continue to welcome us depend on our ethical conduct and exemplary practices.

QUESTIONS FOR DISCUSSION

1. Who is an anthropologist? What are the most relevant criteria for making such a determination: training, credentials, practice? All three of these?

2. What ethical challenges will remain, and which will change with the future development of anthropology in the twenty-first century?

3. How can anthropology develop a culture of ethical conduct of research that is recognized, understood, and practiced by all anthropologists?

Notes

2. WHAT DOES IT MEAN TO "DO NO HARM"?

1. The late Bernard Gert is the philosopher with whom I have most closely worked. I acknowledge with gratitude the many excellent conversations we have had since 1990, when I was selected as the first anthropologist to be a fellow at the Ethics Institute of Dartmouth College. His rendering of universal principles of "common morality" bridges the biomedical and social sciences. His humanism and passion for philosophy framed his long and illustrious career.

2. I acknowledge with gratitude sharing of thoughts and ideas on military engagement and the social sciences with psychologist Jean Maria Arrigo, a founder of Psychologists for Social Responsibility.

3. WHAT DOES IT MEAN TO OBTAIN INFORMED CONSENT?

1. I was asked by the AAA to comment on these recommendations, and I suggested that the AAA add to the list of vulnerable subjects the following: indigenous peoples who have been identified as "at risk" (e.g., by human-rights groups, such as Cultural Survival) and HIV-positive persons from economically disadvantaged countries involved in AIDS research. I recommended language that AAA could transmit to federal regulators to help in the development of the "protection of at-risk, vulnerable, non-Western populations" that anthropologists study (memo from C. Fluehr-Lobban to Peggy Overbey, January 29, 2001; Fluehr-Lobban 2003d).

2. My gratitude goes to anthropologist Lawrence Michelak for summarizing the case.

4. TRANSPARENCY AND DECEPTION IN ANTHROPOLOGICAL ETHICS

1. This section is a tribute to the long and enriching working relationship that I enjoyed with the late Bernard Gert, formerly Stone Professor of Philosophy at Dartmouth College. I was a Mellon postdoctoral fellow in residence at Dartmouth's Ethics Institute between 1989 and 1990 when we began our professional philosophy-anthropology dialogue that continued through his encouraging me to add the subtitle to my 1991 article on informed consent in anthropology, "We Are Not Exempt." Bernie acknowledged the value of this relationship in his *Common Morality* (2004). Our last communication was in 2009 on the subject of secrecy in anthropological research. He passed away in 2012.

5. MORAL AND ETHICAL ANTHROPOLOGY

1. The term *tribal* is in quotation marks due to its essential history and meaning associated with conquered peoples, from the Roman *tribus*—the three areas under the Roman Empire, seen as "tributaries" and subject to paying "tribute" to the center.
2. The film summary is provided by anthropologist Barbara Rose Johnston's notes.

6. INSTITUTIONAL REVIEW BOARDS, ANTHROPOLOGY, AND ETHICS

1. The text of the declaration was kindly provided by Will C. van den Hoonaard.

7. FRAMING FUTURE DEBATES: COLLABORATIVE ANTHROPOLOGY AS TWENTY-FIRST-CENTURY ANTHROPOLOGY

1. Major sections are extracted from my article "Collaborative Anthropology as Twenty-First-Century Anthropology," *Collaborative Anthropologies* 1 (1).

References

AAA Commission on the Engagement of Anthropology with the U.S. Security and Intelligence Communities. 2007. *Final reports*. Arlington, Va.: American Anthropological Association. Available online at http://www.aaanet.org/issues/CEAUSSIC-Final-Report.cfm.

———. 2009. Final Report on the Army's Human Terrain System Proof of Concept Program. Submitted to the American Anthropological Association Executive Board, October.

AAA Committee on Ethics, with Lauren Clark and Ann Kingsolver. 2000. *Briefing Paper on Informed Consent*. Arlington, Va.: American Anthropological Association. http://www.aaanet.org/committees/ethics/bp5.htm.

Abdel Halim, Asma M. 2006. *Sudanese women in the United States: The double problem of gender and culture*. Lewsiton, Maine: The Edwin Mellen Press.

Abusharaf, Rogaia, ed. 2006. *Female circumcision: Multicultural perspectives*. Philadelphia: University of Pennsylvania Press.

Albro, Robert, George Marcus, Laura McNamara, and Monica Schoch-Spana, eds. 2012. *Anthropologists in the securityscape: Ethics, practice, and professional identity*. Walnut Creek, Calif.: Left Coast Press.

American Anthropological Association. 1971. *Statements on ethics: Principles of professional responsibility*. Arlington, Va.: American Anthropological Association.

———. 1990. *Revised principles of professional responsibility*. Washington, D.C.: American Anthropological Association.

———. 1991. Arlington, Va.: American Anthropological Association.

———. 1998. *Code of ethics of the American Anthropological Association*. Arlington, Va.: American Anthropological Association. http://www.aaanet.org/profdev/ethics/upload/ethicscode1998.pdf.

———. 2002. *El Dorado Task Force papers: Submitted to the Executive Board as a final report*; vols. 1 and 2. Arlington, Va.: American Anthropological Association. http://anthroniche.com/darkness_documents/0598.pdf and http://anthroniche.com/darkness_documents/0599.pdf.

———. 2007. *Anthropology and national security threats*. Panel held at a meeting of the American Anthropological Association, San Francisco, November 22.

———. 2009. *Code of ethics of the American Anthropological Association*. Arlington, Va.: American Anthropological Association. http://www.aaanet.org/profdev/ethics/.

———. 2010. Ethics Task Force. *Draft principle: Do no harm*. Arlington, Va.: American Anthropological Association.

American Association of Physical Anthropologists. 2009. *AAPA code of ethics*. Last modified May 27, 2009. http://physanth.org/association/position-statements/code-of-ethics.

The American Heritage Dictionary. 1985. 2nd ed. Boston: Houghton-Mifflin.

American Indian Law Center. 1999. *Model tribal research code.* 3rd ed. Albuquerque, N.Mex.: American Indian Law Center. http://www.nptao.arizona.edu/research/NPTAOResearchProtocolsWebPage/AILawCenterModelCode.pdf.

American Psychological Association. 2013. *Ethical principles of psychologists and code of conduct: Including 2010 amendments.* Washington, D.C.: American Psychological Association. Available online at www.apa.org/ethics/code.html.

The American Psychological Association Presidential Task Force on Psychological Ethics and National Security. 2005. *Report of the American Psychological Association Presidential Task Force on Psychological Ethics and National Security.* Washington, D.C.: American Psychological Association.

American Sociological Association. 1999; reprinted 2008. *Code of ethics and policies and procedures of the ASA Committee on Professional Ethics.* Washington, D.C.: American Sociological Association. Available online at http://www.asanet.org/images/asa/docs/pdf/CodeofEthics.pdf.

ASPSA Committee on Professional Ethics, Rights and Freedoms. 2012. *A Guide to professional ethics in political science.* 2nd ed. Washington, D.C.: American Political Science Association. Available online at http://www.apsanet.org/media/PDFs/ethicsguideweb.pdf.

Association for the Study of Animal Behaviour. 1991. Guidelines for the use of animals in research. *Animal Behaviour* 41:183–86.

Badri, Balghis, Atif Jamal, and Charlotte Martin. 2005. *Inter-communal conflict in Sudan: Causes, resolution mechanisms and transformation.* Omdurman, Sud.: Ahfad University for Women, Building Peace through Diversity Series.

Billson, Janet Mancini, and Kyra Mancini Reis. 2007. *Their powerful spirit: Inuit women in a century of change.* Toronto: University of Toronto Press.

Barfield, Thomas. 2010. *Afghanistan: A cultural and political history.* Princeton, N.J.: Princeton University Press.

Bassett, E. H., and K. O'Riordan. 2002. Ethics of Internet research: Contesting the human subjects research model. *Ethics and Information Technology* 4 (3): 233–47.

Burgess, Michael M. 2009. Proposing modesty for informed consent. *Social Science and Medicine* 65 (11): 2284–95.

Boas, Franz. 1919. Letter to *The Nation*, October 16.

Bosk, Charles L. 2007. The new bureaucracies of virtue or when form fails to follow function. *PoLAR* 30 (2): 192–209.

Caduff, Carlo. 2011. Anthropology's ethics: Moral positionalism, cultural relativism, and critical analysis. *Anthropology Theory* 11 (4): 465–48.

Campbell, Elizabeth, and Luke Eric Lassiter. Forthcoming. *Doing anthropology: Theoretical issues and pragmatic concerns.* New York: Wiley.

Caplan, Pat, ed. 2003. *The ethics of anthropology: Debates and dilemmas.* London: Routledge.

Castellano, Marlene Brant. 2004. Ethics of Aboriginal research. *Journal of Aboriginal Health* (January): 98–114.

Central Intelligence Agency. 1982. *Code of conduct.* Langley, Va.: Central Intelligence Agency.

Chagnon, Napoleon A. 1968. *The Yąnomamö: The fierce people.* New York: Holt, Rinehart and Winston. Rev. ed. 1983.

———. 2013. *Noble savages: My life among two dangerous tribes, the Yąnomami and the anthropologists.* New York: Simon and Schuster.

Chang, Heewon. 2008. *Autoethnography.* Walnut Creek, Calif.: Left Coast Press.

Clarke, Steve. 1999. Justifying deception in social science research. *Journal of Applied Philosophy* 16 (2): 151–66.

Coburn, Noah. 2008. *Qaum: Conceptualizing potters in the Afghan political arena.* Princeton, N.J.: Princeton University Press.

———. 2011. *Bazaar politics: Power and pottery in an Afghan market town.* Stanford, Calif.: Stanford University Press.

Cohen, Patricia. 2009. Panel criticizes military's use of embedded anthropologists. *New York Times,* December 3. http://www.nytimes.com/2009/12/04/arts/04anthro.html.

The Commission on the Engagement of Anthropology with U.S. Military and Intelligence Communities (CEAUSSIC). 2007. *AAA Commission on the Engagement of Anthropology with the U.S. Security and Intelligence Communities: Final report*. Arlington, Va.: American Anthropological Association.

Dauphinee, Elizabeth. 2010. The ethics of autoethnography. *Review of International Studies* 36 (3): 799–818. Abstract available online at http://journals.cambridge.org/article_ S0260210510000690.

DeJesus, Kevin. 2011. Imagining Lebanon: Living on amidst an entangled history in place. Ph.D. diss., York University, Toronto.

Department of Health and Human Services. 1990. *Code of federal regulations: Title 45, public welfare, Department of Health and Human Services; Part 46, protection of human subjects*. Washington, D.C.: Department of Health and Human Services.

Dreger, Alice. 2011. Darkness's descent on the American Anthropological Association: A cautionary tale. *Human Nature* 22:225–46.

Eakin, Emily. 2013. How Napoleon Chagnon became our most controversial anthropologist. *New York Times Magazine*, February 13. www.nytimes.com/2013/02/17/magazine/ napoleon-chagnon-americas-most-controversial-anthropologist.html.

Economic and Social Research Council. 2005. *Framework for research ethics*. Swindon, Eng.: Economic and Social Research Council. 2010 revised edition available online at http:// www.esrc.ac.uk/_images/Framework-for-Research-Ethics_tcm8-4586.pdf.

Edel, May M. [May Mandelbaum], and Abraham Edel. 1959. *Anthropology and ethics*. Springfield, Ill.: Thomas. Rev. eds. 1968, 2000.

El-Dareer, Asma. 1982. *Woman, why do you weep?* London: Zed Press.

Ess, Charles, and Association of Internet Researchers. 2002. *Ethical decision-making and Internet research: Recommendations from the AOIR ethics working committee*. Approved by AOIR, November 27, 2002. n.p.: Association of Internet Researchers. Available online at http://aoir.org/reports/ethics.pdf.

Ethics Rupture: Finding alternatives to formal research-ethics review. 2012. Summit of social scientists, Fredericton, Canada, October 25–28.

Faden, Ruth R., and T. L. Beauchamp. 1986. *A history and theory of informed consent*. New York: Oxford University Press.

Fassin, Didier, ed. 2012. *A companion to moral anthropology*. New York: Wiley-Blackwell.

Fluehr-Lobban, Carolyn. 1987. *Islamic law and society in the Sudan*. London: Frank Cass.

———. 1991. *Ethics and the profession of anthropology: Dialogue for a new era*. Philadelphia: University of Pennsylvania Press.

———. 1994. Informed consent in anthropological research: We are not exempt. *Human Organization* 53 (1): 1–10.

———. 1995. Cultural relativism and universal rights. *Chronicle of Higher Education*, June 9, B1–B2.

———. 2000a. How anthropology should respond to an ethical crisis. *Chronicle of Higher Education*, October 6.

———. 2000b. Globalization of research and international standards of ethics in anthropology. In *Ethics and anthropology: Facing future issues in human biology, globalism, and cultural property*, ed. Anne-Marie Cantwell, Eva Friedlander, and Madeline Tramm, 37–44. New York: New York Academy of Sciences.

———. 2000c. How anthropology should respond to an ethical crisis. *Chronicle of Higher Education*, October 6.

———. 2003a. Darkness in El Dorado: Ethics then and now. In *Ethics and the profession of anthropology: Dialogue for ethically conscious practice*, ed. Carolyn Fluehr-Lobban, 85–106. Walnut Creek, Calif.: AltaMira Press.

———. 2003b. Dialogue for ethically conscious practice. In *Ethics and the profession of Anthropology: Dialogue for ethically conscious practice*, ed. Carolyn Fluehr-Lobban, 225–45. Walnut Creek, Calif.: AltaMira Press.

———, ed. 2003c. *Ethics and the profession of anthropology: Dialogue for ethically conscious practice*. 2nd ed. Walnut Creek, Calif.: AltaMira Press.

————. 2003d. The spirit and intent of informed consent in anthropological research with vulnerable populations. 2003. Presentation at the American Anthropological Association's workshop, Conducting Ethical Fieldwork among Vulnerable, Indigenous Groups, sponsored by the AAA Committee on Ethics, Chicago, November 20.

————. 2003e. Working memoranda on models or characteristics of effective IRBs. Presented to the Social and Behavioral Sciences Working Group on Human Research, Elkridge, Md., July 18–20.

————. 2006a. Advocacy is a moral choice of "doing some good": But not a professional ethical responsibility. *Anthropology News* 47 (October): 5–6.

————. 2006b. *Race and racism: An introduction.* Lanham, Md.: AltaMira Press.

————. 2008a. Anthropology and ethics in America's declining imperial age. *Anthropology Today* 24 (4): 19–22.

————. 2008b. Collaborative anthropology as twenty-first-century anthropology. *Collaborative Anthropology* 1 (1).

————. 2008c. New ethical challenges for anthropologists. *Chronicle of Higher Education,* November 14, B11.

————. 2008d. What does "do no harm" mean for anthropologists who work for the military? *Chronicle of Higher Education,* October 18.

————. 2009a. Anthropology and human rights: Do anthropologists have an ethical obligation to promote human rights? An open exchange. In *Human rights: An anthropological reader,* ed. Mark Goodale, 198–206. New York: Wiley-Blackwell.

————. 2009b. Guiding principles over enforceable standards. *Anthropology News* 50 (September): 8–9.

————. 2012. *Shari'a and Islamism in Sudan: Conflict, law and social transformation.* London: I. B. Tauris.

————. 2013. Anthropology and ethics. In *A companion to moral anthropology,* ed. Didier Fassin, 103–14.

Fluehr-Lobban, Carolyn, and Patricia Marshall. 2004. Working definition of ethnographic research. Memorandum to the American Anthropological Association, February 8.

Frankel, Mark S., and Sanyin Siang. 1999. *Ethical and legal aspects of human subjects research on the Internet: A report of a workshop.* Washington, D.C.: American Association for the Advancement of Science. Available online at http://www.aaas.org/spp/sfrl/projects/intres/report.pdf.

Gert, Bernard. 1988. *Morality: A new justification of the moral rules.* New York: Oxford University Press.

————. 2003. *Morality: A new justification of the moral rule.* Oxford: Oxford University Press.

————. 2004. *Common morality: Deciding what to do.* New York: Oxford University Press.

————. 2006. Advocacy is a moral choice of "doing some good": But not a professional ethical responsibility. *Anthropology News* 47 (October): 5–6.

Gezari, Vanessa M. 2009. *The tender soldier.* New York: Simon and Schuster.

Gitter, Donna M. 2004. Ownership of human tissue: A proposal for federal recognition of human research participants' property rights in their biological material. *Washington and Lee Law Review* 61 (1): 257–344.

González, Roberto. 2009. Embedded. In *The counter-counterinsurgency manual.* Chicago: Prickly Paradigm Press.

Goodale, Mark, ed. 2009. *Human rights: An anthropological reader.* New York: Wiley-Blackwell.

Goolsby, Rebecca. 2012. The winds of politics, change, and social science: Transformation in a military research institution. In *Anthropologists in the securityscape,* ed. Robert Albro, George Marcus, Laura McNamara, and Monica Schoch-Spana. Walnut Creek, Calif.: Left Coast Press.

Graham, Laura R. 2009. Anthropologists are obligated to promote human rights and social justice especially among vulnerable communities. In *Human rights: An anthropological reader,* ed. Mark Goodale, 200–202. New York: Wiley-Blackwell.

Greenberg, Karen L., and Joshua L. Dratel. 2005. *The torture papers: The road to Abu Ghraib.* New York: Cambridge University Press.

Gross, Daniel, and Stuart Plattner. 2002. Anthropology as social work: Collaborative models of anthropological research. *Anthropology News* 43 (8): 4.

Gruenbaum, Ellen. 2001. *The female circumcision controversy.* Philadelphia: University of Pennsylvania Press.

Guha, Sumit. 1998. Lower strata, older races and Aboriginal peoples: Racial anthropology and mythical history past and present. *Journal of Asian Studies* 57 (2): 423–41.

Haggerty, Kevin D. 2004. Ethics creep: Governing social science research in the name of ethics. *Qualitative Sociology* 27 (4): 391–414.

Hamelink, Cees J. 2000. *The ethics of cyberspace.* London: Sage.

Herman, Barbara. 2000. *Lectures on the history of moral philosophy by John Rawls.* Cambridge, Mass.: Harvard University Press.

Hersh, Seymour M. 2004. Annals of national security: Torture at Abu Ghraib. *New Yorker Magazine*, May 10. www.newyorker.com/archive/2004/05/10/040510fa_fact.

Hine, Christine. 2000. *Virtual ethnography.* London: Sage.

Holewinski, Sarah. 2013. Do less harm: Protecting and compensating civilians in war. *Foreign Affairs* (January–February): 14–21.

Humphreys, Laud. 1970. *Tearoom trade: Impersonal sex in public places.* Chicago: Aldine.

Ibeji, Yokotam, and Korowai Gane. 1996. Lower strata, older races and Aboriginal peoples: Racial anthropology and mythical history past and present. *Journal of Asian Studies* 57 (2): 423–41.

Jaschik, Scott. 2009. Anthropologists toughen ethics code. *Inside Higher Ed.*, February 19. http://www.insidehighered.com/news/2009/02/19/anthro.

Johnston, Rob. 2005. *Analytical culture in the U.S. intelligence community: An ethnographic study.* Washington, D.C.: Central Intelligence Agency. Available online at https://www.cia.gov/library/center-for-the-study-of-intelligence/csi-publications/books-and-monographs/analytic-culture-in-the-u-s-intelligence-community/analytic_culture_report.pdf.

King's College and Churchill College. 2012. Ethics at the intersection of philosophy and anthropology. Symposium, London, January 26.

Koppelman, Elysa. 2012. *Federal regulations for animal research.* Washington, D.C.: National Academy of Engineering. Available online at http://www.onlineethics.org/cms/13119.aspx.

Lancaster, Jane B., and Raymond Hames. 2011. Statement on the publication of Alice Dreger's investigation *Darkness's descent on the American Anthropological Association: A cautionary tale. Human Nature* 22 (3): 223–24.

Lederman, Rena. 2007. Comparative "research": A modest proposal concerning the object of ethics regulation. *Anthrosource* 30 (2): 305–27.

Levine, Carol, et al. 2004. The limitations of "vulnerability" as a protection for human research participants. *American Journal of Bioethics* 4 (3): 44–49.

Lucas, George R. 2009. *Anthropologists in arms: The ethics of military anthropology.* Lanham, Md.: AltaMira Press.

Lucas, George, and Carolyn Fluehr-Lobban. Forthcoming. Good anthropologist/bad anthropologist: Human Terrain Teams. In *Human Terrain System*, ed. Montgomery McFate and Janice H. Laurence.

Lykes, Brinton. 1989. Dialogue with Guatemalan Indian women: Critical perspectives on constructing collaborative research. In *Representations: Social constructions of gender*, ed. Rhoda Unger, 167–85. Amityville, N.Y.: Baywood Publishing.

Mackinnon, Katherine C., and Erin P. Riley. 2010. Field primatology of today: Current ethical considerations. *American Journal of Primatology* 72 (9): 749–53.

Malkin, Elizabeth. 2013. In effort to try dictator, Guatemala shows new judicial might. *New York Times International*, March 17. http://www.nytimes.com/2013/03/17/world/americas/victims-of-guatemala-civil-war-eagerly-await-dictators-trial.html.

Mamdani, Mahmoud. 2005. *Good Muslim, bad Muslim: America, the Cold War, and the roots of terror.* New York: Random House.

———. 2007. *Good Muslim, bad Muslim: An African perspective.* Brooklyn: Social Science Research Council. Available online at www.ssrc.org/sept11/essays/mamdani.htm.

Maréchal, Garance. 2010. Autoethnography. In *Encyclopedia of case study research*, vol. 2, ed. Albert J. Mills, Gabrielle Durepos, and Elden Wiebe, 43–45. Thousand Oaks, Calif.: Sage Publications.

Markham, Annette N. 1998. *Life online: Real experience in virtual space*. Lanham, Md.: AltaMira Press.

Marks, Jonathan. 2005. Your body, my property: The problem of colonial genetics in a post-colonial world. In *Embedding ethics*, ed. Lynn Meskell and Peter Pels, 29. New York: Berg.

Max Planck Institute for Evolutionary Anthropology. n.d. Department of Linguisitcs. *Ethics guidelines*. Principle 5. Available online at www.eva.mpg.de/lingua/resources/ethics.php.

McFate, Montgomery. 2005. Anthropology and counterinsurgency: The strange story of their curious relationship. *Military Review* (March–April).

McKinnon, John D. 2009. U.S. offers an official apology to Native Americans. *Washington Wire*, December 22. http://blogs.wsj.com/washwire/2009/12/22/us-offers-an-official-apology-to-native-americans/.

Meskell, Lynn, and Peter Pels, eds. 2005. *Embedding ethics*. Oxford: Berg.

Morenon, Pierre. 2003. Nagged by NAGPRA: Is there an archaeological ethic? In *Ethics and profession of anthropology: Dialogue for ethically conscious practice*, 2nd ed., ed. Carolyn Fluehr-Lobban, 107–40. Walnut Creek, Calif.: AltaMira Press.

National Bioethics Advisory Commission. 2000. *Ethical and policy issues in research involving human participants*. Bethesda, Md.: National Bioethics and Advisory Commission.

The National Commission for the Protection of Human Subjects of Biomedical and Behavioral Research, Office of the Secretary. 1979. *The Belmont report: Ethical principles and guidelines for the protection of human subjects of research; Report of the National Commission for the Protection of Human Subjects of Biomedical and Behavioral Research*. Washington, D.C.: Department of Health, Education, and Welfare.

National Congress of American Indians. 2012. *American Indian and Alaskan native genetics research resource guide: Tool for tribal leaders and citizens*. Washington, D.C.: American Indian and Alaska Native Genetics Resource Center. http://genetics.ncai.org/files/NCAI%20genetics%20research%20resource%20guide%20FINAL%20PDF.pdf.

National Park Service. 1990. *Native American Graves Protection Act: Public Law 101–601*. Washington, D.C.: U.S. Department of the Interior. Available online at http://www.nps.gov/nagpra/mandates/25usc3001etseq.htm.

National Science Foundation. 2013. *Frequently asked questions and vignettes: Interpreting the Common Rule for the protection of human subjects for behavioral and social science research*. Arlington, Va.: The National Science Foundation. Available online at http://www.nsf.gov/bfa/dias/policy/hsfaqs.jsp.

Network of Concerned Anthropologists. n.d. Pledge of non-participation in Counterinsurgency. https://sites.google.com/site/concernedanthropologists/.

Nuti, Paul J. 2006. Ad hoc commission commences. *Anthropology News* (September): 25–26. http://www.aaanet.org/cmtes/commissions/CEAUSSIC/upload/an-sept-2006-nuti.pdf.

Pels, Peter. 1994. National codes of ethics and European anthropology: A call for cooperation and sharing. *EASA Newsletter* (September): 9–10.

———. 1999. Professions of duplexity: A prehistory of ethical codes in anthropology. *Current Anthropology* 40 (2): 101–36.

Price, David H. 2000. Anthropologists as spies. *The Nation*, November 20, 24–27. http://www.thenation.com/article/anthropologists-spies#.

———. 2011. *Weaponizing anthropology: Social service in the service of the militarized state*. Oakland, Calif.: AK Press.

Rawls, John. 1971. *A theory of justice*. Cambridge: Belknap Press of Harvard University.

Resnik, David . 2006. Openness versus secrecy in scientific research. *Episteme* 2 (3): 135–47.

Rhode, David. 2007. Army enlists anthropologists in war zones. *New York Times*, October 5. http://www.nytimes.com/2007/10/05/world/asia/05afghan.html.

Roth, Wolff-Michael. 2009. Auto/ethnography and the question of ethics. *Forum: Qualitative Social Research* 10 (1). www.qualitative-research.net/index.php/fqs/article/view/1213/2646.

Rubinstein, Robert A., Kerry Fosher, and Clementine Fujimura, eds. 2012. *Practicing military anthropology: Beyond expectations and traditional boundaries*. Sterling, Va.: Kumarian Press.

Rudmin, Floyd. 2004. Views and humans: Torture at Abu-Ghraib and the telling silence of social scientists. *Anthropology News* 45 (6): 9.

Rush, Laurie. 2012. Archaeological ethics and working for the military. In Rubinstein, Fosher, and Fujimura, eds. 2012.

Rylko-Bauer, Barbara. 2008. Applied anthropology and counterinsurgency. *Newsletter of the Society for Applied Anthropology* 19 (1). Available online at http://www.sfaa.net/newsletter/feb08nl.pdf.

Salmoni, Barak A., and Paula Holmes-Eber. 2008. *Operational culture for the war fighter: Principles and applications*. Quantico, Va.: Marine Corps University Press.

Scheper-Hughes, Nancy. 2009. Rotten trade: Millennial capitalism, human values and global justice in organs trafficking. In *Human rights: An anthropological reader*, ed. Mark Goodale, 167–97. New York: Wiley-Blackwell.

Selmeski, Brian. 2008. Anthropology for the military masses: A moral-practical argument for educational engagement. Paper presented at the meeting of the American Anthropological Association meeting, San Francisco, November 22.

Shweder, Richard. 1990. Ethical relativism: Is there a defensible version? *Ethos* 18 (2): 205–18.

Silverstein, Leni. 2004. Uncensuring Boas. *Anthropology News* 45 (8): 5–6.

Sipress, Alan. 1995. Egyptian rights group sues sheik on support of female circumcision. *Philadelphia Inquirer*, April 13. http://articles.philly.com/1995-04-13/news/25684816_1_female-circumcision-islamic-law-traditional-practice.

Skloot, Rebecca. 2010. *The immortal life of Henrietta Lacks*. New York: Crown Publishers.

———. 2013. The immortal life of Henrietta Lacks, the sequel. *New York Times*, March 24, p. 4. www.nytimes.com/2013/03/24/opinion/sunday/the-immortal-life-of-henrietta-lacks-the-sequel.html.

Social and Behavioral Sciences Working Group on Human Research. 2003. *IRB best practices*. Workshop sponsored by the Office of Behavioral and Social Sciences Research, with the American Educational Research Association. Elkridge, Md., July 18–20.

Social Science Research Ethics. n.d. *Core issues: Informed consent*. Lancaster, Eng.: Social Science Research Ethics. Available online at www.lancs.ac.uk/researchethics/1-3-infcons.html.

Society for Applied Anthropology. 1949. *Report of the Committee on Ethics of the Ethical and Professional Responsibilities of the Society for Applied Anthropology*.

Spicker, Paul. 2007. Research without consent. *Social Research Update* 51 (Winter). Available online at http://sru.soc.surrey.ac.uk/SRU51.pdf.

Sponsel, Leslie. 2011. Alice Dreger descends into darkness: Scholarship or more obfuscation? E-mail sent April 5. Available online at *Darkness in El Dorado: Archived Document*. http://anthroniche.com/darkness_documents/0617.htm.

Star, Alexander. 2011. Afghanistan: What the anthropologists say. *New York Times Sunday Book Review*, November 18. http://www.nytimes.com/2011/11/20/books/review/afghanistan-and-other-books-about-rebuilding-book-review.html.

Suzuki, Peter. 1981. Anthropologists in the wartime camps for Japanese Americans. *Dialectical Anthropology* 6 (1): 23–60.

———. 1986. The University of California Japanese Evacuation and Resettlement Study: A prolegomenon. *Dialectical Anthropology* 10 (3–4): 189–213.

———. 2009. The activities of anthropologists during WWII in the Japanese American internment camps. Paper presented at 108th annual meeting of the American Anthropological Association, Philadelphia.

Tierney, John. 2007. "Circumcision" or "mutilation"? And other questions about a rite in Africa. *New York Times, TierneyLab*, December 5. http://tierneylab.blogs.nytimes.com/2007/12/05/circumcision-or-mutilation-and-other-questions-about-a-rite-in-africa/.

Tierney, Patrick. 2000. *Darkness in El Dorado: How scientists and journalists devastated the Amazon*. New York: W. W. Norton.

Turner, Terrence. 2001. *The Yanomami and the ethics of anthropological practice.* Ithaca, N.Y.: Cornell University.

Ulrich, George. 1999. Comment to Peter Pels "Professions of duplexity." *Current Anthropology* 40 (2): 126–27.

United Nations. Universal declaration of human rights. New York: United Nations. http://www.un.org/en/documents/udhr/index.shtml.

Walsh-Haney, Heather, and Leslie S. Lieberman. 2005. Ethical concerns in forensic anthropology. In *Biological anthropology and ethics: From repatriation to genetic identity*, ed. Trudy Turner, 121–31. Albany: State University of New York Press.

Washburn, Wilcomb E. *Against the anthropological grain.* New Brunswick, N.J.: Transaction Publishers, 1998.

World Archaeological Congress Council. 1990. *World Archaeological Congress codes of ethics.* Barquisimeto, Ven.: World Archaeological Congress. Available online at www.worldarchaeologicalcongress.org/site/about_ethi.php.

Woodsong, Cynthia, Quarraisha Abdool Karim, and A. Colletti. 2004. *Improving informed consent in HIV/AIDS research: A conceptual framework and supportive materials.* Presentation at fifteenth annual International AIDS Conference. Bangkok, Thailand, July 11–16, 2004.

Zigon, Jarrett. 2007. Moral breakdown and the ethical demand: A theoretical framework for an anthropology of moralities. *Anthropology Theory* 7 (2): 131–50.

Index

Abu Ghraib, 29
accountability in research, 21, 115
American Anthropological Association
    (AAA), 20, 26, 96, 126, 158; AAA
    Commissions on Engagement of
    Anthropology with US Security and
    Intelligence Communities
    (CEAUSSIC), 20, 21, 104; codes of
    ethics, 1, 2, 62, 87, 91, 93, 116;
    Committee on Ethics, 59, 60, 126, 131;
    Principles of Professional
    Responsibility, 11–12, 132
American Association of Physical
    Anthropologists, 5; code of ethics, 6
American Psychological Association, 19,
    38–39, 56, 63; Task Force on Ethics
    and National Security, 18, 19
American Sociological Association: code
    of ethics, 63–64, 90
anthropologists: advocacy, 26, 96, 115,
    116; as "dual professionals," 20;
    employment, 158; ethically conscious,
    25, 35, 40, 44, 52, 141, 157, 161, 163,
    168; in Japanese-American War
    Relocation camps (WWII), 133–134;
    judged as "good" or "bad," 36, 115,
    126–127; majority are women, 26, 165,
    168; paternalism/maternalism of, 26,
    63, 80, 166; from powerful countries,
    31, 134; problem of self-reporting and
    monitoring, 64, 145–146; resistance to

informed consent, 75–76, 80;
    respecting the autonomy of people
    studied, 26; Suzuki, Peter, 134; who is
    an anthropologist?, 2, 19, 158–159; in
    World War II, 133–134
anthropology: biological/physical, 5;
    cultural anthropology as its totality, 4;
    definition of, 158, 159; forensic, 6;
    four-field, 4, 87, 158; future of, 169;
    holism, 4, 136, 158; linguistic, 10;
    "litany of shame," 20, 97, 129; moral
    system for, 27, 136; students and
    teachers dedication, 168; twenty-first
    century, 1; in the United Kingdom, 159;
    "weaponized," 128
antiquities, illegal trade of, 8
The Arab Mind, 29. *See also* Hersh,
    Seymour
archaeologist, 158
archaeology, 6–8, 159; Ba civilization,
    China, 8; codes, 7; Egyptian National
    Museum, 8; World Archaeological
    Congress, 7; World Heritage sites, 8

Baghdad Museum, looting, 8
Barfield, Thomas, 36
Belmont Report, 16, 57, 58, 66, 106, 139;
    basic principles, 58
Benedict, Ruth, 159
beneficence, 23, 24
Billson, Janet Mancini, 165

About the Author

Carolyn Fluehr-Lobban, Ph.D., is professor emerita of anthropology and African studies at Rhode Island College and adjunct professor of African studies at the Naval War College in Newport, Rhode Island. She received her bachelor's and master's degrees from Temple University and in 1973 her Ph.D. in anthropology and African studies from Northwestern University. At Rhode Island College she received both the award for Distinguished Teaching in 1990 and the award for Distinguished Scholar in 1998. She and her husband, Richard, were recognized as 2012 Gallery of Success alumnae for the College of Liberal Arts at Temple University. In 2013 she delivered the keynote address on anthropology and ethics at the annual meeting of the Danish Anthropological Association in Copenhagen.

She spent six years between 1970 and 2009 living and conducting research in the Sudan, Egypt, and Tunisia and uses Arabic as her field language. She has traveled extensively throughout the world, including two trips teaching anthropology with the University of Pittsburgh's Semester at Sea program. Her research subjects cover Islamic law and Islamic society, women's social and legal status in Muslim societies, ethics and anthropological research, human rights and cultural relativism, and comparative studies in law and society. She is a founder and twice past president of the Sudan Studies Association. Her most recent research was conducted in Sudan from 2007 to 2009 and was funded by the United States Institute of Peace.

She is author or editor of eleven books, including the following works on Sudan: *Shari`a and Islamism in Sudan: Conflict, Law and Social Transformation* (2012), *Islamic Law and Society in the Sudan* (1987; Arabic translation 2004), *Historical Dictionary of the Sudan* (coauthor, 1991; 2003), and *Race and Identity in the Nile Valley* (coauthor, 2004).

She is editor of *Ethics and the Profession of Anthropology: Dialogue for a New Era* (1991) and *Ethics and the Profession of Anthropology: Dialogue for Ethically Conscious Practice* (2003) and has authored three textbooks: *Race and Racism: An Introduction* (2006), *Female Well-Being* (2005), and *Islamic Societies in Practice* (1994; 2004). She is also a beekeeper, maintaining hives in both Rhode Island and New Hampshire.